Football and Fascism

The National Game under Mussolini

Simon Martin

Oxford • New York

English edition
First published in 2004 by
Berg
Editorial offices:
First Floor, Angel Court, 81 St Clements Street, Oxford OX4 1AW, UK
175 Fifth Avenue, New York, NY 10010, USA

Berg is the imprint of Oxford International Publishers Ltd.

Library of Congress Cataloging-in-Publication Data
A catalogue record for this book is available from the Library of Congress.

British Library Cataloguing-in-Publication Data
A catalogue record for this book is available from the British Library.

ISBN   1 85973 700 5 (hardback)
        1 85973 705 6 (paperback)

Typeset by Avocet Typeset, Chilton, Aylesbury, Bucks.
Printed in the United Kingdom by Biddles Ltd, King's Lynn.

www.bergpublishers.com

Contents

List of Figures

Abbreviations

ACS	*Archivio Centrale dello Stato*
AdMdAE	*Archivio del Ministero degli Affari Esteri*
AIA	*Associazione Italiana Arbitri*
AOI	*Africa Orientale Italiana*
APEF	*Associazione Proletaria per l'Educazione Fisica*
ASCB	*Archivio Storico del Comune di Bologna*
BA	*Belle Arti*
BFC	*Bologna Football Club*
CA	*Carteggio Amministrativo*
Il Carlino	*Il Resto del Carlino*
CCI	*Confederazione Calcistica Italiana*
CIS	*Commissione Impianti Sportivi*
CITA	*Comitato Italiano Tecnico Arbitrale*
CO	*Carteggio Ordinario*
CONI	*Comitato Olimpico Nazionale Italiano*
ENEF	*Ente Nazionale per l'Educazione Fisica*
ESPF	*Enti Sportivi Provinciali Fascisti*
FASCI	*Federazione delle Associazioni Sportive Cattoliche*
FFGGCC	*Fasci Giovanili di Combattimento*
FIDAL	*Federazione Italiana di Atletica Leggera*
FIF	*Federazione Italiana del Football*
FIFA	*Fédération Internationale de Football Association*
FIGC	*Federazione Italiana Giuoco del Calcio*
FIGS	*Federazione Italiana Giovanile Socialista*
La Gazzetta	*La Gazzetta dello Sport*
GIL	*Gioventú Italiana del Littorio*
GUF	*Gruppo Universitario Fascista*
IFC	*Istituto Fascista di Cultura*
MVSN	*Milizia Volontaria Sicurezza Nazionale*
ONB	*Opera Nazionale Balilla*
OND	*Opera Nazionale Dopolavoro*
PCM	*Presidenza del Consiglio dei ministri*
PNF	*Partito Nazionale Fascista*

PSI	*Partito Socialista Italiano*
RG	*Registro Generale*
SPD	*Segreteria Particolare del Duce*
ULIC	*Unione Libera Italiana del Calcio*
UOEI	*Unione Operai Escursionisti*

Acknowledgements

A trawl through family photo albums during an afternoon that would have been better spent working on this book, revealed the consistent feature of a football. From a back garden in Essex to the *curve* of Rome's Stadio Olimpico, football has guided, if not governed, my mazey dribble through life.

Duncan Shaw's research on Spanish football under Franco, at Queen Mary and Westfield College, London, first exposed me to the game's potential as a revealing and relatively novel area of historical analysis. It was perhaps this work that inspired my doctoral thesis, upon which this book is based. My journeyman Sunday morning football 'career', across the playing fields of Essex and East London, also prepared me well for the demands of historical research; a modicum of ability, grim determination and the inspiration of others can go a long way. In my dream team I would play alongside Diego Maradona, Johann Cruyff and Bobby Moore, while Eric Hobsbawm would be the first name on the team-sheet of my Inspirational XI, and he would wear number 10.

Dave McLean at Abbs Cross School was the first to make the past interesting, while the History department of Queen Mary and Westfield College had the faith to take me on as a slightly mature student with a very average record. Once there, Dr Roger Mettam became my guru and Dr Maria-Sophia Quine helped me discover that there was more to Fascism than men with moustaches. On loan for one season to the Wellcome Institute for Medical Research, Dr Michael Neve entertained and inspired in equal measure, while staff at the School of Slavonic and East European Studies, London, began my postgraduate development.

Dr Jonathan Morris and Dr Axel Körner (University College London) had the dubious pleasure of supervising my doctoral game plan, their substantial advice and criticisms exposing my sometimes naive defending and guiding me through the mists that frequently obscured the goal. Their input was also crucial in obtaining much of the funding that supported me throughout the research for this book. As an undergraduate, I was extremely lucky to benefit from the final three years of the grant system, without which I know I would never have got started. I hope my work goes someway to repaying the Local Education Authority's investment, proves value for money, and demonstrates what is possible with adequate support.

The British Academy followed by the Arts and Humanities Research Board funded my four years of postgraduate study, which was supplemented by individual grants from the Royal Historical Society and the UCL Graduate School. I also received significant support from the Italian Cultural Institute, London. Free language tuition in Italy helped develop the linguistic skills necessary to unpick the stubborn defences of the Italian archives, while two summer bursaries enabled me to concentrate solely on the demands of the work. I hope this generous sponsorship of British students interested in Italy continues, and thank the Director, Mario Fortunato, Signora Silvana Prosdocimo in London, and Gianfranco Renda in Rome. Concluding my thesis was enormously helped by a Scouloudi Fellowship at the Institute of Historical Research, London. I similarly hope this book makes a small contribution to its reputation.

Professor Mariuccia Salvati (University of Bologna) was also instrumental in securing research grants from the Italian government, besides offering encouragement, advice and contacts when away from home. With the thesis completed, Professor James Walvin (University of York) and Dr Stephen Gundle (Royal Holloway, London) offered further encouragement and constructive criticism on the publication of this book, which I tried to incorporate within the limited time and space available. Prof Giuliano Gresleri (University of Bologna) and Professor Tim Benton (Open University) both took the time to discuss my unrefined architectural theories and Professor Pierre Lanfranchi (Leicester De Montfort University) provided some useful early advice. He also put me in contact with Francesco Varrasi, whose impressive work was a regular source of information, inspiration and reassurance. Sergio Giuntini in Milan gave his time, advice, friendship, encouragement and source material freely, in addition to ensuring I saw his AC Milan in the flesh. With the referee poised to blow the final whistle, Lia Antoniou, Rob Mellett, Kate Quinn and Laurence Weeks all took the time to spot the errors of grammar and style that I could no longer see. I naturally take full credit for lapses that remain.

Exploring Italian archives and libraries demanded the attention and patience of staff prepared to interpret my tongue-tied demands and I thank the following institutions: Archivio Centrale Dello Stato, Rome; Archivio del Ministero degli Affari Esteri, Rome; Biblioteca di Storia Moderna e Contemporanea, Rome; Biblioteca Nazionale Braidense, Milan; Biblioteca Universitaria, Bologna; Biblioteca Archiginnasio,

Bologna; Biblioteca Nazionale Centrale di Firenze, Florence; Archivio Storico del Comune di Firenze, Florence. Of particular help were: William Baietti and the staff at the Archivio Storico del Comune di Bologna; Gianfranco La Peruta, FIGC Biblioteca Settore Tecnico Coverciano, Florence, for his bibliographical advice and football talk; Dr F. Fini, Direttore FIGC Fondazione Museo del Calcio, Firenze, for generously putting the impressive contents of the museum at my disposable. Long may it continue to grow.

I should also thank Dr Fini for helping me contact Piero Rava, the last surviving member of the 1938 World Cup winning team. Arranging the interview took persistence, the OK from Signora Rava and the mediation of Mario Parodi, who held the metaphorical keys to their household. I thank them all for their help and welcome. Meeting Piero was probably the highlight of four years research and helped inject some reality into what sometimes seemed like a surreal world of make-believe. A man of achievement and humbling modesty.

Academic research is often a very lonely business, although studying Italian football has opened many doors to friendships and acquaintances that entertained me and taught me much about contemporary Italian life. It would have been impossible to conclude it without the friends and colleagues who helped, supported me and made me laugh in their own ways. Among those back home who advised me, took the trouble to stay in touch and sometimes visited were Torbun Attrup, Bob Blenkinsop, Tony Callaghan, Paul Dossett, Simon Kuper, Chris Martin, Paul Riley, Mike Rivers and Wendy Sumpton. Ron Nicholls also put his patience and technical skills at my disposal when Microsoft frequently got the better of me.

My first research trip was eased by Massimo Cutini and his family who took me in as the lost, linguistically challenged Inglese that I was, and made me feel one of their own. I was also fortunate to meet the Pitonzos: John for becoming another brother and holding me up when I needed it, Paola for her knowledge of *calcio*, Marianna for being Marianna and Dorina for always welcoming me with a smile on the frequent occasions I invited myself to stay. Thanks to Uncle John in England for introducing me to Sharon, Richard, Rhian and Bethan Thomas, in Milan, who regularly put their welcome, house and refrigerator at my disposal and ensured I maintained my more English talents. I cannot thank you all enough.

Always in need of friends, Mario Lazzaroni and Andrea Gagliardi, who I met in Brussels through Lucy Hillier, never let me down in any city I lived in. Besides showing me aspects of Neapolitan life that I could not have imagined, they introduced me to Germana Guzzardi and Diana

Letizia, who, like so many others, welcomed me unconditionally into their lives.

My time in Florence was enhanced by Cat Antoniou, Gherardo Bonini, Monika Fraser, Mikael Jalving, Neil Lewin, Louise Littmann, Luca Lunghini and Bjorn Thomassen, while Mario Paolini and Isabella Tosi kept me sane and in touch with humanity during a difficult, isolated trip to Bologna. Seven entertaining months in Rome were in no small measure due to Barbara Bellisari, Deep Sandhu, Maria Teresa Fancelli, Sonya Morozow, Massimo Izzi, Tonino Sabaudo and the Roma branch of the Messina Supporters Club. A very special mention to Ed Nadalin, the skateboarding technical genius who endlessly fed, 'watered' and entertained me and saved my thesis when all seemed lost. The boy done good!

Above all, I have to thank my parents, who unceasingly encouraged and supported me through the good times and the bad, tolerated my mood swings and embarrassed me with their pride. I could not have done this without them. Always ready with the bucket and sponge, they never once threatened to brandish a yellow card (when a red might have been justified), asked how long this game would last, or questioned the high price of their tickets to the show. Thanks so much! I hope it was worth it!

–1–

Introduction

Whether beyond or within the borders, sporting or not, we Italians . . . shook, and still shake with joy when seeing in these pure thoroughbreds, that overwhelm so many noble opponents, such a symbol of the overwhelming march of Mussolini's Italians. Now the 'Tour' [de France] awaits us: the footballers shirts are in the cyclists' bags as moral support and certain lucky charms. But the strongest sign of the third, desired, hoped for, predicted victory is in the unshakeable will with which, outside the country, Italy's athletes struggle and win in the name of Mussolini. L. Ferretti, 'Uno, due . . . (e tre?)'

The 1938 World Cup victory in France was the zenith of sporting achievement for Fascist Italy. As Lando Ferretti, Mussolini's press officer and one of Fascism's most prominent theorists of sport, suggested, such successes were uniting the Italian diaspora behind the regime and symbolized the rise of the Fascist Italian nation.

Until this point, 'Italy' was a more accurate term for the geographical area united by the 1861 *Risorgimento* (Unification) than the 'Italian nation', which remained a disparate, disconnected entity, in need of physical and psychological integration. Post-unification governments lacked a critical sense of legitimacy among Italian citizens, who were alienated by geographic, economic and linguistic barriers. Their legitimacy was also severely impeded by the restrictive franchise and the failure of electoral turnout to register any more than 60 per cent between 1861 and 1886, which resulted in governments that 'represented' only a tiny minority of the population. There was a desperate need for something capable of tying the new nation into a communal identity.

Geographically and psychologically Italian society was estranged from itself as much as from the state, while analyses of the physical condition of the 'united' nation failed to improve the picture. Not surprisingly, for the malnourished masses, who were employed in backbreaking labour for gruelling hours, lived in desperately unsanitary conditions and experienced high rates of infant mortality, the pursuit of sport and physical recreation for health or leisure purposes was a low priority. Among the working and peasant classes there was simply not the time, money or will to consider the pursuit of any sporting activity, as the majority concentrated their energies on merely staying alive. Only the financially comfortable aristocratic, bourgeois and often Anglophile members of society were in any position to take an interest in sport, be that as active participants or passive supporters and enthusiasts.

There was a huge gap in the market and a lack of provision that became increasingly more evident as the fruits of modernity – material goods, leisure time and to a certain degree disposable income – began to spread throughout mass society. This gap between demand and provision expanded rapidly due to the failure of the various liberal governments, the Catholic Church, and the Socialist/Labour movement to respect sport and physical recreation, and appreciate their potential for achieving the type of mass socialization of society that was so desperately needed.

Although Fascism preferred more classical, scholarly sports, such as fencing, and the modern sport of motor racing, unlike its liberal, Catholic and Socialist predecessors the regime was quick to appreciate the mass appeal of football (*calcio*), even if it questioned the game's merits as a sporting activity. The regime institutionalized *calcio* as a Fascist game in 1926 after which it was exploited domestically as a political soporific to develop a sense of Italian identity, and internationally as a diplomatic tool to improve the standing of the regime in the global arena. Under the Fascist regime, which came to power on 28 October 1922, sport in general and football in particular were awarded a level of importance previously unseen in united Italy. Financial and organizational investment quickly and dramatically improved results at the Olympic Games. Moreover, Fascism's intervention in *calcio* not only removed the threat of implosion, but also resulted in a more disciplined structure capable of producing well-honed, technically outstanding footballers that raised the Italian national game to the highest international level.

To achieve this, Italian football had to reach and surpass the standards already set by those countries behind which the regime realized it was lagging. Outside of South America where Argentina and Uruguay possessed strong international reputations, English football was also widely recognized as one of the strongest in the world, despite the FA's chauvinism that limited the team's international appearances. In central Europe, the Austrian, Czechoslovak and Hungarian federations possessed national teams of considerable repute, while Spain was also a regular, if albeit underachieving, favourite at the international tournaments that were establishing an unofficial hierarchy in world football.

Besides its desire to break into this established international elite, the regime had other reasons for intervening in *calcio* in 1926, which this book establishes through analysis of its implemented changes and their effect upon the cities, club teams and stadia of Florence and Bologna, plus the national team. In doing so, it draws conclusions as to the coexistence of apparently contradictory local, national and Fascist identities. Furthermore, it also contributes to the debate regarding the regime's attempt to manufacture consent through the political direction and exploitation of the leisure time of the masses, with an original examination of a mass popular activity that has so far not received the type of attention reserved for others.

The formation of the first national league in 1929 contributed to the emergence of a number of teams that dominated European competition in the following decade. Internationally, the Italian team won the 1934 World Cup, held in Italy, the 1936 Olympic soccer tournament in Berlin, and retained the World Cup trophy in France in 1938. Yet, despite the arguably successful attempt to construct an imagined community by politicizing this form of mass popular culture, on occasion, the regime's projected Italian identity met serious resistance that exposed some of the real and unavoidable conflicts and contradictions within Fascist society and the state.

While contributing to the cultural history of Fascist Italy, this book draws overall conclusions that suggest the regime's attempt to use sport to form identity actually forced it to recognize existing tensions within society, thereby permitting the existence of the type of diversity and individuality that is not naturally associated with Fascism. Consequently, while the regime promoted its ideal of an organic, patriotic, nationalist and united nation through football, the reality was often very different. Although *calcio* was an effective vehicle for promoting and disseminating the idealized Fascist, national community, occasionally it also drew considerable attention to the strong regional identities that existed throughout the peninsula.

Besides the benefits derived from the centralization of *calcio*, one of the regime's principal objectives following the takeover was to make it more adept at producing footballers and teams capable of representing the new political order and society. By 1934, as Carlo Levi argued under the pseudonym of Ettore Bianchi in the socialist and anti-Fascist publication *Giustizia e Libertà*, the regime's direction of football and sport in general had created: 'a great industry, where all the results are accurately recorded, catalogued, utilised and exploited. The press and schools serve propaganda: they feed the young a vain pride in some sporting successes . . . and together they excite that passion . . . that holds no danger. Sport co-operates in the most efficient mode to hold the country in blissful infancy.[1]

Yet, rather than make national pride reliant upon the endeavours of an individual athlete, as was often the case with Olympic events, the successes of football teams at all levels reasserted the individual's important role in the organic whole, under the tutelage of a single leader figure. As the contemporary football magazine *Il Calcio Illustrato* pointed out: 'being a collective sport accentuates the purely social value of football. Football exists, fundamentally, from collaboration. Individuality is allowed and demanded, as leaders and the best players are needed in societies, but neither are less talented players any less important.'[2] It confirmed what the 1927 *Carta del Lavoro* had earlier stated: 'The Italian nation is an organizm having ends, a life, a means superior in power and duration to the single individuals or groups of individuals composing it . . . it is a moral, political, and economic unit which finds its integral realization in the fascist state.'[3] Developing the earlier work of Mabel Berezin,[4] Jeffrey Schnapp used this statement as a basis for his discussion of the regime's attempt to carve a central niche for theatre within the cultural life of the masses. Although unsuccessful, it was almost certainly inspired by Fascism's earlier and more successful exploitation of *calcio* which, as argued here, enabled it to truly reach out to mass society in a manner and on a scale unachievable through any other cultural medium.

While this study makes an obvious contribution to sports history, it is primarily a cultural study of life under the regime through the prism of football. Drawing conclusions about the game's impact upon Italian identity and the attempt to manufacture consent through the exploitation of mass culture, it reflects and further contributes to the existing historiographical debates by considering the following broad themes: identity, consensus, national and racial regeneration, plus culture and modernity.

When speaking of identity I refer to the possibility of three coexisting yet differing types: Fascist, national and local. As one of the key themes explored, *calcio* shows how the Italian Fascist identity, as constructed and disseminated by the regime, both reflected and contradicted the national and local identities that were also intensified by Fascism's takeover and politicization of the game. Besides considering how these differing identities were expressed through *calcio*, establishing their peaceable coexistence reveals much about the regime's attitude to identity itself. While it promoted an idealized Italian Fascist model in an attempt to form an albeit imagined community, there was also considerable room for differing local and national expressions that were often far removed from the party vision, but still acceptable to the regime. The breadth of these reflected the various sources of the regime's inspiration, which partly explains why such apparently contradictory identities were often allowed to coexist.

As will be demonstrated, the thematic issues identified above remain interconnected throughout the study and cannot be treated as isolated areas of investigation, due to the particular nature of football and its mass, cross-societal appeal. While this is the first specific investigation into the nature and importance of Italian football under the regime in English, other studies of Fascist mass culture have highlighted the way that consensus, modernity, national regeneration and identity are all intertwined.

Ruth Ben-Ghiatt's study of culture and modernity, which discusses Mussolini's intention to 'make Italians' and 'remould behaviours and bodies', has already shown how each of the four broad themes that underpin this work were instrumental in this process.[5] If the regime was to physically, mentally and spiritually change Italian society, then the Fascist makeover had to do more than merely paper over the cracks of the liberal facade of nation.

Establishing an Italian Fascist identity among citizens required a physical and psychological process of renewal and regeneration, which the regime attempted to achieve through a positive programme of physical education and a more negative eugenics policy to identify and isolate 'social ills'. Despite containing unquestionably racial implications this was more social horticulture, which was not uncommon in western Europe at the time, than a Nazi-style radical re-engineering of the bloodline.[6] Yet, if it was possible to physically regenerate bodies, minds also needed specific attention. For this reason, as Tracy Koon's work illustrates, Fascist education policy also had a crucial role to play in directing the future generations.[7]

However, had the regime concentrated solely on the future it would have abandoned those already mature Italians, which accounts for its complementary intervention to instruct, guide and direct the adult population. By examining Fascism's exploitation and manipulation of workers' leisure-time activities, Victoria de Grazia demonstrated how such a flagrantly anti-working class regime attempted to socialize the masses and thereby establish a degree of legitimacy and consent for its rule.[8] While the Opera Nazionale Dopolavoro (OND; After Work), Opera Nazionale Balilla (ONB; Fascist Youth Corps), local organized recreational circles and social clubs were important avenues into the everyday lives of the masses for the regime, they remained relatively unpoliticized and never attracted the interest or involvement of more affluent members of society. De Grazia's work was complemented by that of Koon, who similarly concluded that despite its best efforts, the regime was never able to rid itself of the 'basic contradiction between rhetoric and reality'.[9]

De Grazia's work, in particular, also encouraged the further investigation of many issues in broader cultural contexts, such as Stefano Cavazza's research into the regime's rediscovery and restoration of popular, folk-type festivals and activities.[10] Further contributing to the regime's attempt to establish consensus through the development of myths and rituals that created some sense of common community, Cavazza attributed the resumption of these old, folk-type activities to the 'effect of the acceleration of the processes of modernization and of the technological transformation in the world of work'.[11] Above all, his study draws attention to how the regime's deliberate restoration of such activities was designed to invent a tradition of shared identity. However, this constructed sense of community and belonging was essentially artificial, which casts a logical and unavoidable doubt upon the allegedly 'popular' nature of the activities, as promoted by the regime.

In many respects the artificiality, or otherwise, of these traditions, festivals, myths and rituals is less important than the regime's actual attempt to use them as a form of social glue. In this respect, Cavazza's work develops Emilio Gentile's theory about the regime's use of festivals, rituals, myths and cults, centred on the sacralization of the state, to present Fascism as a lay political religion.[12] As futurists and nationalists, such as Enrico Corradini, promoted the restorative powers of war and death, combat and struggle became both real and metaphorical features of life in Fascist society. Motivated by such irrational and mythical thoughts, Gentile identified how the masses were encouraged to join this imagined group by communing in acts of collective public worship. His argument clearly relates to Gustave Le Bon's nineteenth-century theory of crowds, in which he suggested the mind of the mass collective could be manipulated and politically directed by the astute leader figure.[13]

Building upon both Le Bon's and Gentile's ideas, this book suggests that the regime also tried to mobilize Italian society through an occasionally subtle and sometimes very unsubtle use of the aesthetic in building works, design and art. While the various local parties went about restructuring their urban city life, a national construction programme resulted in a huge number of new and imposing buildings that symbolized Fascism. Containing often controversial aesthetic features that provoked contemporary debate about the nature of Fascist art, which remained definitively unresolved, these numerous public works projects were also integral to the battle against unemployment that further contributed to developing a sense of community action.

Most importantly, these projects symbolized Fascism's physical regeneration of Italy, which Gentile argued was intended to further sacralize the regime and develop consensus among the masses. New regulatory town plans drawn up in cities across the peninsula, contained new buildings designed to signify the strength and identity of the regime by imposing an unmistakable change in style from liberal structures. Somewhat ironically, the construction projects that symbolized the various city expansions also contributed to the regime's attempt to de-urbanize society, by moving the masses from the overcrowded and disease-ridden centres into the peripheries. This regenerationist theme was further underlined by land reclamation projects, such as the construction of the new town of Sabaudia from marshland south of Rome and the Foro Mussolini project on the flood plain of the Tiber.

The latter also demonstrated how the regime manipulated its broad interpretation of culture and modernity to formulate something that appeared intrinsically Fascist, thereby contributing to the establishment of a national culture that many deemed to have been lacking since unification. Designed to stimulate and develop physical education and sporting excellence, the project's neo-Roman style mediated the regime's historic imperial influences with its modernistic leanings. This formed a third way that was also visible in other cultural formats, such as the attempt to establish a theatre of masses for the masses which, as Schnapp explained, was designed to break down the old, exclusive, liberal bourgeois medium, in favour of one that was more inclusive and better represented the ideals of the regime.[14]

Berezin also described how, through the propagation of myths and rituals in productions, theatre was thought to have been a medium that could 'generate emotions that would make all participants incorporated into a fascist collectivity'.[15] To enable this attempted metamorphosis of an essentially bourgeois institution into one for the masses, Fascist culture remained undefined and thus more inclusive than exclusive. Not only did this negate the need for difficult theoretical choices about the nature of Fascist theatre, art and architecture, for example, it also avoided the consequent exclusion of cultural practitioners and theorists who may not necessarily have been in accordance with the regime, but still had something of value to offer. As Marla Stone illustrated in her study of politics and culture:

> the official culture of Italian Fascism is best defined by its diversities, contradictions and ambiguities . . . For the greater part of the Fascist era, the regime sought the cooperation and consent of artists, and the association between art and the state was one of mutual recognition and legitimation. The Mussolini dictatorship allowed artists to work and be supported without direct censorship (so long as they were not explicitly anti-Fascist). A large cross section of Italian artists and architects reciprocated by accepting the Fascist regime's patronage.[16]

Much can be said about the regime's various attempts at establishing consensus through the construction of a national community, albeit one that was imaginary and did not necessarily reflect reality. However, while the various issues already mentioned contributed hugely to the establishment and development of a number of debates within the historiography, no one topic of study has thus far been capable of encompassing the four key themes of identity, consensus, national/racial regeneration, plus culture and modernity. As a mass popular activity and spectator sport that crossed social and class barriers, arguably like no other, *calcio* provides the perfect opportunity to consider how the regime attempted to use culture to construct and establish a sense of national community among mass society, from which it hoped to gain some legitimacy and consensus.

To assess how the regime undertook this challenge and its success, or otherwise, this book is separated into the following thematic chapters that reflect the principal issues of identity, consensus, national regeneration and culture. Chapter 2 considers liberal Italy's sporting bequest and Fascism's response to its minimal inheritance. Only bourgeois elitist circles and societies had provided any sort of structured sport prior to Fascism, which left an obvious opportunity for both the Catholic Church and the labour movement to mobilize the support of the masses. However, theoretical barriers and divisions within each presented Fascism with an 'open goal' that Mussolini converted with aplomb. Once securely in power, the regime attuned its cultural influences towards creating a new sense of national community through sport and leisure-time recreation.

Chapter 3 both establishes and analyses the reasons for the regime's specific and radical intervention into *calcio*. As a growing mass participatory and spectator sport, the game possessed a cross-national appeal that demanded Fascism brought it under control so as to demonstrate its authority, to end the chaotic events that were punctuating almost every season, and to portray its new vision of society. The opportunity that *calcio* provided to reach out to the masses really was an offer that Fascism could not refuse.

After reforming and revitalizing the structures, organization and management of *calcio* along Fascist lines, the regime set about providing facilities worthy of the new order and the Italian national passion. As Chapter 4 suggests, the national stadium-building programme that was launched with Bologna's Littoriale arena in 1926, possessed a significance beyond simply providing impressive stadia for club teams. In Berezin's words, they were arguably the most striking '"hypernationalization" projects' in which public political spectacles became 'the dramatic enactment of fascist community and the expressive crucible in which fascist identity was forged.'[17]

First and foremost, massive stadia symbolized the regime's national campaign to regenerate bodies and buildings, for which it was to provide a stadium in every commune of the peninsula. Open to the public, these stadia were intended to further encourage individuals to participate in physical education, thereby giving them a serious propaganda role that extended beyond merely convincing the domestic audience of Fascism's ability and desire to deliver its promises. Demonstrating Fascist Italy's cutting-edge engineering skills and architectural ambitions, stadia were specifically designed and regulated to challenge practically and aesthetically the former architectural orthodoxy of such buildings, thereby, in the process, stamping the regime's identity upon every structure in sometimes apparently contradictory ways.

Chapter 5 develops these themes through consideration of the city, stadium and club of Bologna, which forms the first of two comparative case studies. Besides launching the regime's stadium-building campaign, the Littoriale also expressed and mediated the apparently contradictory identities of the regime and the locality. While making a significant contribution to the local party's reorganization and expansion of the city, it also conformed to the demands of the regime's national regeneration programme in every respect. Furthermore, the Littoriale became the spiritual home of Bologna Football Club. Its achievements further highlighted the stresses between the various identities in Fascist Italy, as the provincial side that intensified the local sense of belonging acquired an international fame that resulted in it being seen as a direct representative of the regime.

Following the construction of a new railway line through the Apennine mountains, Florence became a rival more than a close neighbour of Bologna, the contrasting experiences of this city, club and new stadium, in Chapter 6, showing how diverse the nature of local Fascism could be. Lacking a single representative team like Bologna FC, Fascism's restructuring of national football encouraged leading Florentine political and cultural figures to form AC Fiorentina. Although the club never achieved the success and fame of its Bolognese rival, the city's pride in its team was no less passionate. Only five years after the Littoriale's completion, Florence's Giovanni Berta stadium opened to the public. It was as aesthetically different to the Littoriale as could possibly be imagined. Yet, for reasons explored in Chapter 4 and further developed here, it was more than just a source of great international pride for the regime and the radical local party, as it also demonstrated the broad parameters of acceptability in Fascist architecture, thereby further indicating the scope for cultural diversity under the regime.

As shown in Chapter 7, both stadia also made significant contributions to *calcio's* international importance for Fascism by hosting matches during the 1934 World Cup tournament. A perfect propaganda opportunity, it was the government's chance to sell the merits of its methods of rule to the domestic and foreign markets. Besides the stadia, the Italian national team provided the most convincing evidence of the regime's successful national regeneration programme, which contributed to the creation of a generation of players that dominated international football in this era. However, even this unparalleled success uncovered fissures within Italian society. Questions were raised about the nationality of some members of the team, while the regime's politicization of the game also created problems for the national team and clubs when competing abroad, as they increasingly became the foci of anti-Fascist activities.

As a study of Fascist, national and local identities, this book draws on a variety of primary source material. The local state archives in Bologna and Florence hold considerable information, although not everything, relating to the construction of the respective cities' stadia. This source material that addresses many questions raised from the local perspective was complemented by an investigation of the Archivio Centrale dello Stato – central state archive – and that of the Foreign Ministry, both of which contained information relating to the international significance of *calcio*.

Unfortunately, some private archives remain closed, such as that of the national team coach Vittorio Pozzo, while it has been equally difficult to access any professional club's holdings. Aware of such access problems at the beginning of this project, the research was designed to circumvent such obstacles by assessing primarily the type of information that was deliberately made available to the masses, principally through published books and the printed media, the sports press in particular. Naturally this requires deconstructing if the real meaning and intention of the sources is to be understood, such were the regime's censorship powers. As will be seen, even a superficial glance at the sport-specific press in this period, clearly indicates the bias of a media that was compelled to conform to this glaring abuse and restriction of freedom. Nonetheless, for those fans unable to attend matches, newspapers and magazines provided a wealth of detailed, descriptive information.

As Tracy Koon states in her study of youth and Fascist education, it would be unwise to ignore the regime's use of the media 'to push a whole series of myths that were, by virtue of repetition and familiarity, more real to many Italians than the philosophical musings of Gentile or Rocco or even the universally quoted, quasi-inspired articles on fascism by Mussolini himself'.[18] Consequently, it is within these myths, as propagated through the semi-official channels of the sports media, that we can uncover a view of the regime's idealized Fascist society and how it attempted to establish this as the desired norm for the aspirations of the masses. Uncovering this idealized national community and the various methods by which the regime attempted to impress this upon the masses is a consistent feature in the work of Koon, De Grazia, Gentile, Cavazza, Berezin, Schnapp and Ben-Ghiatt to name but a few. It is hoped this book further contributes to this.

If we are to assess and understand how the regime presented itself to the masses, then the print media is an unavoidable, key source of evidence and information. Consequently, this project was more concerned with what was portrayed to the masses than necessarily determining the exact truth behind the potential myths and legends.

Although newspapers were undoubtedly crucial sources of power for the regime between 1922 and 1924, they were controlled by a combination of informal partnerships with owners and financiers[19] and outright *squadrismo*-style intimidation. Following the murder of the Socialist deputy Giacomo Matteotti, in 1924, Fascism's control of the press became more systematic through coordinated and complementary legislative controls, intimidation and agreements with paper proprietors over the heads of editors. Although the need for strict censorship laws was reduced by the equally muting threat of forcible closure, the 1925 Press Censorship Law supplemented earlier legislative powers, in which Prefects could 'warn' editors and ultimately sequester 'disloyal' papers, by extending this authority to the public prosecutor.

The law also established the Order of Journalists that all professionals had to belong to if they were to work,[20] although there were so few ideologically Fascist journalists that the regime was in no position to purge the profession of those who had trained under the auspices of the liberal free press. However, as Günter Berghaus has outlined with specific regard to artists, but which also applies to the majority of cultural practitioners, even membership of the Syndicate did not necessarily have to restrict an individual's work: 'Most artists found it expedient to adapt to the political changes by going through the necessary motions of indicating loyalty to the régime and then carrying on in their habitual mode of production . . . they joined the syndicates, issued a few pro-Fascist statements, and took advantage of the subsidies and gratuities purveyed by the régime.[21]

Nonetheless, journalists were supervised and standardized by Mussolini's Press Office, under the tutelage of Lando Ferretti from 1926 to 1928, which was a personal instrument of censorship that developed into the Fascist Propaganda Ministry.[22] Thereafter, the press was expected to publicize positive news that varied from promoting the achievements of the regime to playing down negative news such as natural disasters and train crashes.[23]

Sport was a very good news story in this era, so much so that national triumphs were not just restricted to the sporting press but also covered by mainstream dailies like *Il Popolo d'Italia*, Mussolini's personal symbol and the official vehicle of the party. A relatively moderate paper it publicized the regime's more conventional plans, often leaving the more extreme/radical ideas to *Il Tevere*. Despite the mainstream press's growing interest in Italy's athletic ambassadors, the sport-specific press naturally possessed a huge role in raising awareness of the sporting achievements of the nation, or the regime. Between 1924 and 1934 it expanded massively with a number of weekly and monthly publications complementing *La Gazzetta dello Sport* and the *Corriere dello Sport* (*Il Littoriale* from 1927) that sold, on average, 150,000 copies per day and over 300,000 at the weekend.[24] As the party's leading promoter and theorist of sport Ferretti was made director of *La Gazzetta*, after which he turned the paper more towards the needs of the regime. Besides these national publications, most cities also had their own local sports paper – often more than one – such as the Florentine *Lo Stadio* and Bologna's *La Voce Sportiva*.

By promoting the various achievements of Italian sport on a daily basis, the press contributed to the creation and affirmation of the regime's idealized image of Fascist Italy. Consequently, journalists were almost as important as the champion athletes, many becoming household names themselves through their extremely prominent, nationalistic, triumphal and occasionally xenophobic accounts of Italian international victories in the Fascist epoch: Bruno Roghi, Emilio Colombo, Vittorio Varale, Emilio De Martino, to name but a few.[25] It was not only the triumphal writing of Italian journalists that filled column inches, as albeit unsubstantiated praise from across Europe was regularly brought to the reader's attention in an effort to show how the regime's policies were apparently winning European recognition and prestige.

Essentially, this was the ultimate rationale behind the regime's takeover of sport and its restructuring of *calcio*; the acquisition of international respect from sporting success that it was hoped would develop a shared a sense of national achievement, experience and identity. In the ways that have been outlined in this introduction and that will be expanded upon in detail in the following chapters, *calcio* was a conduit for the subtle and psychological dissemination of the national myths, rituals and behaviours that were intended to accelerate the regeneration and nationalization of the masses. This was supported more directly by the development, exploitation and politicization of physical education, sport and football in particular, all of which contributed to the creation of a real and imagined sense of community that was capable of pulling together the cracks in

Fascist Italian society, before papering over them. As the nation's largest mass popular leisure-time activity, *calcio* almost certainly provided one of the best opportunities to achieve this, if indeed it was ever realistically possible.

–2–

'Mens sana in corpore sano'

Making the Italian people idealistic and physically perfect was a task for sport in its many forms, as it demands discipline, order, rigour, sacrifice, a spirit of dedication and healthy morals, while engendering in the individual a desire for the struggle for victory . . . It was necessary to restructure the institutions, co-ordinate their, often chaotic activities, overcoming the reluctance of individual governors [while] building sports grounds in those areas in which their absence impeded serious preparation. *Il Popolo d'Italia*, 'Come il Fascismo ha potenziato lo sport italiano'

Celebrating ten years of Fascist rule, *Il Popolo d'Italia* credited the regime with physically, morally and spiritually regenerating Italian society through sport, thereby rectifying the failures of liberal Italy. Fascism's investment in the nation's sporting life ranged from encouraging the mass pursuit of leisure-time activities to a radical intervention in the education system.

Exploiting the Socialist and Catholic failures to mobilize Italian society through sport, Fascism took control of the 'opium of the masses' and redirected it towards regenerating mass society. Traditional attitudes to 'high' and 'low' culture were rethought, bringing sport and football, in particular, into the mainstream fold of Fascist culture, which included architecture.

By 1932, urban landscapes increasingly featured massive stadia in addition to the smaller sports grounds that every commune was promised.[1] By encouraging the pursuit of physical exercise these facilities contributed to the regime's demographic campaign that was intended to replenish and revitalize Fascist society. Fitter bodies and occupied minds were not only distracted from the class struggle that threatened the regime and the organic collective, they were also primed for mobilization through the party's organization of leisure time. In return for the regime's investment in health and physical education, its provision of leisure-time activities and facilities, plus the reorganization of 'professional' competitive sport, the utmost loyalty was demanded from all participants. The result was the politicization of Italian sport at every level.

Socialism 0   Catholicism 0

A latecomer to industrialization, Italy showed few signs of social and economic upward mobility until the early 1900s, when technological advances, leisure time and disposable income began to stimulate the development of Italian sport and recreation.[2] So apparent were the changes by 1910 that Ivanoe Bonomi, the Reformist Socialist and future Prime Minister (1921/2, 1944/5), reflected upon harder times of misery and famine when the revolutionaries commanded support in rural Lombardy and Emilia-Romagna:

> Peasants went about barefoot and watched with irritation the first penny-farthings that passed through the dusty streets. They were a great luxury those bikes, expensive and needing a lot of time to learn how to ride them. Between those rich middle class cyclists and the barefooted peasants there was an abyss that was thought to have been insurmountable. Today, it is no longer so. The peasants of the flat plain of Padania . . . are no longer barefoot. They dress like citizens, read newspapers, use trains and . . . horror! they buy bicycles. The 'machine' has been democratised . . . it has become the instrument of a new democracy . . . it has evened out the classes: everybody goes by bicycle today, rich and poor, the farmer that goes to supervise the peasant, the artisan and the lord, the man and the woman. There are no more sexes, there are no more classes. This is the triumph of the bicycle.[3]

As Bonomi suggested, it was those peasants who had seized the higher standard of living and taken an interest in sport that were the true radicals, not the young idealists.[4]

More than just an opportunity for recreation, the bicycle was a liberating means of transport that increased physical and social mobility. Although Bonomi's assessment was almost certainly romanticized, the bicycle's social revolutionary role was connected to the considerable lifestyle and status changes that came with ownership. Padania was also an extremely important area in the development of Italian sport, as it included the booming industrial triangle of Turin, Milan and Genoa, where the bourgeoisie established the factories that employed the masses who would become the spectators and participants of the future.

Had Italy followed the English model[5] where the modern form of association football was developed and evangelized by employers and priests in the working-class industrial centres, then competitive sport might have found a spiritual home within the labour movement and religious circles.[6] However, individual and historical circumstances lent no consistent pattern to the development of sport in other countries.

Socialism and Catholicism were the two principal players in those sporting and recreational opportunities that existed in pre-Fascist Italy, both having established societies to develop an 'alternative culture' that would contribute to their members' personal development and cement their loyalty. While their aims and interests differed, they both competed with existing private middle-class clubs and state-sponsored, liberal bourgeois institutions that viewed sport merely in terms of developing patriotism and military strength.

In fact, it was the inability to promote and develop sport for the masses by successive liberal government administrations that gave both the Left and the Church a perfect recruitment opportunity. Despite the apparent disinterest in sport, some attempts were made to introduce physical education into schools, the essayist, literary historian and politician Francesco de Sanctis[7] being one of the few to positively promote gymnastics and athletics. As one of the first to conceptualize the *Italiano nuovo*, his 1878 law made the teaching of gymnastics in all schools compulsory. However, despite support in the house, it failed to make a great impact on Italian youth due to the difficulty in training teachers, apathy within the profession, a lack of equipment and no effective national supervision.

An attempt to address many of the law's failings was made in 1909, but the continuing disbelief in the benefits of physical over mental exercise maintained the disparity between teachers of physical education and those of more traditional subjects. It did, nonetheless, compel all primary age children to undertake one half-hour of activity per day, with three hours per week for those in middle school, with all trainee teachers having to undertake an authoritative course of instruction before they could obtain their diploma. However, despite such governmental inability to integrate the masses through sport, Socialism and Catholicism both failed to fully exploit the opportunity.

The Catholic Church had a close relationship with sport from the mid-nineteenth century, with schools, colleges and oratories employing physical education to improve the discipline, morality and health of pupils. Thereafter, it formed its own societies to recruit and retain young people while educating them in the pathways of religion, through exercise and other means.[8] With many individualistic activities condemned as distractions from religious practice Father Giovanni Semeria,[9] one of the founders of the Catholic sports ideology, extolled the educational value of team games that contributed to the formation of group spirit. However, instead of aiding the spread of cycling and football, which were considered Anglo-Saxon, Protestant activities, the Church preferred its own brand of repetitive gymnastics.[10]

Up until 1903 there was no significant political aspect to Catholic sport societies, but this changed after 'Fortitudo' of Bologna and 'Voluntas' of Milan were refused entry into the Italian Gymnastic Federation due to their confessional and political nature. With the support of a few conservative Catholic deputies, elected following the Pope's tactical decision, in 1904, to relax the *non expedit* decree that outlawed Catholic participation in national politics, Giolitti retained control of parliament. Although he then pressured the gymnastic federation into rescinding its earlier decision, the government re-emphasized its opposition to these Catholic societies in 1906. In response, they formed the Federazione delle Associazioni Sportive Cattoliche (FASCI) – Catholic Sports Association – the initial sixteen societies growing to over 200 by 1910 with over 10,000 members.[11] Despite this, the FASCI was unable to establish a monopoly over Catholic sport and from 1918 onwards, many new societies sought recognition from the official sporting bodies.

Although weak, the FASCI still delayed the Fascist centralization of sport and physical education, for while the regime was endeavouring to reach a coexistence agreement with the Church (finalized by the 1929 Lateran Accords), it was unable to repress the Catholic associations brutally and decisively. Instead, it chose to slowly and indirectly erode them with the Ente Nazionale per l'Educazione Fisica (ENEF) – National Organization for Physical Education – in 1923, and the Milizia Volontaria Sicurezza Nazionale (MVSN) – National Voluntary Security Militia – in 1924, which had exclusive responsibility for providing physical education. Supported by the Fascist youth organization Balilla, these institutions undermined the FASCI until 1927, when the regime practically liquidated it with a measure that restricted its actions to mere oratory.[12] Rather than wait for the final blow, the Catholic associations disbanded voluntarily.

The Church's alienation of a natural source of support might have paved the way for socialist sport to make significant inroads into the rural and urban working class, but for different reasons it too proved equally unsuccessful. Some leisure-time activities for the working and peasant class masses did exist in the middle of the nineteenth century among the mutual aid societies of Piedmont and Liguria,[13] but despite the 1907 formation of the Socialist Sports Union, a branch of the Workers International, the leisure time of the masses remained unstructured and apolitical.

Socializing the masses was not helped by the delayed and limited nature of Italian industrialization. The earlier and more rapid process in Germany had resulted in a mass, relatively united working class that provided the market for an alternative socialist culture.[14] Yet, by 1900, it was still unrealistic to refer to Italy as an industrialized nation, which resulted in a correspondingly small and disparate working class. This barrier was further reinforced by ideological Marxist interpretations, as some viewed sport and leisure as opiates of the masses that inhibited the development of class-consciousness among the young, thereby distracting them from the class struggle. Others, such as Gramsci, argued that it was the combination of culture and the state, thus cohesion and coercion that maintained the current state of affairs.[15] Rather than explain historical change Gramsci interpreted why the status quo remained intact, redefining 'the state as force plus consent to hegemony armoured by coercion in which political society organized force and civil society provided consent'.[16] According to this model, the control and direction of culture, which included sport, football, leisure and recreation, had an integral role in maintaining the hegemony of the ruling class.

Slow to embrace sport, socialism even went so far as to recommend direct action against what it saw as a preserve of the rich. In one example the daily newspaper *Avanti!* of which Benito Mussolini was the director during his socialist period, openly invited readers to sabotage cycle races by littering the streets with nails.[17] In 1910, the third national congress of the Federazione Italiana Giovanile Socialista (FIGS) – Young Socialist Federation – also took an intransigent stance against sport, arguing that it debilitated and destroyed the human body and generally contributed to the degeneration of the species.[18]

Others appreciated the dangers of such a position, arguing that the FIGS was rejecting an opportunity to influence the development of sport. Ironically, some members of the industrial bourgeoisie also recognized this and began to form corporate societies, to which the socialists responded in the only manner they knew how – another polemic in *Avanti!* Irritated by the inability of the young revolutionaries to recognize the opportunities that sport and cycling in particular provided for social change, Bonomi questioned their physical and mental capacity for revolutionary activity:

> You cannot be young and call yourself a revolutionary if you don't have an irresistible urge to sacrifice yourself to others; to throw away your life in a beautiful gesture for something great and good . . . You don't die on the barricades because at the first gunshot, even the revolutionaries show a clean pair of heels . . . What remains? What remains is the struggle against the forces of nature; the great moral gymnastics of conquering an inaccessible peak, driving a frenetic motor race, or flying over the mountains or the sea.[19]

Yet, while Bonomi suggested the young revolutionaries were no longer worthy of the name, he also identified both a cause and a solution: 'Who does not know how to train his body to resist inferior self-centredness, does not truly know how to open his soul to the joy of courageous victory, he is not a revolutionary, he is only an incompetent and an idler.'[20] Although generally agreeing with Bonomi's idealistic vision, the socialist Giovanni Zibordi suggested he had overestimated sport's capacity for revolutionary change:

> The generation under 20, entering a world of relatively good conditions, finding the way paved by the older citizens, neglects our organization, associations and papers, giving itself excessively, uniquely and madly to sport . . . the bourgeoisie undoubtedly intends to spread through its newspapers, the contagious microbe of feverish sporting infatuation, an illness far from the healthy sport practised as one of the aspects of human existence and vigorous youth.[21]

Despite his reservations, Zibordi still recommended that socialism embrace and utilize sport as part of an alternative culture, rather than reject it as a bourgeois evil. In response, the Russian PSI member Angelica Balabanoff attacked the newspaper for wasting important space on such 'a secondary issue as sport',[22] arguing that races and prizes were a moral and spiritual danger for class solidarity as they represented the proletariat's struggle for the price of a loaf of bread in a capitalist society. 'The preoccupation of sport . . . is taking youngsters away from the organizations and buying sports newspapers is almost always a sure cause and effect of their non participation in the class struggle.'[23]

Perhaps in response to such debates, some examples of socialist sport began to appear. In 1912 a group of 'red cyclists' was formed to reclaim the fidelity of the masses through cycling trips and excursions. Wearing distinctive uniforms, they crossed the plain of Padania organizing rides and distributing pamphlets before moving onto the next town.[24] There was also an increasing working-class interest in trips to the countryside and the mountains, which led to the formation of the Unione Operai Escursionisti (UOEI) – Italian Workers Excursionists Union – in 1911. Campaigning against alcohol and promoting a programme of activities designed to improve workers' mental and physical health while encouraging an interest in the outdoors, the UOEI claimed 40 sections and over 10,000 members by 1914.[25]

Despite these pre-1914 initiatives, socialism only began to acknowledge the virtues of sport formally in the years following the Great War. In 1917 the Unione Libera Italiana del Calcio (ULIC) – Free Italian Football Union – was formed in Milan to defend the game for the less wealthy classes. Completely contravening the statutes of the Federazione Italiana Giuoco del Calcio (FIGC) – Italian Football Association – ULIC held liberty from the FIGC, no taxes or fines as its political and economic foundations, organizing as many tournaments as possible under these auspices. Despite its ideology, the organization never assumed a class-based character and by 1920 was seeking a rapprochement with the FIGC that was formally concluded in 1926.[26] Thereafter, ULIC became an autonomous section of the FIGC that was still responsible for the diffusion of the game, albeit under the Federation's control.[27] It was a classic example of the regime's preference of taking over and redirecting problematic organizations, rather than abolishing them.

Despite these initiatives, intellectual soul-searching over the role of sport continued to prevent the Left from reaching even an acceptable compromise solution. Incredibly, in 1923, with the Fascist government firmly in power, similar arguments were still raging in the socialist press. Fanning the flames and expanding the argument, Grospierre drew attention to the increasingly popular and even more dangerous practice of spectating that enabled the bosses to exploit the workforce further: 'the workers could not find long-term satisfaction . . . watching the movements of a ball under agile feet, when terminal misery awaits them at the exit. These youths need to realise that tomorrow will be the same for them as it was for their fathers . . . Long live sport, but also long live the struggle for bread.'[28]

Suspicions were also raised about narcissistic, personal, physical development that was thought to have negative implications for a fully socialized society, but Giancinto Serratti[29] suggested that socialism merely guard against these maladies rather than oppose, discredit or combat sport. Indicative of the changing political climate in Italy, his comments were made in *Sport e Proletariato*,[30] the weekly 'internationalist' publication of the Associazione Proletaria per l'Educazione Fisica (APEF) – the workers' association for physical education – that attempted to diffuse sport as an instrument of class struggle.[31]

Despite concurring that sport had become the principle means by which the dominant classes had secured the loyalty of young workers, Serrati believed that physical recreation could prove 'a valid instrument of organization, propaganda and class struggle', but it was 'necessary to know how to use it'.[32] By 1934 that knowledge was still lacking, Carlo Levi arguing that the mania for sport had depoliticized the masses who were 'reduced to interesting themselves, like babies, in the gratuitous bounce of a ball.'[33] In this way, the Fascist government had exerted political control through sport: 'The man who jumps, chases after a ball or swims like a frog does not have time to think of politics: therefore sport is his favourite. But left free he could become dangerous: it is necessary for him to be regulated, ordered . . . except to raise a special class of champions to put in the window for the glory of all.'[34]

Perhaps, as Serratti argued, it was important to differentiate between 'good' and 'bad' sports, which he loosely defined as those that did and did not train the individual for the benefit of the mass: 'To avoid every vice and corruption it is necessary to develop only those sports that give the individual more energy [and] do not isolate him from the collective . . . Like group gymnastics, rowing, football, which at the same time as developing the individual, attune singular with social actions and exercise the spirit of discipline.'[35] His summary, albeit unwittingly, sketched a blueprint for Fascist sport that was further embellished by another *Sport e Proletariato* contributor who espoused the domestic and international importance of sportsmen.[36] Rather than aid the proletarian collective, Fascist sports policy would develop athletes for the good of the national organizm.

Having already called for the formation of an Italian Workers Sport Federation to defend and emancipate the proletariat,[37] Serrati recommended reforming the UOEI into the Gruppo Socialista Amici dell'Arte – Socialist Group of Friends of the Arts – to extend its aims and make it 'the nucleus of a bigger association for the education of the working classes.'[38] However, by 1923 it was too late for Serrati, the magazine, or any organized socialist sport movement to combat Fascism. On 10 December 1923, following the publication of an article announcing the imminent formation of the Italian Workers Sport Federation, *Sport e Proletariato*'s printing offices, which also served *Lo Stato operaio* and *Sindacato rosso*, were destroyed by Fascist squads and its production suspended.

Italian socialism was too slow to embrace sport and the workers sport movement that was a truly international organization capable of developing health, solidarity and culture among working-class men and women. The 1924 Worker Olympics in Frankfurt emphasized this; the 150,000 spectators that came to watch competitors from over nineteen countries[39] reflecting how German and Belgian socialists had better appreciated the opportunity to mobilize the working class through sport. Restricted by limited industrialization, dogma and narrow minds, Italian socialism failed to harness and mould this potential hotbed of support.

Fascism, however, did appreciate sport's ability to create community and on securing power, embraced it as a medium through which its vision of society could be disseminated throughout the peninsula. This perhaps best explains why, unlike in England, *calcio*'s boom corresponded more with the Fascist epoch than the early years of Italian industrialization and the growth of the workers movement.[40]

Fascism 1   Rest of Italy 0 (The Fascist Attitude to Sport)

Lando Ferretti derided both the description of sport as a 'mania' and the old arguments that connected it with the decline of Italian thought. Contrary to European intellectuals that linked the decline of the ancient Greek and Roman empires to an increase in games and sporting activities over more cerebral pursuits,[41] he suggested that periods of artistic and intellectual decadence had never coincided with the greatest veneration of physical education. In fact, he argued that Greece reached its artistic and intellectual apogee during the fifth century, when the Olympic Games also showed the empire at its physical peak. Rather than one impacting negatively upon the other, Ferretti believed that intellectual, scientific and physical pursuits flourished and declined symbiotically. Consequently, it was intellectual decadence that had led to the development of games at the Roman Campo Marzio, where participants competed for money rather than in veneration of strength and for the benefit of society, civilization and the motherland.[42]

As Ferretti clarified, Fascist sport was not just about spectacular boxing matches that created huge takings and even bigger celebrities, it was also there to 'reflect, penetrate and elevate the masses. The mass is its sole objective, not the individual.'[43] Nonetheless, sporting champions were still important role models, embodying what could be achieved through intellectual and physical pursuits that began with the united, organic, psychophysical system of virile education, as conceived and implemented by the regime.

Others still believed that competitive and spectator sport had contributed to the degeneration of the nation. The huge success of Italian cycling might have created a massive fan base that encouraged *La Gazzetta* to launch the 'Giro d'Italia' race in 1909, but despite its democratic origins, cycling and superstar cyclists came increasingly under suspicion. As the journalist Vittorio Varale suggested in one of his regular contributions to *Lo Sport Fascista*, it was important that 'the events, or the "glories", of these and other champions be contained within just limits and that the mass of the young speak in more measured terms in keeping with the needs of the day'.[44] Giuseppe Ambrosini expressed similar concerns in the same sports monthly, noting how even idols like Alfredo Binda were causing concern: 'Binda is a great champion and worthy of the predecessors, but he is the purest expression of rationalism applied to sport, which is the absolute negation of his spiritual and moral content . . . From "girardenghismo"[45] we have fallen into "bindismo".'[46]

His remark demonstrated the regime's concern about the emergence of idols and superstars that were the unavoidable by-products of Italian successes in mass popular events. This was intensified by the emergence of idolized individuals from team sports, most notably the national game of *calcio*. If the centre forward who scored the goals that effectively won matches for a successful team became more important than the collective, this threatened to undermine the regime's organic, national ethic. Consequently, creating and controlling champions became one of the regime's primary contradictions.

As competitive events expanded, the demand for victory continued to raise individual profiles to the point where they were said to have begun rivalling the popularity of the Duce himself.[47] This concern contributed some fundamental principles to the Dopolavoro movement, most notably in the abolition of classification, ranking and victory prizes from sports practised by the masses.[48]

More threatening was sport's alleged contribution to societal decadence that was first identified following a number of European military failures that highlighted declining physical standards among army recruits.[49] The ensuing pseudoscientific obsession with this apparent degeneration of the species accused sport and its related 'vices' of competition, alcohol, gambling and spectating of worsening the situation, forcing further comparison with the Roman and Greek empires.

In France, Benedict Augustin Morel had concerned himself with the hereditary nature of degenerative ailments, diseases, disorders and how they corrupted the moral and physical make-up of individuals, families and society as a whole. Classifying this pattern of heredity and pathological change as *degenerescence* (degeneration), his treatise, which also considered the potential to regenerate society through programmes of spiritual and physical education, was more than just a negative assessment of society's ills.[50]

The Italian criminal anthropologist Cesare Lombroso introduced the concept of anthropometry to this type of anatomical study. By precisely measuring the dimensions and relations of parts of the body, he believed it was possible to identify and manage potential dangers to organic society. Viewing the body and conduct of the criminal as an 'atavistic' throwback to the evolutionary past, Lombroso suggested that it was possible to freeze evolution and isolate the inherited backwardness that plagued the state and nation.[51]

Although Fascism responded to the theory of degeneration to some extent, it conflicted with liberal opinion as to how the problem should be identified and overcome if the race was to be strengthened. Rather than some form of medical intervention, it was the 'new man' that would confront and overcome the sources of degeneration, rebuilding the nation in the process. Refuting the 'bread and circuses' theory, Ferretti argued that culture now had to be seen as both physical and spiritual; that being the psychophysiological. Whereas sport and culture had previously pursued their apparently mutually exclusive interests, Ferretti's new mantra was: 'fascist sport and fascist culture for fascist Italy'.[52]

Fascist Culture

Despite Ferretti's pronouncement, it is still difficult to establish what exactly Fascist culture was or consisted of, so heterogeneous were its influences. As Vito Zagarrio has suggested, 'culture' could have a number of alternative interpretations:

a) the degree to which cultural life was either autonomous of or dependent on the dictatorship.
b) the new form assumed by culture in a mass society, in which culture also comes to mean customs and collective behaviour.
c) the regime's cultural policy.
d) the creation of a cultural plan by the Fascist intelligentsia aimed at the development of a new ruling class.[53]

Even before the regime formed its first administration many intellectuals believed that liberal Italy had become a 'cultural colony', left to the mercy of dominant foreign traditions.[54] For this reason, Fascism had to develop its own national culture to mobilize society behind the movement and the party. However, as Victoria de Grazia has argued, despite its attempt to acquire 'a measure of cultural legitimacy' by adopting the intellectual elite's traditional disdain for the mass popular format and reinforcing the class divisions of 'high' and 'low' culture,[55] it could not permanently ignore its eclectic melting pot of inspiration.

The heterogeneous cultural influences of Futurism, the avant-garde and neo-classical *romanità* (romanness, that of being Roman) reflect Fascism's pragmatic streak. Partly explained by its lack of doctrinal direction, this mixture enabled the regime to include many useful thinkers and creators within society, who might otherwise have felt or wished to be excluded. As Günter Berghaus has explained:

> Mussolini was not like Hitler when it came to artistic matters. He had little interest in the arts and kept himself out of the aesthetic debates of the period . . . He only issued general orders and left it to his functionaries to implement them or translate them into concrete directives . . . The result was

the promotion of a rather vague conception of Fascist art that left artists considerable leeway in their choice of subject matter, style, composition, format etc.[56]

At the national level its practitioners and purveyors were a diverse mixture of personalities and party functionaries, while lecturers and teachers worked the localities. By deliberately monumentalizing traditional forms, teachers protected and reinforced their positions as the purveyors and interpreters of culture. As Zagarrio, Berghaus and Marla Stone have all suggested, rather than doctrine, it is better to speak of a general plan for the organization of consensus through culture in which relative autonomy was given in return for subservience to the regime.

However undefined, culture was undoubtedly one of the key areas through which the regime envisaged constructing a Fascist civilization that would reflect its sense of continuity and community of ideas and thought. Key to this was the consistent reference to Imperial Rome and the cult of *romanità*: 'For fascism, the discovery and restoration of Roman ruins was mainly "symbolic archeology", inspired by a mythical attraction to a "sacred centre" and a desire to come into contact with its "magical power".'[57] As Mussolini stated himself:

> Rome is our point of departure and our point of reference; it is our symbol and, if you like, our myth. We dream of a Roman Italy, an Italy that is wise, strong, disciplined and imperial. Much of the spirit of Ancient Rome is being born again in Fascism; the Lictorian fasces are Roman, our war machine is Roman, our pride and our courage are Roman too.[58]

Yet, this unquestionable commitment to spiritually and physically recreating the Roman Empire was also complemented by modernistic cultural policies. The most obvious example of this in action was the regime's approach to architecture, where neo-classical and modernist visions peaceably coexisted, such as the traditional Biblioteca Nazionale (National Library) and the modernist Giovanni Berta stadium. Both built in Florence by the local party, they demonstrated Mussolini's prevarication, inability or lack of desire to commit to one particular style, the contradictions of which will be considered in later chapters.

Sport soon became one of regime's metaphorical battlegrounds. Yet, despite accusations of physical degeneration and the lack of a governing body to supervise its development, the nation's performances in the 1908 and 1912 Olympic games were remarkable. Arguably deriving from De Sanctis's apparently ineffective attempt to introduce gymnastics and virile education into middle schools, his cocktail of spiritual and physical education became a key component of Fascist education that was symbolized by the *Libro e moschetto* – book and musket. As Ferretti observed, sport exercised the body, inflamed the spirit and stimulated discipline, all qualities that came to the fore in 1915 when Italy finally entered the Great War.

> When the long awaited news arrived in that late twilight of May, and the doors of the schools closed as everybody left for the war . . . we truly felt like knights of a great ideal. Sport had prepared us to confront each battle.
> Fossati, captain of the national football team; world rowing champion Sinigaglia, fell heroically in the front line. And in the universities, when peace was concluded, many who left on 24 May were missing . . . but, prepared in body and spirit by virile games, beyond and against the spirit and methods of school . . . they confronted and wanted to make the supreme sacrifice to create with blood, the beautiful and great Italy of today.[59]

As he explained for many years in a variety of different publications, war was the 'crucible that effected the metamorphosis of Italian identity, where the men of the old generation found the purification of spirit in the blood dedicated to the motherland'.[60]

Satisfaction with the army's wartime performance was not universal, others arguing that Italy's 'mutilated victory' was a result of the moral and political failings of the education system. When assessing the Italian military performance Ferretti carefully avoided the pitfalls, contradictions and dilemmas that lay in wait. Criticizing the armed forces was no manifesto for a party reliant on support from ex-servicemen's organizations, even if their efforts had often amounted to a display of considerable ineptitude. By administering praise through the medium of sport he avoided giving the old liberal regime any credibility, while outlining the fundamentals of Fascist sport policy in the process: individual physical and mental fitness for the benefit of the organic whole.

War without the Shooting

A burgeoning number of young Italian Futurist writers shared Fascism's faith in the merits of a physical culture that blended tradition and modernity in the restoration of gymnastics and an appreciation of the machine and speed. Although games such as football were less admired, their potential contribution to the creation of the *Italiano nuovo* was still recognized. As George Mosse has explained, they hoped this new Fascist man, who was disciplined and loved combat and confrontation, would 'proclaim Italy's glory through his personal drive and energy. Futurism took the concepts of manliness, energy and violence, and sought to tear them loose from the historical traditions in which conventional nationalist movements had anchored them.'[61]

Through this synthesis of virility, violence, combat and struggle, it was hoped the *Italiano nuovo* could spiritually and physically regenerate the nation, thereby completing the 'moral' unification that the Fascists accused the liberal state of failing to achieve. Besides inspiring the Fascist movement, the Great War was also a crucial event in the evolution of the 'new man', as it was 'precisely the experience of war that, according to Fascism, forged veterans capable of leading the new men of the future'.[62] As only those who had faced death could understand the meaning of sacrifice, it was entirely appropriate that Fascist society existed in a state of permanent war where battles, struggles and fights were applied to national issues varying from money and births to internal enemies and sport.

Fascism's ability to draw from complex and often contradictory ideological roots enabled it to employ Futurist ideas of renewal and rebirth that focused on the glory of sacrifice, rather than dwell on the military disasters of the past. Even the failed imperial exploits in Africa in the liberal era had positive aspects, as those who were killed/sacrificed were said to have shown their personal qualities in addition to those of the nation.[63] A huge percentage of Great War army conscripts came from sports clubs and societies that had lost 50 per cent of their members just prior to the Italian entry, after which full mobilization apparently accounted for the remainder.[64]

Recording individual acts of bravery and courage by sporting soldiers that usually culminated in their glorious death and posthumous decoration, was the type of nationalistic writing that became *Lo Sport Fascista*'s trademark. Inspired by the motto, 'the programme, the faith and the flag: Loyalty',[65] the monthly magazine's remit was to showcase Fascism's overhaul of Italian sport and influence contemporary and future society by permanently recording the regime's reawakening of its youth.[66]

Through the submissions of well-known journalists, national sporting figures and members of the political hierarchy, the magazine's sole obligation was to document the regime's development of Italian sport. As stated in the October 1929 editorial: 'We lay out our simple words . . . in homage to the cause of national rebirth. This is true liberty . . . this is healthy independent journalism.'[67] However, the PNF Secretary Augusto Turati's praise of the magazine, for being perfectly in tune with the Fascist spirit, hardly reinforced its claims of independence.[68]

Endorsing the regenerative powers of struggle and death, Fascism mythologized those amateur and paid sports stars killed in the Great War. This 'cult of commemoration', as Berezin has labelled it, reinforced the link between 'Italian political generations and ritually attacked all enemies of the Patria – liberals, bolsheviks and capitalists.'[69]

The cyclist Carlo Oriano, one of the first Giro d'Italia winners, was joined in death by weightlifters, athletes, climbers and mountaineers – who were indispensable during combat in the Alps – rowers, gymnasts and footballers, to name but a few. Among the many footballers were Dr Canfári, ex-player and president of the Associazione Italiana Arbitri (AIA) – Italian referees association; Dalmazzo, Croce, Corbelli and Colombo, all of Juventus; Virgilio Fossatti, captain of the national team and Milan's Internazionale who died at Montefalcone in 1916; and his national team colleague Attilio Trere, who was a mutilated survivor.[70]

According to *Lo Sport Fascista*, those who died in combat were 'heroes in the purest sense of the word; heroes whose memory and example will last long in the history of Italy; heroes that left reality to immortalise themselves in legend.'[71] In this way, the magazine reinforced the memory of those heroes in the minds of contemporary athletes and their fans: '"Always present!" was the password of sportsmen. Always present! When the homeland calls its sons to defend it against external and internal enemies . . . sportsmen always arrive at the double.'[72] Although not on the scale of the Great War, 1930s athletes were still expected to risk their lives on the battlefield when not dedicating them to the sports field. As Ferretti clarified prior to the 1936 Berlin Olympics, they were all role models and ambassadors for the regime, paying debts of respect to their fallen heroes:

> Like us, like all sportsmen, like all Italians, the athletes at Berlin remember and see the heroes; they feel them nearby, sharing the anxiety of the conquest until the joy of victory . . . this time, to be worthy of Mussolini's Italy, it is no longer enough to compete with all your strength; it is necessary to go further, to give more, to reach the finishing line exhausted.[73]

By the mid 1930s, enough soldiers had died during the imperial campaign in North Africa for the President of the FIGC's 7th Zone to establish the Coppa Emilia, a *calcio* tournament 'to honour the memory of footballers, gloriously fallen in the AOI' (Africa Orientale Italiana).[74] Comprising of eight teams, the trophy was awarded to the winning squad's section of the Associazione Famiglie Caduti – Association for the Families of the Fallen,[75] with prizes donated by the various regions awarded to all participating teams.[76] Yet, without diminishing the glory attached to those sportsmen martyred and wounded in the Great War, it was no longer enough merely to sacrifice oneself or to die in vain. Fascism now demanded victories.

Of course, renewal and regeneration did not require death per se, which was especially applicable to the sporting arena where the natural passage of time limited a champion's reign at the top. Having achieved supremacy, the athlete set the standard to which others aspired. Metaphorically, they were there to be shot at, which resulted in fierce competition and a continual turnover and improvement in top-level athletes in every sport. In his contemporary biography of Arpinati's career, the respected Fascist Marcello Gallian made just such an observation about a former long jumper: 'champion for one hour, hero for a minute; tomorrow he will return to his job: another will win the next Olympics and he will pass into the world of the unknown ... What can be more beautiful than that champion who returns to his job and will give to another a way of surpassing him.'[77]

Besides *Lo Sport Fascista*, nationalist and politicized sports writing came increasingly into vogue in general, as the regime sought to disseminate its message to the massive market of fans. In 1925, the Bolognese weekly *La Striglia Sportiva* headlined its first edition: 'Sportsmen, give ONE DOLLAR to the motherland.'[78] Encouraging fans to play their part in the 'battle for the Lira', the editorial's vision of sport in the nation's future was more akin to a political or party newspaper: 'For us, we do not see sport simply as a method of physical education or entertainment, but above all as a method for the improvement and harmonization of the body and morals to put oneself at the service of the motherland when and however it chooses to call.'[79]

Referring to the crisis of Italian sport that had corresponded with the nation's poor military performance during the First World War, the first editorial of Bologna's *La Voce Sportiva* established it as a weekly in which Italian athletes would be strongly defended and censured when necessary. Demanding physical and moral strength, the paper called for a spirit of sacrifice that would contribute to the 'good name of Italian sport, for its victory is each and everybody's'.[80] Furthermore, with the nation of primary importance, it astutely warned against the potential dangers of regionalism as local city-based clubs intensified their rivalries. 'Regionalism does not need to be, nor can it be, parochial and partisan: but only a source of spiritual emulation, a potent inspiration to greater things.'[81]

In 1929, with the regime fully aware of sport's potential market and impact, Arpinati's *Il Littoriale* took sports journalism beyond just nationalism and into the realms of political direction, by imploring its readers to support the Duce's nominations for national representatives (former parliamentary deputies). With the usual sporting activities cancelled for the 'elections', the editorial asked fans to demonstrate their love for the country by contributing to the organic mass and affirming 'national unity' at that Sunday's plebiscite.[82]

Yet there was more to Fascist sport than simply promoting the regime and preparing individuals for war, as the combination of physical and spiritual education with the synthesis of sport and culture was intended to create the 'new man' that Giovanni Gentile and others had been discussing for some time: 'In the process of its continual formation, our body is our own script, the same that is said of will, intelligence, sensibility . . . spiritualization; and in this sense the body is educable . . . the body is what we make it: and the more we spiritualise it the more we make it our own and revive it.'[83]

According to Gentile, the combination of exercise, sacrifice and spiritual control would make the morally and physically able youth generally capable of resistance and self-sacrifice, but particularly in times of war.[84] The mental and spiritual aspects of fitness had become as important as the physical, as the novelist, playwright and arts critic Massimo Bontempelli also noted: 'sport is something more than simply physical education. The spirit of sport represents in itself a complexity, a balance, a harmonious blend of different forces . . . The sporting spirit begins, first of all, where the competitive element and instinct, enters the field.'[85]

Contrasting with earlier class-based governments that stimulated competition among society, the Fascist regime wanted to arouse the energies of the individual and the collective, thereby reflecting the new interventionist role of the state.[86] As the journalist Ubaldo Grillo argued in *Il Littoriale*, maintaining or developing an interest in exercise and improving physical fitness among the entire adult population would benefit the race as a whole.

> The rebirth of our people coincides – and it could not be otherwise – with an exuberant flowering of every sporting manifestation. Sport, helped and encouraged, wisely imposed, of course, by the vigilant foresight of the Fascist Government, is winning over the strata of society most reluctant to the novelty and pace of life that characterise our times.[87]

The moral and physical education of this strata included self-sacrifice, struggle and obedience to human and divine laws that would theoretically see the emergence of a healthy man: the *Italiano nuovo*.[88] As Leandro Arpinati later clarified when president of the FIGC:

> Sport, in short, is understood not only just as athletics, as competition between champions, but as an indispensable physical education of the masses, an exercise that may do some good to the body and spirit . . . For the

physical improvement of the race, nothing is as useful as sport that teaches everybody an amount of discipline and moulds muscles with character.[89]

However, power came with uncertainty, and the new Fascist government was suddenly unsure of the most effective way to educate and spiritualize the nation. The former ease and confidence with which its theorists had outlined various roles for sport disappeared, as the party faced the dilemma of whether to abolish the old organizations and substitute them with new ones, or to use them and instil a new spiritual content under PNF supervision.[90]

The Battle for Bodies

Fascism rejected outright a return to the methods of democratic Italy that were incapable of serving the new order. As *La Gazzetta* argued, sport needed to be 'designed as an instrument for the Imperial education of the youngest Italians'.[91] Rather than abolish those societies that pre-dated Fascism, the regime chose the more pragmatic option of restructuring them and imposing its own sense of spirit and discipline while developing their technical and political aspects. As noted by Augusto Parboni, one of Fascist Italy's most prominent journalists, sport became a new method to penetrate and educate the masses physically and spiritually, thereby helping the regime insert itself firmly into the life of the nation until it became indispensable.[92]

To achieve this, Parboni identified four underlying principles beneath the Fascist intervention in physical education:

1) The fusion of the classical Greco-Roman concept of physical education with the medieval element of warlike preparation.
2) To solve the problem of propaganda with the creation of large stadia (Littoriale, PNF stadium, Milan Arena and the Mussolini stadium).
3) To penetrate the masses with the creation of numerous gymnasia and sports fields.
4) To no longer leave teaching in the hands of exponents of old style gymnastics, but to entrust it to the young who were strong and ready, not only physically.[93]

The most obvious area for the regime to begin this process was in the field of state education,[94] but there was so little substance to pre- and post-unification sport. Some pre-*Risorgimento* societies had existed but patriotism was more important than physical activity. Post-unification governments were no better, tolerating sport as little more than a means for Italy to defend itself. Muscles were honed to produce fit soldiers rather than athletes, George Mosse observing how the statutes of each sport society or federation were designed to make 'the young agile and strong, and thus more useful to themselves and to the homeland'.[95] Consequently, one of liberal Italy's legacies to the Fascist era was an impoverished sporting culture and infrastructure that caused the parliamentary deputy for Novara, Ezio Gray, to question what little was being done to maintain and improve the nation's position in the world.[96]

Unfortunately, many parents did not concur with the merits of physical exercise and failed to encourage their children to participate, often providing them with medical certificates to exonerate them from activity. Vittorio Costa, the schools gymnastics inspector for the Commune of Bologna noted Arpinati's recollection of schoolboy boredom with the old-style repetitive gymnastics that 'they all followed like automatons, and was certainly more adept at containing nascent forces than developing them.'[97] He was supported by Lando Ferretti who equally lamented how 'the Italian school had closed its doors to physical education'.[98]

A prolific public speaker, writer and journalist, Ferretti's career included spells as co-director of *La Gazzetta dello Sport*, from 1919 to 1924, and editor of *Lo Secolo* and *Lo Sport Fascista*. After participating in the March on Rome, he became a member of the Fascist Grand Council, a Member of Parliament, an officer in the Militia and head of Mussolini's press office from 1928 to 1931. In this last role he extended the regime's control over the press while becoming one of the principle synthesizers of sport and Fascist culture, reconciling them with politics in a manner that reflected the regime's ideals.[99] He was also the instigator of the first Fascist youth organization and President of the Comitato Olimpico Nazionale Italiano (CONI) – the Italian Olympic Committee[100] – from 1925 to 1928, where he appointed Arpinati to oversee the FIGC's restructure.[101] As *Lo Sport Fascista* proudly proclaimed, its editor not only appreciated sport's prominent force in the modern world in general, but also its particular resonance for the national politics of the new Fascist state.[102]

Arguing that Italy had been suffocated by German culture and philology, Ferretti questioned the achievements of the 1878 and 1909 laws, as exercise of the body was still deemed vain and all that was considered useful was 'to study, study and study to pass exams'.[103] The situation was apparently no better in the universities or society in general, where those participating in sporting activity were considered carefree time wasters. Scorn was also poured upon university professors, particularly those who had not fought in the war and were consequently unable to understand the Fascist revolution. Ferretti raged against the profession that: 'cursed sport

[and] the new youth bursting onto the battlefield of Italian life, through the most authoritative, most heard and consequently most responsible voice: that of Benedetto Croce.'[104]

Many intellectuals saw only a negative and contradictory relationship between sport and culture; the former blooming as the sun set on the latter. Giovanni Papini da Bulciano, the Futurist co-founder of the influential review *La Voce* who later joined the Catholic fold,[105] was another who believed Italy's former greatness had always been founded in the pre-eminence of spiritual things. For this reason he objected to modern heroes no longer being 'the great artists or even the conquerors . . . but the boxers . . . the "kings of the pedals" who have no other rivals in the favour of the millions'.[106] Yet, in his 1915 collection of essays entitled 'Maschilitá' (Masculinity), Papini argued that the 'new man' would be built on the somewhat contradictory foundations of discipline and spontaneity, both of which sport could develop. His ideas imparted serious influence on Fascist thought, with perhaps the most important being his organic theory that the combined majority of the population had an inseparable spiritual and physical power.[107]

Yet many of those who criticized the education system for woefully neglecting its responsibilities during the liberal era, were even less convinced of its ability to make a significant contribution to Fascist society. Giovanni Gentile envisaged a new Fascist intelligentsia emerging from a restructured, authoritarian and elitist education system.[108] Two of his close associates were Ernesto Codignola and Balbino Giuliano, who responded to the education system's apparent inability to select, educate and develop strong enough nationalist sentiments among a new Fascist elite, by forming a splinter section of the Fascio di Educazione Nazionale – national teachers association – soon after the conclusion of the war. They located the source of the problem in the expansion of high school and university education. Not only had this integrated middle-class students with the petty bourgeois and working-class masses, but it had also reduced the institutions to 'a machine for supplying diplomas and certificates to a horde of petty-bourgeois status seekers,' precisely the sector of society that Codignola believed was 'incapable of acquiring true culture'.[109]

Gentile became Mussolini's first minister of public instruction in 1923, at the apogee of the crisis of physical education in schools. His response was an immediate education act that Tracy Koon has described as 'the foundation upon which later ministers of education constructed the complex superstructure of school and party organizations aimed at socializing Italian youth'.[110] The law introduced more militarism and extreme nationalism into the curriculum, plus tougher selection for secondary schools. By further restricting access to education and university entry, it reinforced traditional class distinctions in response to the Right's fear that the 1859 Casati law had opened up higher education too much. As Lyttelton also suggests, Gentile's reform drew a distinct line between elite education and popular instruction: 'Free culture and the totalitarian State were not, for him, incompatible ... The reform of education was to encourage at the same time individual and national integration.'[111] Quite simply, it was the breeding ground for the citizen-soldier.

Despite Mussolini's endorsement of the act as crucial for the creation of a Fascist ruling class, one party member decried it as 'more reactionary than Fascist', while Futurists opposed its exclusivity, demanding that education be made more practical with a greater emphasis on industrial techniques and sport.[112] Gentile's reform also removed the responsibility for providing physical education from middle schools and gave it to the ENEF,[113] which Patrizia Ferrara describes as a complete failure.[114] Ending the state's role within the teaching of gymnastics, it forced many of the system's oldest and best teachers to retire while also failing to address the need for public gymnasia.

Despite its faults, the drive to establish physical education in schools resulted in over 150 teachers in Bologna receiving rudimentary athletics training at the new Littoriale sports complex. In a series of eight, two-hour lessons, they were given theoretical instruction in general sport and physical education, followed by practical coaching from recognized athletes. Aware that two hours of gymnastic activity per week could only have a limited effect, staff were taught simple daily exercises that pupils could carry out each morning and evening.

To assess teaching standards and ensure the physical education programme was reaching its intended goals, all pupils took a test at the end of the third year. Consisting of a military-type exercise, a game, long jump and a run, it catered for all abilities from the weakest to the strongest with pass rates set according to ability. At the end of the school year, both boys and girls came together to compete in a week-long athletics competition staged in the Littoriale. By 1928, Bologna boasted over 15,000 graduates.

Praise was not only given to those successful children, but also to their families and the sporting infrastructure in general. While individual excellence was an important propaganda weapon in the regime's armoury, no one person was bigger than the team, as *Lo Sport Fascista* noted: 'We certainly praise the little champions, but our minds need to rest above all on the mass of pupils, teachers, on the fathers and mothers of the family taken over by physical education, by sport and above all by athletics.'[115]

Despite the positive aspects of participating in competitive sport, some critics were still concerned about its negative side-effects.

Rumours circulated as to the moral and physical effect of sport upon the nation's youth, while female participation continued to receive little encouragement, partly due to Church protests but also in fear that it might lead to further calls for emancipation. As noted by Victoria de Grazia: 'Ultimately, childbirth was the best exercise, of course.'[116] Such doubts even extended to a minority of doctors who thought sport could impair the physical development of young people, while others were concerned that the devotion of extra time and energies to physical education might have a negative impact on students' general education. Despite such claims, there was already a firm belief in the benefits of sport and recreation for the population, so long as potentially harmful side-effects were monitored. Thus, to supplement the attention given to athletes' mental health, their physical well-being during events within the Littoriale stadium was monitored by a team of doctors, who also pooled their knowledge and skills to develop a new specialization in sport science.[117]

The Institute for Sports Medicine was another of Arpinati's initiatives. Based at the Littoriale, the physicians conducted research varying from anthropometrics and eugenics, to more mainstream enquiries into biomechanics, biometrics and tests on the effects of nutrition, tonics, stimulants and hormones.[118] While by modern standards it may have constituted a crude and invasive format, it was an innovative centre of research that, incidentally, had the full 'cooperation of Italian and German-financed pharmaceutical firms like Bayer'.[119] Designed specifically to benefit the development of Italian athletes with injury prevention and cure, the Institute's anthropometric research also contributed to the advancement of general medical science. As *Il Littoriale* made clear: 'the most important duty of the medic [is] not that of creating champions and specialists, but it is raising the average physical development for the benefit of individuals, but better still to the advantage of the collective.'[120] It was something that Arpinati also recognized, when head of CONI: 'I repeat, it is necessary to distinguish the sporting aspect from that of the collective interests for the improvement of the race. I need champions because the champion is the banner of sport, but I am also interested in sport contributing to, indeed it might be the best factor, the improvement of the race.'[121]

The drive to improve the nation's health through sports medicine extended throughout the peninsula. This was illustrated by the 1929 conference to defend the concept of sport and discuss injury prevention, convened by Arpinati at the Casa del Fascio in Bologna, which attracted participants from as far as Milan and Bari. Above all, this first conference was intended to pool the collective wisdom and enthusiasm of the medical profession from all over Italy. It was essentially a national networking opportunity that, according to *Il Resto del Carlino*, officially encouraged doctors who 'had been almost alienated from the sports field, to enter through the main gates, with all the weight of [their] authority and specific knowledge'.[122] As Arpinati expressed in his opening address: 'The impulse given by the Fascist Regime to the development of sport is the most wonderful thing, but it could also be dangerous if the doctors do not tell us where the limits of progress end and those of harm begin.'[123] Key speaker Professor Giovanni Pini similarly argued that medicine could no longer afford to isolate itself from the physical and moral athletic development of the coming generations, if Italian sport was to aid the physical regeneration of society.[124]

The type of medical research carried out in Bologna also ensured that the health of both amateur and elite athletes came firmly under the control of the regime. What had formerly been considered an essentially private issue, had now become public and a state responsibility. As David Horn states in his study of the social body that was Fascist society, such interventionist practices 'redrew the boundaries between the public and the private that had characterized the liberal problematic. In the name of social defense and the promotion of the population, previously private behaviors were made targets of a permanent governmental management.'[125]

The needs of collective society were further enhanced by the opening of a sports training institute for men in Rome, in 1928, which eventually gained university status in 1939. Students were selected from party members who met strict selection criteria and had passed aptitude tests, after which they undertook courses on mysticism and Fascist legislation as part of their three years of teacher training. Boarding at the institute, students lived in six vast dormitories and benefited from a library, baths, barbers, plus medical and training facilities. Completely immersing the students in this world of Fascist education was designed to create sports teachers and 'new men' who would set the correct examples, encourage and educate society's youth that, according to *Lo Sport Fascista*, would otherwise withdraw from sport if continually ignored:

> Abandoned to themselves, or worse still, badly guided, these youngsters waste precious energies in efforts unsuited to their physical means that ruins their physique. We need to teach them technique, to control their exertions in order to succeed and get the maximum benefit from the minimum effort. And here CONI includes in its utilization programme for the stadium [*Stadio Nazionale*] theoretical-practical courses for instructors.[126]

Physical exercise and sport also strengthened the regime's complementary campaigns against alcoholism, tuberculosis, malaria and infant mortality,[127] which contributed to its pronatalist drive to breed fitter and more politically malleable future generations. While there was initially a genuine belief that pronatalism could regenerate Italian society, it was also considered important not to ignore the existing elements, to make the best of the liberal era's bad job. However, as pronatalism proved increasingly fruitless, the benefits of improving the health of the existing population assumed an increasing significance.

This was further augmented by the regime's organic view of society as the sum of its individual parts, the needs of the former being prioritized over those of the latter, which resulted in it being diagnosed as either healthy or diseased, normal or pathological.[128] According to Horn, this categorization of society as a social body which, 'like physiological bodies, could be cured, defended, and made objects of an ongoing prophylaxis,' was part of what Mussolini and others in interwar Italy described as 'medical' art.[129] Social and medical sciences now had the responsibility for diagnosing, preventing and curing society's ills.

A break from the liberal prioritization of the individual over that of the collective, it also made any personal, physical or behavioural 'defects' a potential threat to the generic, social body. Thus, the reduction of the individual to one constituent part of the entire social organizm had profound implications for personal freedoms and liberties. Alfredo Rocco, one of the founders of the Italian nationalist movement and justice minister from 1925 to 1932, similarly interpreted the new role of the Fascist state as one in which social and national interests were pursued over those of the person. Yet, individuals were still subjects as opposed to merely objects and therefore able to impact upon the social body, which caused Rocco to argue that state intervention in the health and welfare of the population was necessary to protect and develop the social body as a whole.[130]

While the early years of Fascist rule were characterized by repression, as the regime fought to establish and secure its position, by the mid to late 1920s preventative work was more common as part of the 'normalization' campaign.[131] From this point onwards the regime became less interested in penalizing crime, preferring instead to identify, anticipate, contain and prevent risks to the social body. In short, to protect society, the state awarded itself the right to take preventative action in areas that had previously been considered the private responsibility of the individual.

One example was the introduction of social insurance, which was arguably intended to protect society from its individual component parts. The 1927 *Carta del Lavoro* removed the individual's previously understood right to work, redefining it as a task that the state would assign. Welfare provision also changed from providing for individual needs to addressing those of society as a whole, a practice that Umberto Gabbi termed 'political medicine'.[132] While preventing social disease, this new attitude towards protecting the organic being extended to improving the physical and hygienic condition of the future generations. Despite the state's new invasive powers, personal responsibility for health and welfare was also increased, as illness or lack of fitness would prevent the individual from making a full contribution to the social body, be that quantified in terms of work, productivity or fertility. Personal welfare had become a social duty. This prioritization of the organic collective was often portrayed in the successes of the Italian football teams, which provided a perfect allegory in which individuals were depersonalized and lost within the identity of the collective.

On 26 May 1927, Mussolini delivered his Ascension Day address[133] in which he assessed the physical health of the population and explained how it would be regenerated. Contrasting sharply with the laissez-faire 'suicidal theory' of pre-war liberal governments, he stated that: 'in a well-ordered State, taking care of the health of the people was of primary importance.' As 'the clinician', he promised not to 'neglect the symptoms'.[134] His remarks were indicative of a new paternalism in which Fascism would take the necessary hygienic measures to protect the national stock. Horn has also suggested that the demographic campaign was in fact a reaction to a culturally assembled problem: 'a specifically *modern* construction of the demographic and medical needs of the biological population that called into question the relations between the individual, the social, and the political.'[135] Through the demographic campaign in all its guises, the regime intended to revolutionize social relations between the individual and the state.

Certainly, Mussolini held both genuine and imaginary concerns about the national stock, particularly following the substantial losses during the Great War and 600,000 deaths from the flu epidemic of 1918.[136] There was good reason to improve the health of those remaining citizens that had an integral role in nation's future, but unlike the northern European and Nazi eugenics policies that were aimed at racial purification, it was quantity and quality rather than racial purity that preoccupied the regime. Differing from Nazism's racial fundamentals, Italian Fascism preferred the concept of national stock, which was reflected in its population policy up until the introduction of the racial laws in 1938. In fact, Morel's theory of mixing the genetic gene pool to regenerate the race, was arguably a strong source of Fascist inspiration. As the liberal, social theorist Vilfredo Pareto had suggested, a biological free-for-all could invigorate both the race and the political elites.[137] The 1934 World Champion football team that possessed no less than five players who were *oriundi* or first-generation Italians from South America, again provided interesting supporting evidence.

The declining birthrate was a symptom of disease that Fascist doctors, social engineers and teachers were all charged with curing, even if there were considerable concerns about racial fitness and population decline throughout Europe at the time, most notably in France and Britain. As Morel argued, the principal causes were modernization, industrialization and urbanization, which caused people to move into expanding urban centres where disease, unemployment and crime were rife. Consequently, Fascism was forced to look beyond pronatalism to regenerate society. If a positive birth rate could attend to the numerical problems, physical education, sport and urban regeneration could strengthen its existing members. Besides improving the physical and moral condition of society, they also provided the regime with tailor-made opportunities to control or interfere in a major part of the nation's private life.

Although the successful examples of sports development in Bologna and at Farnesina contributed to the expansion of physical education in Italian schools, there were still considerable gaps in the albeit limited provision for children. It was hoped that youth groups and the ENEF would identify and make up this deficit, but the new body lacked the funds and facilities. On 3 April 1926, the growing number of groups were united and granted legal status under the auspices of the ONB. Its days clearly numbered, the ENEF was finally suppressed on 18 October 1928, as Balilla took complete responsibility for the physical education of under eighteens.

Harnessing Hearts and Minds

Much to Starace's chagrin, the ONB was more dependent upon the state than the party. Enthusiastically led by Renato Ricci who cared little for traditional hierarchies,[138] he tried to prevent national bodies outside of the ONB from using its sporting facilities. With forty-five *Case di Balilla* built by 1933 and many more in progress, in addition to the construction of the Foro Mussolini (Italico), Ricci possessed a strong argument had Mussolini wanted to reproach his deliberate isolation of the ONB from the main body of the party. Either way, the Duce was unable to permit the inevitable conflict that arose between schools, CONI and the various sports federations.

Ricci also opposed the ideology of *campionismo* (the primary importance of winning) among those under the age of 18, fearing the moral and physical damage the child might incur. However, the 1930s saw a shift in the regime's thinking away from merely integrating the classes and mobilizing the masses through the ONB. Fascism now demanded champions whose achievements and victories would earn it cultural capital.

Prior to this the ONB had been separated into Balilla (8–14 years), which focused on general physical activity, and Avanguardie (15–18), which concentrated on sports activities. Although both were established for recreational-hygienic and physiological purposes that reflected Ricci's coeducational programme for the development of Italian youth,[139] they also possessed a distinctly militaristic flavour. Between the ages of 18 and 21, young men joined the Fasci Giovanili di Combattimento (FFGGCC) – the premier youth group – where they could participate in the selection process to join the ranks of the PNF and the militia. The Balilla, Avanguardie and Fasci Giovanili became the three essential steps by which an individual could reach the threshold of the party, although membership was still a reward that individuals had to earn, rather than a natural right of passage.[140]

In 1928, the *Carta dello Sport*[141] added a competitive element to sport and gave the ONB responsibility for organizing physical education for all children aged 6 to 18. Adolescents over the age of 14 could enrol directly into CONI organizations, but this was subject to their prior membership of the ONB.[142] Balilla recruitment was carried out through schools, with membership reaching 5.5 million by 1936, of which over 3.7 million were actively participating in physical exercise. When the Gioventú Italiana del Littorio (GIL) replaced the ONB in 1937 and expanded its age group from 6 to 21, its membership increased to 7.5 million overnight.[143] By forming the ONB and taking control of young people's sporting activities, one of Fascism's three initial sporting objectives was achieved.

Playing Political Games

Having seized the means of moulding the next generation, the regime turned its attention to adult society, which was less malleable but equally important to its immediate survival. While it was unrealistic to attempt to regenerate the entire adult population, the regime did try to make the best of what it had. Even if adult bodies were beyond redemption, their minds certainly were not. Giovanni Gentile was once again called upon to establish a framework to ensure their support and in 1924 he formed the Istituto Fascista di Cultura (IFC) – National Fascist Institute of Culture – to establish some common aims between traditional academic culture and the activism of the new Fascist intelligentsia.

Reformed in 1929 by Alessandro Pavolini, the IFC moved to Florence where he was *podestà* (mayor). Although there were no dramatic changes in its aims, the body's work was redirected towards the masses, as demonstrated by Article 2 of its new constitution, which defined its role as boosting and diffusing culture 'among every social stratum, with particular regard to the middle and popular classes'.[144] The IFC established study centres, conferences, courses, libraries and exhibitions, in addition to promoting almost any other cultural activity, but as Victoria de Grazia has observed, the majority of lower social classes were 'incapable of "directly assimilating doctrine"'.[145] This forced Fascism to attack its two remaining goals of gaining control over recreational sport associations for industrial workers, plus sports societies affiliated to national sports federations.

In 1925, following poor international results, CONI was charged with producing a sporting elite worthy of representing the regime in international competition, while another commission of experts was assembled to consider how Fascism could best diffuse the practice of physical education in Italy.[146] The solution to both problems was the expansion of sport among the masses. The various sports federations were compelled to join CONI, while Lando Ferretti's appointment as CONI chairman symbolized the beginning of its complete loss of autonomy. By the following year it was a virtual arm of the party that could appoint executives to the various federations and had imposed the *fasces* on the badges of all members. Thereafter, as *La Nazione* commented, CONI oversaw the 'discipline and co-ordination of the various sporting activities from the political and benevolent point of view'.[147]

Although the Olympic Committee's achievements were assessed by the performance of Italian teams in international competition, it was also expected to secure a more prominent Italian presence in the various European governing bodies that tended to be dominated by the French. With over fourteen of the thirty international sporting bodies based in France, Italian sport had something of an inferiority complex. Only Alberto Bonacossa, head of the International Federation of Motorcycle Clubs, was in a position of influence, although even his office was based in England. Augusto Turati's appointment to the International Olympic Committee, in 1930, was the type of international presence that Guido Beer, Secretary of the Council of Ministers, had earlier hoped would help bend the allegedly corrupt system in Italy's favour:

> It is necessary to send influential people abroad . . . to substitute them for people absolutely unknown outside of Italy. Too often we believe we have been victims of organized juries, when instead, we have almost always been victims of our own meagre moral and material preparation. It is necessary to intervene at the congresses, to know the men that compose the international

bodies, to have our representatives in all the bodies of the big competitions, because it is too evident that when results are even, the judges always side with the colours of their own nation.[148]

A national sports office maintained links between CONI and the party, while provincial party secretaries ensured that the *Enti Sportivi Provinciali Fascisti* (ESPF) – local sports organizations – were equally well coordinated. Their role was to oversee provincial sport and take direct control, when necessary, of those activities that were considered important but lacked the necessary financial and material resources to develop. With this brief, the work of the ESPF was divided into four main areas: politics, propaganda, organization and finance.[149]

Politically, they were responsible for creating, fusing and dissolving sports clubs. Aspiring societies needed to demonstrate how their activities conformed to the new Fascist legislation, that being their contribution to the development of the new national spirit. The ESPF helped to develop this spirit by encouraging municipalities to establish sports facilities and societies, especially in the south where poverty continued to impair their development. Popular and healthy sports that had been neglected in the past were generally aided, while existing events, such as the Mille Miglia car rally, were also reorganized. As Parboni argued, wherever sports events took on a popular, local character, they would receive the help and collaboration of the party to improve them.[150]

Despite his claim, the ESPF failed as organs of propaganda and were dissolved in 1930, their responsibilities being placed directly in the hands of the party's provincial federal secretaries. As the ultimate, provincial sporting and political authorities, they were theoretically free to bypass unnecessary bureaucracy and better serve the development of sport.[151] Of course, the reality was a further centralization of sport in the regions.

In a circular informing the various secretaries of the changes, Turati emphasized two principal areas in which they needed to concentrate their work: financing the poorest, most popular and most useful sporting activities, plus the political control of the directors of societies and agencies active in propaganda.[152] As Carlo Levi later lamented, the control and future of Italian sport had been brought firmly under the auspices of the party: 'Sport is no longer considered a free activity but a political interest, its value moved away from the sporting human being to the mechanical result; considered a value in itself. Inside a particular sport a hierarchy develops, an association of governors and servants: sport takes on the moral nature that characterises the regime.'[153]

Prior to their dissolution, the ESPFs propaganda work was supported by the Dopolavoro, which the regime hoped would structure the common man's leisure time and recreation. Although separate to CONI, the OND still shared a common interest in developing sport for the masses. By encouraging corporate paternalism and the establishment of company sports and social clubs, it was hoped that workers could be tempted away from rival socialist and Catholic organizations. In many respects, the OND embodied the socialist fear of organized sport and leisure as a distraction from the class struggle. Yet, somewhat ironically, its structure resembled the earlier ideas of left-wing thinkers who proposed the socialization and politicization of the working class through just such an organization. It only further underlined the Socialist Party's missed opportunity.

Although there was little debate about the exact role of the OND prior to the 1928 *Carta dello Sport*, the new legislation gave it a firm direction that eliminated the conflicting ideas around physical education and competitive sport that had impeded its work. Physical education was now directed towards making the mass of young people healthy while educating the social body to strengthen itself. Sport, on the other hand, was for athletes contesting primacy, the struggle for life among men who had been blessed with the best physiques, will and ability to sacrifice themselves to training. These distinctions defined the respective roles of CONI and the OND; the former concentrating solely on competitive sport, with the latter on sport, among other activities, as a mass popular leisure-time activity.

As Ferretti further clarified: the concept 'that inspires the sporting activity of the Dopolavoro is not that of creating champions, but of offering the masses physically and morally healthy recreation after long hours of work'.[154] Contemporaries were soon able to observe the ONB and OND spreading and diffusing the passion for sport on a mass basis. One contributor to CONI's 1930 annual publication claimed this was uniting and reawakening the national spirit to produce athletes who would truly represent the entire nation while showing the world its future.[155] Realistically, champions were unlikely to emerge from the OND because, in general, the masses had not been blessed with the skills and talents of top sportsmen, but this in itself was deemed neither a problem nor a reason not to promote sport for all among society. As noted in a memorandum from the Prime Minister's secretary, it was necessary to distinguish between physical education and Olympism: 'Physical education lifts the masses, it creates champions from which Olympic super-athletes will be selected . . . The sporting strength of a nation is given especially by the mass of good athletes, not by the number of Olympic victories.'[156]

The lottery of life had forced the masses to work for a living and restricted their participation at the top level to that of spectators.

However, this in itself attained a greater significance in the eyes of the regime that hoped spectating might distract them from increasing social, political and economic problems. Despite the masses' sporting limitations, the OND nonetheless tried to instil personal pride by helping individuals explore their own abilities in a given field, thereby confirming the validity of their participation.[157] According to Fantani, the Dopolavoro also had equally important national benefits, as leisure-time sport and recreation enabled the individual to rest physically and mentally, thereby helping them attain their maximum productivity in the workplace.[158] As *La Nazione* pointed out, the OND was one organ in the body of institutions designed to promote a love of sport among society that would help improve the nation's physical condition.[159]

Once workers had been recruited into the OND it was hoped, in contrast to the IFC, that it would impart simple and accessible doctrinal information supplemented by general ideas of Fascist culture, which often contained a dominant nationalist theme with negative images of liberal democracies abroad. While nationalist ideas were both easy to convey and comprehend, the OND was not intended to develop a strong political consciousness. In fact, it kept traditional ideas of political education to a minimum, preferring a 'moral education' or 'elevation'.[160] In fact, it strictly avoided monopolizing leisure time, with many clubs, cafés, meeting places and organizations continuing to exist outside of its aegis. Nonetheless, it unquestionably enabled the regime to take more control over the free time of workers and students, while establishing a Fascist hierarchical organization among sporting and recreational associations. Echoing Gramsci, Levi saw sport as a double-edged sword for the government to wield: 'a release on one hand and a method of control on the other.'[161]

Companies within the industrial triangle were slow to appreciate the potential benefits of establishing OND groups and the initiative was soon taken over by the Fascist trade unions. Membership began to increase following the introduction of the eight-hour day in the industrial sector and in 1927–8 it actively began recruiting within the countryside and among emigrant communities abroad, although its strength was among the growing urban population. Reflecting upon the Dopolavoro's achievements in Florence ten years after the revolution, the local sports weekly *Lo Stadio* hailed it as a categorical success for the physical development of local workers, among whom it had apparently established 'a fervour, absolutely without precedent, in favour of every type of sport'.[162]

Certainly, the restructured system gave many Italian citizens the opportunity to practise some form of physical activity from childhood into adulthood, if they wished, but the failure to achieve this equally throughout Italy contradicted those who suggested that the OND had helped develop an organic sense of nation. In reality, not only had it failed to mask society's inequalities, it had also reinforced and even highlighted class differences in some cases. Moreover, it was the working and lower middle classes that took most advantage of the facilities and opportunities on offer, as the bourgeois, landed and professional members of society continued to practise elitist sports such as hunting, tennis and golf.

With Mussolini portrayed as the number one sportsman in the press to stress the importance of moral and physical personal development,[163] ONB and OND membership rose to over seven million within five years.[164] Fascism had seized the initiative and moulded sport into a modern, mass phenomenon, the regime having apparently realized that sport could invigorate physical energies and stimulate economic productivity, while improving the morality and spirituality of the Italian people.[165]

Besides invigorating society, sport also offered the regime an opportunity to interfere in the social politics of the nation, through science, art, medicine and hygiene. The social function of the Fascist state was to invest in all areas of the individual's life – because individuals were considered a part of the state – supervising and protecting them from conception into adulthood, according to its organic vision. To achieve this, Fascism entered all agencies involved in physical education, which included the Gruppo Universitario Fascista (GUF) – Fascist University Group – ONB, OND, sports federations, schools and CONI. This commitment ranged from training teachers and building stadia, to educating the young and old in military discipline and the joy of physical exercise, which, it was thought would help them confront their responsibilities.[166]

A long and costly commitment, Ferretti already recognized the fruits of the interaction between the various organizations connected with physical education, in 1935: 'From the formation of the *giovanili*, universities, sporting societies to the Dopolavoro, the Party has forged, from technique and physical exercise, a force of virile Italians that had been protected and wrapped in a passive ideal for too long.'[167] This virile generation was now expected to promote the regime's achievements with 'champions that will give prestige to the nation in international competition'.[168] Thus, if the regime was to gain the maximum benefit while meeting Mussolini's demand that sport become firmly identified with Fascism, it had no choice but to give it the utmost attention. No longer a frivolous pastime, it had become a symbol of the nation's new-found fortune, spirit and rising status.[169] More than simply athletic endeavour, sporting trials of strength and technique against other competitors had become a true 'battle of the races'[170] that Fascist Italy needed to win on every occasion.

As Ferretti explained to the young generation charged with defending and promoting the regime's honour in muscle, energy, spirit and thought: 'sport for us is an instrument of propaganda and authority of the nation'.[171] His message was regularly repeated throughout Italy, as in an article on Florentine football published in the commune's monthly magazine in 1934: 'You youngsters have been given the honour of representing Mussolini's Italy in the sporting arena. In this name and with this task is your dignity. Sport demands seriousness, sacrifice, responsibility, exemplary physical and moral conduct.'[172]

As representatives of Mussolini's Italy, the political loyalty of all sportsmen had to be beyond question, but in 1926 this did not appear to be the case. While the regime's political opponents were excluded from the various sports federations and thus denied the opportunity to compete, there was still concern that not all of those sportsmen who claimed to be Fascist actually were. As the journalist Adolfo Cotronei argued in *La Gazzetta*, there were still 'cheats, greedy and shady characters' within sport, from which the regime and the nation needed to free themselves. Only once these were 'liquidated' could Fascism hope to form a secure national force, 'a militia armed only with fortified hearts'.[173]

Improved results at the 1932 Los Angeles Olympics emphasized the impact of the regime's contribution to sport and the international importance it placed on victory and success, however they were defined. These achievements also drew considerable comment from the foreign press that *La Gazzetta*, in particular, was always keen to publicize domestically. One such example was a long article on the development of Italian sport and the recent successes of Italian athletes that was apparently published in the Hungarian *Magyar Hirlop* in 1934: 'It is marvellous to realise . . . the extraordinary development of Italian sport. The young are stimulated by the example of the leaders who willingly restrict themselves to a severe mode of life, just to get what is the ambition of every Italian today: the acclaim of the Duce.'[174]

In his 1934 essay, Carlo Levi gave perhaps one of the most eloquent descriptions of the manner and extent to which sport had been consumed by the needs of the regime. Levi had no ideological objection to the masses' passion for sport and even saw it as a potentially dynamic force, if it were left alone. However, aware of the stealthy methods by which the government had asserted its will over the people's passion, he attacked its Fascist format:

The action of the government, even indirectly, first causes this excessive passion for sport, it then returns to intervene, this time directly, by turning it to its needs and reducing it to a vain and non dangerous hero-worship. That is, it grants the people enough entertainment to distract them from less innocent concerns, but it prevents them from developing an autonomous, uncontrolled sporting activity. At the same time it is used as a controlled activity for the purposes of the government, police, propaganda and prestige.[175]

As the relationship between Fascism and sport intensified, so the various teams were increasingly seen more as representatives of the regime than the nation. 'When Italy is playing, the new, sporting Italians are always members of the Fascist squads, even in foreign fields.'[176] Gallian's statement in 1928, was also an early indication of the increasing militarization of the sporting lexicon that was employed among the highest echelons of the PNF, such as Party Secretary Augusto Turati:

> In some years, when the legions of young that will have been able to train in all of our cities and regions have reached physical maturity, Italy will be able to count on a mass of wisely prepared athletes that, in international competitions, will hoist the tricolour up the flagstaff of the Olympic Stadium; and it will have an army of men in which desire and courage will equal military force and virtue.[177]

The net effect was twofold. Diplomatically, representative teams faced increasing anti-Fascist activity when competing abroad, especially as Italian foreign relations began to deteriorate. On the home front, victory became increasingly important for the regime, as noted by one *Lo Sport Fascista* contributor who described how the young carried 'in their hearts, the hopes and fears of everybody, the support and applause of the government that knows how to domestically organize and incite'.[178]

Yet, as Arnd Kruger has pointed out, if we are justifiably to refer to the domestic and diplomatic image of elite sport as a form of national representation, it is necessary to look for concrete events that demonstrate how 'there was not only talk about national representation through sports, but also action'.[179] In Italy, there was both talk and action as sport quickly came to represent the regime and the nation in a variety of ways. Most visible were the facilities that leaders throughout the peninsula were encouraged to build, in order to provide the infrastructure that was gravely lacking. Almost overnight, stadia, swimming pools and gymnasia rose to form exciting new features of urban and rural life that provided organizations such as the ONB and OND with the necessary means to fulfil their roles. They were the weapons with which Mussolini was fighting the maladies of urbanization.[180]

However, the greatest and arguably most enduring impact of the new stadia was their symbolic representation of the drive to regenerate society through exercise. As the Under-secretary of State, Giacomo Sguardo, told all prefects in 1927, they would comply with 'the government's constant effort to make the new Italian youth, through daily exercise, physically and morally prepared to take on the jobs that await them'.[181] The following year, in a circular to leading sporting figures within government and society, Turati further explained how such sports grounds had to contain everything required for all activities 'arranged by youth groups, schools, Dopolavoro, Balilla, avanguardisti, etc thus favouring the spread of sport among the youngest part of the nation'.[182]

As the regime's show piece stadia, the Littoriale and the Giovanni Berta in Florence were also intended to inspire Italian society that had been promised an 'easy and inexpensive to build' sports ground in every commune.[183] Their scale was such that they made an immediate impact upon local identities and while many were designed to accommodate a variety of events, their primary function was as venues for the increasingly popular mass spectator sport of *calcio*. These stadia gained even greater national prominence in 1929, when teams from the major Italian cities began competing in a single national league for the first time. The organizational change was part of a continuing process following the regime's intervention and subsequent takeover of *calcio* in 1926, which was specifically designed to bring order to the game, improve the national team, mobilize the masses and develop a sense of Italian identity throughout the peninsula.

As will be seen, the Fascist takeover of *calcio* was generally considered to have been successful, improving standards at all levels while contributing to the development of a culture of physical fitness among the population. In fact, it was so successful that it began to undermine its contribution to the development of national identity, by intensifying the local rivalries that were a by-product of city based clubs competing in the national league. It was one of the many contradictions exposed by *calcio* that Fascism failed to adequately resolve. Although this indicated the regime's problems when trying to exploit football to create a sense of national identity, its success should not be underestimated either; as following the restructuring of the game, *calcio* took the regime to the pinnacle of international sporting achievement.

–3–

Fascist Football Foundations

Sport is that fatal art that gave the ultimate strike against the old conservative and backward mentality: if pure fascism exists today, it has its triumph in the gymnasia and the stadia. M. Gallian, *Arpinati politico e uomo di sport*

By the mid-1920s football had become a national institution to which the regime needed to dedicate serious attention. Despite its original disinterest in competitive sport, the sheer weight of numbers involved in *calcio*, either as players, spectators, or merely followers of the expanding sport-specific press, demanded the regime look closely at the game's organization and the Italian sporting infrastructure as a whole. Far from the only game in Italy, the journalist Filippo Muzzi declared it: 'a calling card that will help the understanding of other sports that do not have the sympathy of the crowd'.[1]

The desire to unite the nation culturally and politically prompted the regime's restructuring of *calcio*, in 1926, after which it symbolized Fascism's new-found confidence and desire to spread its new identity among the masses. The intervention came as Augusto Turati took over as the PNF secretary, which Jeffrey Schnapp suggested signified 'a move towards party discipline, hierarchy, and coordination from the center',[2] which was reflected in the regime's takeover and administration of the game during the following decade.

Calcio-chaos: The Road to Viareggio

Formed in 1898, *calcio*'s original governing body, the Federazione Italiana del Football (FIF) became the Federazione Italiana Giuoco del Calcio in 1909. As in much of post-1918 Europe the Italian game experienced a massive growth in popularity; the sixty-seven clubs competing for the title in 1919 increasing to eighty-eight within two years.[3] This expansion sparked calls for structural reform from the biggest clubs that wanted a smaller, elite championship and greater voting rights in the Federation. However, as the championship grew so did the power of the smaller clubs. The inevitable conflict between the big and small teams erupted in July 1920, following the move of the Federation's administrative centre to Milan, against the wishes of forty-seven clubs that included the Ligurian and Piedmontese power brokers. The dispute resulted in a schism and the formation of the Lega Italiana del Gioco del Calcio – the Italian Football League. The threat worked and the FIGC was united again by October, albeit with the concession of a reformed championship.

Vittorio Pozzo, who had already taken the Italian squad to the Stockholm Olympics in 1912, was assigned to oversee the restructuring. His model for reform was inspired by the English league's two regional divisions of twenty-four clubs, the winner of each competing for the overall title of league champion. Pozzo, who became one of the most revered names in *calcio*, was also a technical director of Torino Football Club. Arguing that his reform favoured the bigger teams, the smaller clubs that still possessed majority voting rights rejected the plan, causing the minority of bigger teams to rebel and form the alternative Confederazione Calcistica Italiana (CCI) – Italian Football Confederation. For the first time, the 1921–2 season resulted in two Italian champions; Pro Vercelli the dominant club of the era winning the CCI version, with the lesser-known Novese claimed the FIGC title. Nonetheless, lacking the necessary support and recognition from the Fédération Internationale de Football Association (FIFA) – the world governing body – the CCI was forced to seek a compromise with the FIGC.

Voting restrictions upon the smaller clubs and the expansion of the league to thirty-six teams united the FIGC once again. However, the uneasy peace was soon damaged by another dispute, this time between the Commissione tecnica della Lega Nord – technical commission North league – and the FIGC Federal Council, after its Commission of Thirteen drew up a new federal charter without seeking the agreement of the clubs themselves. The FIGC worsened the situation in 1926 by imposing a special one-off payment upon all clubs to make up the deficit in its accounts. It was a sign of the FIGC's perilous financial situation and the beginning of the crisis that would change the face of Italian football.

The FIGC had been on the verge of bankruptcy the previous year and was only saved by money obtained from an infamous championship decider between Genoa and Bologna, that conveniently required five replays. The deficit partly derived from the cancellation of a number of international matches from which the Federation had expected to replenish its funds and some over generous subsidies, such as the 50,000 lire given to an international football congress at Rome. A further illustration of the Federation's unwieldy, inefficient and uneconomical structure was the controversial Commission of Thirteen that had cost 30,000 lire for work that many of the leading clubs disapproved of,[4] plus the expenses incurred from the many meetings of its diverse commissions, councils, leagues and committees. Although the various regional leagues were required to provide an annual budget showing how the costs of the season would be met, the reality was that expenses were always greater than the individual societies and clubs could afford.[5]

In an effort to raise the 150,000 lire[6] required to stave off the crisis and meet any unforeseen future costs, the normal rate of taxation levied upon each club was increased. However, the argument still remained that it was not so much the weighty costs of the game as the bureaucratic Federation itself that prevented the financial issues ever being tackled with any degree of authority and efficiency.[7]

The conflict between small and big clubs also continued to cause problems; the former accusing the latter of restricting their ability to compete by hoarding the best players. Although a genuine issue, the growing importance of league football and the Italian championship intensified self-interest among *all* clubs. Concerned at what he saw Bruno Roghi asked 'What will become of Italian Football?', before prescribing a 'tonic of discipline, to free matches from the incendiary hyperbolic passions, to make it a healthy and chivalrous game that tempers the energies of the race'.[8]

As *calcio*'s popularity increased, large and sometimes volatile crowds became regular features, with some fans encouraged to travel to away matches by subsidies from the clubs. Supported by improved infrastructure and transport links, football tourism began as a popular if not always economical leisure activity.

Following Bologna's defeat to Verona in April 1925, the local sports newspaper *La Voce Sportiva* suggested the lack of Bologna supporters had been an important factor in the loss. Arguing the club should have helped fans attend the match by offering them half-price tickets, the paper suggested that an investment of 2–3,000 lire would have resulted in over 400 supporters going to Verona to counter the intimidating cries of the locals.[9] The following year 'thanks to the interest of Leandro Arpinati', according to *Il Resto del Carlino*, a special train service discounted by 50 per cent was organized for the Lega Nord final in Turin.[10] Indicating the team's growing status and cross-regional support in Emilia-Romagna, it stopped in Modena, Reggio, Parma and Piacenza to collect a huge number of fans whose 'enthusiastic and passionate support will be truly impressive and will be testimony to the discipline and strength of our glorious club.'[11]

As these burgeoning crowds began to impact upon the control and outcome of matches, refereeing standards became one of the most contentious issues of the day. Confronted with hostile and disruptive interventions from players, fans and officials, their ability to control matches was questioned for the first time.[12] In 1925, the third Lega Nord play-off match between Genoa and Bologna, demonstrated the extreme pressure to which they were increasingly subjected. Leading 2–1 with only two minutes remaining, a shot from Bologna's Muzioli was deemed by the referee, Giovanni Mauro, to have been saved by the goalkeeper and a corner kick awarded to Bologna. Although widely considered to have been the best referee in Italy at the time, Mauro was far away from the incident in question, which intensified the Bologna fans' conviction that the ball had crossed the line for a goal. Among those supporters was the leader of the Bolognese Fascist Federation and future mayor, Leandro Arpinati, who, apparently, led a pitch invasion with his *squadristi* that culminated in shouting, pushing, threats and some skirmishes.[13] Choosing personal safety over conscience, Mauro reversed his decision and awarded a goal. He also asked the Genoa captain, De Vecchi, to control his players on the understanding that he would invoke FIGC Rule 50 pertaining to dangerous circumstances, which De Vecchi interpreted as Mauro recognizing the legitimate 2–1 scoreline as final.[14] The match continued purely to avoid further trouble and with no more goals the Genoa players assumed they had won both the tie and the championship. However, Mauro recognized the 2–2 scoreline and ordered extra-time. The Genoa players refused, Bologna claimed the title and chaos ensued.

The Bolognese press was quick to reinforce the legitimacy of its team's victory, *La Voce Sportiva*'s claiming that the team had won the championship: 'on the pitch and by a unanimous plebiscite of the public.'[15] Members of Italian football's aristocracy attending the game were also quoted as having concurred that the goal was indeed just, although one post-match interviewee, without questioning its legitimacy, agreed that the decision had been made due to the pressure of the crowd.[16] However, the suggestion that the crowd had pressured the referee was rejected on the basis that the match had been played on a neutral ground, although the development of football tourism clearly made this possible. Having already appreciated the advantages of vocal, travelling support, it was no surprise that Bologna FC had subsidized thousands of supporters to make the journey to Milan in special trains.[17]

In a final act of parochial provocation, *La Voce Sportiva* patronizingly excused the Genoa fans for their understandable anger, but it could not 'approve the un-sporting gestures'.[18] The Bolognese press's decision to award its team the championship was presumptuous; perhaps deliberately so in an attempt to sway the Lega Nord. Apparently following a further intervention from the Bolognese Fascists,[19] Mauro chose to declare the match null and void and a fourth game was convened to decide the title, which suited the empty FIGC coffers if neither of the clubs. Not only had Bologna FC been denied the title, *La Vita Sportiva* claimed the decision had also created: 'a disagreeable and un-sporting precedent that could be repeated tomorrow by people who intend to use the complaints process as an indispensable weapon to satisfy their ardent partisanship, more than the legality of the battle on the field of play.'[20]

Against this background of complex issues that the FIGC was struggling to contain let alone resolve, the ultimate crisis erupted after the Casale-Torino match on 7 February 1926. Almost replicating the Genoa-Bologna incident the previous year, referee Sanguinetti failed to award Torino a goal when the players were convinced they had scored. Although *La Gazzetta* questioned if anybody could possibly have determined the truth with any degree of certainty,[21] Torino blamed Sanguinetti for their defeat and the result was referred to the Council of the Lega Nord. After considerable deliberation and following ratification from the Federal Council, the league annulled the match on the basis that Sanguinetti's control had lacked the necessary 'perfect serenity of spirit'.[22]

Given the continuing splits between clubs in the league, any majority decision was unlikely. Moreover, the two-and-a-half-month delay cast further doubt on the wisdom and efficacy of the Lega's competence to manage the game's. As *La Gazzetta* noted: 'When you want to cleanse the football world of the germs of indiscipline and intolerance that are the most serious threats, you need to rid the field of protests and cases that infuriate. Resolved three months ago, the Casale-Torino complaint would already have been forgotten.'[23]

Further undermining the committee's decision, *La Gazzetta* questioned what exactly constituted 'a match that was not directed by the referee in the perfect serenity of spirit' and the reason for such linguistic ambiguity.[24] Whereas referees' authority had previously been unquestionable, this incident brought the conduct of all into the spotlight. An ambiguous statement that contributed more to conjecture than clarity, the Lega's decision was deemed to have lacked legitimacy and raised questions about its 'real' motivation.[25] Besides the issue of Sanguinetti's dignity there was also the wounded party of Casale FC, which was supported by a number newspapers. Having won the initial, disputed encounter, *La Gazzetta* encouraged Casale to win once again for the good of sport,[26] but Casale was denied the opportunity by the decision to play the match behind closed doors. Fearing this unpopular choice would only inflame the situation further the authorities vetoed it completely, *La Gazzetta* ironically recording a small crowd that had gathered outside the ground to generously applaud the arrival of the Torino team.[27]

Responding to the continuing publicity surrounding the Sanguinetti case and the Commission of Thirteen's earlier decision entitling clubs to reject up to 8 per cent of the nominated list of referees, the AIA chose to defend its member stoutly.[28] A council meeting of the Association was convened on 30 May 1926 to discuss the status of referees in general, but with direct reference to Sanguinetti. It concluded that the lack of any clear censure of his conduct had authorized almost anything and undermined the position of referees as a whole.[29] In the light of this affront to the dignity and authority of its members, the AIA asked them to return their identity cards to the Sports Commission. Renouncing the body that was no longer protecting either them or the written laws of the game, the AIA effectively proclaimed a strike.

While many sympathized with the referees, there was considerable concern about the effect of this course of action upon *calcio*. What had originated as a number of loosely connected issues relating to the management of football had developed into a crisis that threatened the notion and nature of the national game. *La Gazzetta* demanded a solution to the problem at all costs: 'in honour of the flag, the athletes and the crowds, the championship needs to restart next Sunday.'[30] Its plea was fortified by *La Vita Sportiva*, which demanded central government intervene and forcibly resolve the crisis.[31] Coupled with the FIGC's inefficient, bureaucratic system there was, quite simply, *calcio*-chaos.

The protracted season also only highlighted the stark division between the wealthy and poor clubs. A rich minority capable of winning the title had emerged but the demands placed upon them had also become more exacting as supporters demanded stronger squads, which required more money to attract the best players. Many games had also become unattractive mismatches between the rich and poor, the real business of the season commencing only once the play-off positions had been decided. Unable to break into the league's elite due to their financial limitations, the poorer teams were left with little to fight for other than survival.

Although it may have been possible to delay the game's restructuring, change had become inevitable and essential if *calcio* was to be saved. Bruno Roghi proposed a championship that placed teams in smaller divisions, to reflect and strengthen their technical abilities: 'It does not only provide a champion resulting from exciting, close, sold-out matches, but it is also the basis for a thriving coexistence among all the Italian clubs and the stimulus to break the current deadlock.'[32]

With the league reduced in size, teams could be more rigorously selected and matched according to their ability, while those clubs that were relegated or found themselves in lower divisions would benefit from a more appropriate level from which they could launch a more prosper-ous future. While increasing attendances, he also believed the reduced championship would stimulate more discipline, mutual respect and loyalty among the clubs. Football would be the winner.

There were also alternative suggestions, one of which proposed that league football revert to a more regional basis because of poor facilities.[33] Yet, whatever the solution, there was notable concern that any changes might intensify local rivalries. Even the game's biggest supporter, *La Gazzetta dello Sport*, recognized the inevitable consequence of *calcio's* popularity, categorizing it as: 'a drug that arouses passions accordingly as the distance in kilometres between the two teams is reduced.'[34] Whether the championship was structured on a specifically regional basis or as an all-embracing national competition, it was impossible to neuter the passionate game that thrived on local rivalries or *campanilismo*.

If the crisis was a chance for referees to improve their lot and newspapers their sales, it was also an opportunity for the regime to intervene in a national institution. On the announcement of the referees' strike the CONI President, Lando Ferretti, implemented an action plan that began with a meeting between AIA President Giovanni Mauro and other leading figures in the administration of Italian sport. Having established a formal date to begin mediation and a cooling off period, Ferretti drew a concession from the AIA that its members would continue to work out of love for the game. The second meeting, convened by Ferretti at the expressed desire of the PNF secretary Augusto Turati, established a compromise whereby all parties accepted that the Sanguinetti decision was not an attack on the dignity and subjectivity of referees, nor could it be interpreted as one. Both clubs in question and the AIA accepted that the match had been annulled for 'sporting reasons'.[35]

Contentious as these reasons were, the brokered agreement seemed to suit all parties, although the AIA later endorsed the complete honourability of Sanguinetti. More importantly, the interests of the aggrieved parties and the FIGC had been subordinated to CONI in the national sporting interest, during what Ferretti later referred to as a 'temporary regency' period.[36] Significantly, *La Gazzetta* recorded the meeting's conclusion with a vote of thanks to Turati for his interest in the sport and a pledge to serve the nation unconditionally.[37] Although the crisis had been temporarily averted and the championship restarted, *La Gazzetta* claimed the decision had seriously weakened the Federal Council.[38] With attention turning towards the phase of reconstruction, CONI, which had already been reordered along Fascist lines, was given a free hand to establish a new directorate to reorganize the Football Federation.

Ferretti's blueprint for the future of *calcio* still had to mediate between the needs of the game and the desires of the regime. As Roghi noted, the new championship 'needed to find a point of harmony between the superior rights of the sport as a racial gymnasium – gymnasia of discipline, courage and solidarity – and the rights of the clubs to affirm and consolidate their sporting apprenticeships in the long term'.[39]

In what was arguably the most significant act in the history of *calcio*, Ferretti appointed a panel of three experts, on 7 July, radically to restructure the statutes of Italian football in accordance with the realities and demands of the new political era. *Calcio* needed to subordinate its activity to Fascism's new concept of physical education, while the clubs themselves had to impose more self-discipline to end the sort of incidents that had stimulated the crisis in the first place.[40] If this could be achieved he anticipated more peaceful contests that would neither result in rancour among the winners and losers nor inflame the causes of *campanilismo* that contradicted the spirit of Fascist fraternity. If this proved impossible, Ferretti's alternative was stark: 'Football would be fatally condemned to degenerate into the trick of a money grabber, worthy of repressive police measures and the contempt of the citizens . . . Because it is a grave problem we are setting about resolving it in a Fascist manner: that is seriously.'[41]

The Roman Fascist bureaucrat and future Prefect Italo Foschi, engineer Paolo Graziani and lawyer/referee Giovanni Mauro were appointed to discuss the organization of the next championship; assign clubs to the various divisions; classify players; organize taxation and establish the hierarchy of the governing body.[42] Their work was completed by 2 August, when Ferretti was handed the Carta di Viareggio that, according to Zanetti and Tornabuoni, reordered football to reflect 'a general and revolutionary concept of government'.[43]

The Carta di Viareggio

The Carta substituted the old Federal Council with the theoretically elected Direttorio Federale, although the board of governors was selected by the president of CONI for the first two years, after which a further reform established that all federation heads would be appointed by an assembly nominated by the Duce.[44] In effect, the president's role was to approve rather than nominate officers,[45] the FIGC having been subordinated beneath CONI that was already an organ of the party. The FIGC president and the Direttorio Federale now exercised absolute power and authority over all football matters, this transition to Fascist sport illustrated by the addition of the *fascio* to the Sabaudo Shield that was the crest of all CONI members.

A new complaints procedure established that any matters regarding the condition of the pitch should be raised before the start of the game, while those resulting from incidents during the tie now had to be submitted directly to the referee within 30 minutes of the final whistle. No doubt with the Casale-Torino contest in mind, Ferretti explained how these regulations were specifically intended to cure Italian football of the 'protest mania' that had enabled some clubs to get victories at the adjudicator's table that stronger teams achieved on the pitch.[46] Complaints among teams competing in the National League and Division I went directly to the new board of the superior divisions. Division II was governed by a board of the Northern and Southern Leagues, with authority for the third resting with regional committees. Having consulted these bodies, any club that remained unsatisfied could appeal directly to the FIGC directorate that had been appointed by the regime.

This directorate included the Syndicate Board, responsible for all FIGC administrative and financial matters, plus the *Comitato Italiano Tecnico Arbitrale* (CITA) – referees association – which assumed responsibility for overseeing referee discipline, selection and training in the internationally accepted rules. Although CITA was governed by the Direttorio Federale, crucially, it was given unquestionable authority over the dismissal of referees for technical reasons.[47] Despite this concession, the replacement of the former independent referees fiduciary/representative by CITA regional directors meant that by 1930, the new class of referees was also firmly under control.[48] No longer meriting the ire of the supporters or the scowls of the regime, crowds and clubs were now expected to accept their expertise. As *Il Bargello* announced: 'today the class of referees is as the regime wants it: honest and competent. Whoever does not want to understand it will do well to keep quiet.'[49]

Having taken control of the political aspects of the game the charter continued to fascistise *calcio* in other areas. The most significant act of the restructuring was the formation of the first national division, which had been mooted for some time.[50] The new Lega Nazionale comprised of twenty teams: sixteen from the old Northern League, three from the Lazio and Campagna divisions of the Southern Leagues, with the final position being established by a play-off. They were then divided into two divisions according to economic and geographical considerations, with the new national champion determined by a series of play-off matches among the top three teams in each. The last placed team in each was relegated to Division I, with the corresponding winners promoted. It was a change that Ferretti hoped would place more significance on the 'national' element of the competition by bringing the two strongest clubs from the capital, plus Napoli, directly into competition with teams from the north, thereby giving 'new horizons to the sport in the south'.[51]

Economic and geographical considerations restricted Division I to an interregional basis. With three leagues in the northern section and one in the south, the overall winner was again decided by play-off matches. Division II was smaller and interregional, with a third division restricted to a regional competition with interregional finals. In essence, league football had not changed beyond recognition, but the principle of a truly national competition had been established, even if it was still contested on a north-south basis. It was the first step in the regime's unification drive, which culminated in the formation of a single national division within two years, in which only the best teams from the length and breadth of the peninsula would compete.

In addition to league football, a number of cup competitions were also introduced. The Coppa d'Ora (Gold Cup) was established for the fourteen clubs in the national division that failed to qualify for the play-off matches, with the Coppa Italia (Italian Cup) reintroduced to ensure the smaller clubs received a full complement of fixtures, in addition to the opportunity of competing against the bigger, lucrative teams. The introduction of cup competitions was Fascism's attempt to protect both big and small teams, while bringing the composite pieces of the puzzle closer towards an integrated national picture that would further develop the Italian game.

Footballers themselves were not exempt from the Carta's scrutiny either. Divided into amateur and non-amateur categories, the individual's status was decided by a CONI commission. CONI also assumed responsibility for strictly imposing the rules governing amateurism, with the harshest sanctions possible levied against those players and clubs in contravention. Amateurs signed one-year contracts for their club but were permitted to become 'non-amateurs' at any time, although any return to their old status required two years of inactivity. 'Non-amateur' players were similarly committed to their clubs for a period of twelve months and despite not being considered professional, they were allowed reimbursement for any expenses or loss of income incurred through playing football.[52] Players could transfer between clubs from 1 July each year but they were not able to play for two different teams in the same season, although at the FIGC's discretion clubs were able to replace players called up for national service.

The introduction of 'non-amateur' status was a significant move towards establishing and legalizing professionalism. In the new charter the FIGC's definition of 'non-amateur' status reflected Article 113 of FIFA's rules, which established that a non-amateur player was one reimbursed for the loss of earnings.[53] Only weeks earlier a FIFA commission had failed to reach such an agreement, arguing instead that players who made up their losses in earnings were to be considered professionals.

Ultimately, according to *La Gazzetta*, FIFA passed the responsibility onto the individual football associations, leaving each one 'free to resolve the problem in a manner that reflected the principles of amateurism'.[54] For Italian football it was left to the Carta di Viareggio to provide some definition to the blurred borders of amateurism. It was also hoped this would improve the nation's football prowess by forming, within the first and second divisions, a nucleus of genuinely amateur players capable of striving for future Olympic teams.[55] True amateurism supported by the spirit of fair play was an endearing image that the regime was keen to promote, especially when confronting nations that it considered less honourable.

The principle of amateurism itself was also strongly supported as a foil against increasing professionalization that was thought to have been threatening the morality of the game. While *calcio* was acknowledged as having progressed enormously some, such as the Prime Minister's secretary Guido Beer, believed this had come at a moral cost.

> The capital problem of the Italian sporting life is that of slowing the enormous development of professionalism that is most dangerous to the nation. The professional must call himself so, because while it is not a dishonour, it is when you call yourself amateur when you regularly receive large sums (see footballers), or if you are kept all year by the management of great hotels, or if you travel in first class and sleeping carriages.[56]

Unfortunately, this increasing professionalization of the game had not improved the financial position of the individual clubs, which had been a key factor in the 1926 crisis. As Leone Boccali noted in *Lo Sport Fascista*: 'the public that pay their ten or fifteen lire to watch a football match from the popular areas are amazed to hear all the societies, big or small, complain annually of disastrous balance sheets. Counting the large takings, evidently disposes clubs to spend cheerfully.'[57]

Part of this expenditure was accounted for by the increasing importance of the players themselves and the development of a transfer system. In 1930 some footballers were reputed to be earning an average wage of 500–600 lire per month, while those who moved away from their home town or city were remunerated with up to 1,000 lire relocation expenses.[58] Some of the smaller clubs that attempted to buy themselves a position in the national league found themselves unable to afford to keep their best players. The result was the emergence of the transfer list that Boccali described as: 'a form of sporting slavery that fed and prompted markets'.[59] Yet those who noted the faults of the transfer system also appreciated its inspirational merits for talented players that might emerge from the masses. For those players capable of winning the toughest international matches, the transfer was an incentive and reward for their efforts to reach their maximum potential.[60] Those that failed to attain this standard of excellence remained duty bound to their clubs where they were expected to give their all.

The clubs tried to protect themselves against their 'investments' leaving to play for other teams, but there were still a number of routes by which players could obtain a move. Enticed by attractive offers, they would often neglect to train properly, demand extras and exaggerate injuries. In essence, they were exercising their empowerment from *calcio*'s increasing professionalization, albeit occasionally disreputably. One example was the alleged case of the player who refused to represent his team unless the club directors settled a significant gambling debt incurred the previous night.[61] It was such incidents that were held up as examples of the damage being done to the morality of the game and Italian sport in general, Boccali identifying money as the source of evil in *Lo Sport Fascista*.[62] While there was no suggestion that these 'professional' players had lost their love of the game, their lifestyle was thought to have generally reduced their combative instincts that were only truly called upon for decisive or international matches.

The ultimate danger was the example this set to the nation's youngsters, especially as the FIGC's legislation dictated that every registered player needed 'to have a clean record and be an unquestionable example of arduous activity in their private and professional life'.[63] It was a hopeful measure intended to discourage those who thought football was a relatively easy game for which players were well recompensed. In organic Fascist society, there was no room for team members looking for the easy option. Boccali's view on the degenerative effects of the game was supported by other journalists, such as Vittorio Varale, who argued that praise for champion athletes needed be contained within acceptable limits if the mass of youngsters were to talk about their heroes in a more restrained manner. Undoubted inspirational examples for the stars of the future, they could also portray the worst possible example to those that looked up and admired them.[64]

It was such ideas that led some, like Boccali, to reconsider the benefits of high profile sporting activities. Arguing that *calcio* had imposed too high a price for its contribution to propaganda, he declared it: 'an enemy of healthily intended and practised sport; worse still, an enemy of society that distracts rich energies by turning them into drop-outs: youngsters from 28–30 will need to restart their existence all over again'.[65] His fears were echoed by the journalist Giuseppe Centauro who believed that sport's primary role should be to guide the young spiritually 'onto the lawful platform of life: work. Here is the programme. Sport must not forget this imperative need of man: to work.'[66]

Reflecting the game's recent history, Boccali called for intervention from the highest authority to restore its health for the benefit of Italian sport as a whole. The restorative tonic that he and others had been proposing for some time was to prevent footballers from joining clubs outside of their region, province of birth or place of permanent residence. In an interview in 1929, Arpinati was asked what dangers he foresaw in such a measure, especially for southern regions such as Calabria and Basilicata. His primary concern was the potential impact on the game's propaganda role, with particular reference to how the regime expected it to contribute to the nation's psychological and physical unification. Whereas foreign players had once been the main sources of strength and education at many clubs, some considered the technical development of the Italian game sufficient to have rendered them superfluous, with their roles now fulfilled by the best Italians.

Acknowledging the measure's potential for reducing the professionalization of *calcio*, Arpinati feared it would also arrest the game's technical development and its propaganda role. Restricting the movement and transfer of players between regions might remove the element of competition and, thus, the incentive to improve skills and achieve the highest standards. More importantly, he was concerned the proposed measure might prevent some regions from raising their playing standards sufficiently to compete with any other in the country, thereby destroying the equilibrium 'that is indispensable to the fortunes of the national game'.[67] Consequently, any law preventing clubs from purchasing players from outside of their region might have inhibited the ambitious ones from improving.

The degree to which the Italian game had raised its standards nonetheless contributed to the misguided notion that it no longer needed or could benefit from the influx of foreign players. This desire to Italianize *calcio* was responsible for one of the Carta di Viareggio's more short-sighted rulings, which banned clubs from signing foreign players. With many having already made commitments, the 1926–7 season was designated a transitory period in which clubs were permitted to sign two foreign footballers, although only one was able to play in each match. The following season there were none and by 1928 the FIGC's annual publication was able to clarify the formerly grey area: 'In the Italian championship only players of Italian nationality and citizenship are allowed to compete.'[68] It was an indisputably xenophobic and opportunistic measure with which the regime nailed its colours to the FIGC mast by arguing that foreigners could not contest an 'Italian championship'.[69] According to Tornabuoni and Zanetti, in their book on the FIGC legislation, the restrictions were both timely and necessary in the interests of the national spirit, to ensure 'the Italian championship did not become a faded subsidiary of the Austrian or Hungarian; and so that it did not impede the more important claims of Italian players'.[70]

The pragmatic compromise during the transition period when all foreign players were supposed to have been released, resulted in some confusion even within government circles. Having asked for clarification from the Prime Minister in 1928, the Minister for the Interior was informed that: 'Footballers of other nationalities are not authorised to participate in the Italian championship. Societies affiliated to the Italian Federation can only appoint foreign coaches when they cannot find anybody suitable in the motherland.'[71]

Yet the law on foreign players was pointless at best; if not outright damaging to the prospects of Italian football. As intended, it did successfully increase the number of northern Italian footballers playing for southern teams in the 1929–30 season, although this came at the loss of those foreign players that had originally raised technical standards. The counter-productivity of this myopic measure was illustrated by the achievements of the Uruguayan and Argentine national teams at the 1928 Amsterdam Olympics, which alerted the regime not only to its mistake but also to the pool of South American talent with strong, Italian genealogical links.

The ban on foreign players soon became one of the more unpopular aspects of the charter for the clubs and the regime, as both appreciated the opportunities they were missing. While there was no official reform, the legislation was bypassed on a technicality as the sons of first-generation ex-patriot Italians, primarily from Argentina and Uruguay, were welcomed back to form the basis upon which the golden era was built. It is difficult to defend this aspect of the law against charges of racism, although Zanetti and Tornabuoni's interpretation was more nationalist than racist. While arguing that it was impossible to allow 'anti-national' players to compete within any branch of Italian sport, they also correctly identified how the Fascist concept of nationality was more dependent upon an individual's commitment 'to the national ends' than their blood and birth.[72]

Some foreign coaches were allowed to work in Italy, although they too were eventually attacked by the Carta's xenophobia. As CONI *Commissario Straordinario* (Extraordinary Commissioner), Augusto

Turati publicly disapproved of foreign coaches and imposed a limit on the number permitted to work in the country. In the future, clubs that wished to employ them were obliged to first seek permission from the CONI secretary, before making any offer of employment.[73]

The policy was as short-sighted as the restriction upon players, as many coaches, such as the Austrian Hermann Fellsner and the Hungarians Hugo Meisl and Arpad Weisz, had contributed hugely towards the modernization of the Italian game. In fact, cruelly disregarding his contribution to the development of *calcio*, Weisz, who was a Hungarian Jew, was forced to resign from coaching in January 1939 following the introduction of the racial laws. He was later deported and eventually died in a concentration camp.[74]

At the time, the Danubian countries dominated continental football and while the overall number of foreign coaches in Italy was reduced, pragmatism enabled the best to continue working and thereby developing the Italian game. To increase the number of suitably qualified Italians, a coaching school was established in 1933 as part of a 'university' of Calcio. Although the 'university' concept was short-lived, a one-week summer residential course was established in Rome to train future Italian coaches.[75] It was, according to the Florentine sports weekly *Lo Stadio*, an 'excellent initiative, a most desirable institution that will take Italian football away . . . from the intrusive foreign technical direction'.[76] In his opening address to the first intake of coaches in 1933, Arpinati also drew attention to the way that foreign influence was said to have contributed to the game's moral decline. As he explained to the aspiring coaches, they needed to teach the Italian youngsters how 'to play with openness and discipline, and not to wait for the right moment to foul and cheat when not seen by the referee'.[77]

Coaches wishing to train at the new institution needed to have reached a requisite educational standard in addition to having played football at a respected level. Both elements were considered crucial due to the various demands of the position that required the individual to be the trainer, coach and technical director. So diverse were the qualities demanded of an excellent coach that *Lo Stadio* suggested the term was no longer appropriate and that the position should be called *Maestro*.[78] By further erasing the game's English origins that had introduced trainer and Mister into *calcio*'s lexicon, it was indicative of another facet of the Carta di Viareggio: linguistic nationalism.

In effect, the Carta merely rubber-stamped a process that had already begun prior to the official changes. At a conference on sport in the Fascist state in 1925, Ferretti announced that the Roman salute would be obligatory before the start of all matches. The replacement of 'Hip. Hurrah' with the more romanesque '*Eja, Eja, Alalà*'[79] demonstrated how the nationalization of the game also extended to the players. As Zanetti and Tornabuoni noted: 'When the player enters the field, he represents the Federation more than just the society to which he belongs; he needs to control himself according to the principles of dignity, chivalry and courtesy that the federal laws and customs prescribe.'[80]

The nationalization process was also reflected in the regime's attempt to Italianize or manufacture a new history of the game through words and symbols. In 1925, the journalist and author Amerigo Bresci took up this theme in his book on the question of Italian identity in *calcio*.[81] Attacking foreign words that had become an inherent part of the language of the national game, he railed against members of the press who used terms such as corner, team and penalty, demanding they promote what he believed was an inherently Italian game. It was an argument often employed during the Fascist era, whereby the roots of football were attributed to the ancient sport of *calcio Fiorentino* or *calcio storico*, a traditional folk game of the Middle Ages, which was also restored to prominence by the regime.[82]

To educate the readership and reinforce the modern game's Italian identity, Bresci assembled a glossary of foreign words and their 'correct' Italian counterparts. These ranged from standard terms such as goal kick (*calcio di rinvio*), forward (*attaccante*) and 'kich-off' [*sic*] (*calcio d'inizio*) to the more bizarre or specialized plungeon (*tuffo: uno dei caratteristici movimenti del portiere per impedire che la palla entri in porta*) and daisy-cutter (*tiro radente, o raso terra*).[83]

As the era's famous voice of football, Niccolo Carosio's radio broadcasts also contributed to the Italianization of *calcio*'s language and the regime's exploitation of the game. His style was distinguishable by his replacement of many of the traditional English words with the preferred and sometimes cumbersome Italian alternatives, even occasionally inventing expressions of his own that became a permanent feature of *calcio* culture.[84] A talented and famous broadcaster, he brought the game to life for those masses that collected throughout the country for their Sunday ritual, many of whom had never even kicked a ball or seen a stadium. His nationwide fame was courtesy of the regime's investment in radio, which, up until 1928, had experienced considerable difficulties with live broadcasts.[85] Once these problems were overcome Carosio became the perfect propaganda vehicle that the regime exploited by, apparently, pressuring him to adopt the Italianized language of *calcio*.

Calcio goes South

On the eve of the 1926/7 season Italian football had changed to meet the needs of the modern game and the regime, but not beyond recognition. There was of course the introduction of a national league with promotion and relegation from interregional and regional divisions below, none of which were perceived to have had too negative an effect. It was also appreciated that first and foremost, the structural changes were intended to develop the national aspects of football, which not only included the improvement of the Italian national team but also the relationship between northern and southern Italy. With matches between teams from the north and south previously restricted to just the national play-off final, they were now both unavoidable and of critical importance for the development of the game and the nation. By standardizing the laws CONI established uniformity, thereby removing one of the hurdles that had prevented the full integration of the south into the national football structure. To achieve this, CONI accommodated those southern societies that had previously not only felt excluded from the system but had also been unable to assert themselves due to insurmountable geographical, economic and transport difficulties.[86]

Although national integration was important, there was no single underlying motive behind the restructuring of football. In fact, the changes were forced by a number of interrelated demands, many of which were included in Vittorio Pozzo's personal definition of what a championship should be:

> The championship is the most egotistical manifestation in sport that one can imagine. Its purpose should be to provide a solid and irremovable base to the work of the big and small clubs and to confer regularity on the season . . . Its mission . . . should be that of recalling and capturing the attention of the public, of always forming, preparing and developing new players, of creating fresh energies, while maintaining and improving the existing forces.[87]

If 'to serve the needs of the regime' had also been included in his description at some point, it would have perfectly described what emerged as *calcio* in a black shirt.

Reflecting on the events of 1926, Ferretti declared the crisis as one of authority as much as finance. While the referees' strike had brought a number of issues to a head, he argued the clubs had already shown themselves to have been in open rebellion with their deliberately small financial contributions to the FIGC deficit which, by 30 June, had reached 20,000 lire.[88] That a further 50,000 lire were raised in the month of July alone, suggests they were either deliberately withholding their financial resources in protest or that the intervention of Ferretti, on behalf of the regime, had 'encouraged' them to support the national institution. Either way, the FIGC's financial position was in recovery, which was further helped by restricting the costs and frequency of the numerous Federation meetings and pruning its duplicitous bodies. As Pozzo reflected in 1928:

> Who can forget those famous meetings that started at nine in the evening and ended at four in the morning without concluding anything; those discussions that took five, six, seven hours to decide what one person could have done in ten minutes; those struggles that degenerated into even more ignoble uproar than one can imagine?
>
> . . . This used to happen once. The Regime, intervening energetically, introduced swift and practical systems, revitalising the environment.[89]

Using his extraordinary powers acquired during the 'regency period', one of Ferretti's first moves was to make Leandro Arpinati president of the FIGC. According to the CONI secretary, his energy, intelligence, authority and love of the game was above and beyond any praise he could bestow upon him.[90] With his appointment, the Federation's central office moved from Turin to Bologna, the seat of Arpinati's power. Undoubtedly it suited him, but it also seems to have been part of a deliberate attempt to move the headquarters of the game closer to Rome. Besides undermining the original Italian capital and *calcio* power base of Turin and minimizing the cost of relocating members of the Federal Board, the move was intended to further integrate the south into the national game; Bologna was merely a political staging post before the Federation's final move to the capital.

In response, the northern press launched an aggresive campaign against the decision, which was replicated in Bologna in 1928 when the FIGC finally moved to Rome, prompting the Bolognese sports paper *La Pedata* to announce the move under a bitter headline: 'We affirm the right of Rome to pocket the Football Federation and the two towers, the [piazza] Neptune, the Littoriale and the rest.'[91] The FIGC's transfer to the capital coincided with Arpinati's appointment as under-secretary to the Interior Ministry, but realistically this was just another pragmatic centralizing opportunity, after which the office never moved again. In the space of three years, the Federation had been stealthily, if not unnoticeably, relocated from its original northern periphery to the new centre of the nation, exemplifying what the Carta di Viareggio had been designed to achieve.

Unquestionably nationalist and patriotic, one journalist likened the Carta to a 'surgical operation' that would morally and sportingly revitalize the national game within a year.[92] Although it introduced the fundamentals necessary to achieve this, it soon became clear that revolutionizing and Italianizing the system would be an ongoing process. Evolution, experimentation and perpetual change being the modus operandi by which the regime believed perfection could be reached and maintained in all fields. This certainly applied to the world of sport that, according to *Il Bargello*, had shown its readiness to 'confront new organizational problems and experiment with new formulas, for only through practical experience is it possible to perfect a great task of work that encapsulates everything about our sporting movement'.[93]

The next stage of *calcio*'s metamorphosis came in 1929, with the amalgamation of the northern and southern divisions into a single national league. For the top eight teams from the northern and southern divisions that merged to form Serie A, the new structure represented a better way of determining the national hierarchy and developing the Italian game. *La Nazione* praised the initiative for providing football with 'a new impulse, organizing, encouraging and giving it robustness and meaning'.[94] Yet, while clubs in Serie B had the opportunity to secure promotion to the top division, life in the lower league was a harsh economic counter-blow. Expenses increased due to the demands of national fixtures at the same time as gate receipts declined following the loss of the most attractive matches.[95]

Their desperate financial situation led to calls for reductions in their tax payments to the FIGC, in order to 'equally favour the development of football in all regions of Italy'.[96] To ease the financial burdens imposed by extensive national travel, others suggested the division revert back to a regional basis of four smaller leagues, which seemed to defeat the object of the changes in the first place.[97] However, on closer inspection, this contained aspects that could also have contributed to the regime's nationalization of football and continued to introduce fresh teams and energies into Serie A each season. Of more interest was the way the proposed system would have not only guaranteed permanent southern representation in the top flight that was lacking under the existing order, but also the opportunity to continually increase the number of southern clubs in Serie A, so long as none were relegated. The one snag with this system was that it did not guarantee the promotion of the strongest four teams in Serie B.

The south also remained a key factor in the restructuring further down the football league pyramid, as the regionally based Division I – the rung below Serie B – was enlarged to include more southern clubs. As Arpinati explained in *Il Littoriale*: 'We wanted to enlarge the first division above all, to help the south, which, besides benefiting from a 50 per cent reduction in match taxes, will save a notable amount in travelling costs.'[98]

The formation of Serie A also signalled the final defeat of the smaller clubs, which had long punched above their weight in the FIGC structure and resisted all attempts to reduce their status. Moreover, the change to a single, national division represented more than just an effort to raise the technical standards of the game that were thought to have been suffering under the strain of such a long season.

Such was the belief in the merits of the new national league structure that on news of the imminent changes, even the Florentine Fascist weekly *Il Bargello* publicly supported it, despite its negative effect on the Tuscan clubs of Fiorentina and Prato. *Lo Stadio* also championed the national league and opposed its expansion into two regional divisions of eighteen, despite how the latter scenario would have ensured top-flight representation for Fiorentina and its close neighbour. Disregarding the potential damage to the region's prospects in the name of the national game, *Lo Stadio* recommended a reduction of the number of teams competing in Serie A and B to a final figure of fourteen.[99] It was supported by Vittorio Pozzo and Emilio Colombo who both believed that a smaller championship would improve the national team.[100]

While there were technical merits to such a proposal, the idea of restricting the national division to sixteen teams caused great consternation as it would have excluded Triestina (Trieste), Lazio (Rome) and Napoli (Naples), with the obvious implications for the desired national league. Consequently, all three teams were admitted into Serie A for the first season, *La Nazione* declaring the decision: an 'act of great sporting justice, greeted with enthusiasm by all the nation'.[101] On what authority the newspaper spoke for the nation is difficult to imagine, but its pronouncement showed how the Fascist daily both accepted and promoted the regime's desire to subsume local desires beneath national needs.

Yet the decision to expand the league was calculated on a far deeper basis than merely sporting justice, as Arpinati explained in an interview. While agreeing that sporting reasons had prevailed in many cases, he explained that propaganda had also been an important factor, especially when considering the benefits to the national game of including those big cities that still did not have a single team capable of competing at the top level.[102] In the future, as Arpinati clarified, any smaller cities that wanted to secure representation in the national league had to decide which of the many existing local teams they would support: 'I need to say with complete frankness that if in two cities like Trieste or Florence bodies had not already existed that vowed to succeed in becoming worthy of competing with the best squads in Italy, it would have been necessary to create them.'[103]

The inevitable result was that some small and medium-sized clubs were prevented from entering the top division by their more illustrious neighbours, despite their respective abilities. After finishing in an equivalent position to Fiorentina in its section of the old first division, Ternana (Terni) claimed the right to join the national league, while Fiume argued that having finished one place above Triestina, it too had earned the right to join Serie A. Neither club succeeded, thereby exposing a selection criteria that was based upon more than just playing strengths and what Arpinati described as a 'minimal difference in final league table position'.[104]

A talented team needed the support of both the club and the city if it was to compete on a national basis, such as the Società Sportive Modenesi (Modena), which was created by the merger of the local teams of Panaro, Fratellanza and Modena FC. Despite conforming to the Fascist blueprint, prior to the official ratification of this new society the prefect still requested Arpinati's sanction as minister of the interior.[105] Such mergers, however, were not always popular with the fans themselves, the prefect of Bari apologizing for a complaint made direct to Mussolini that was said to have qualified as dissent towards the Fascist provincial secretary's decision to merge the Società Sportive 'Ideal' and Bari.[106]

This desire to raise football onto a truly national level was reinforced by the way the regime took the game south, in every respect. On 25 March 1928 the national team played in the capital for the first time. According to the journalist Leone Boccali, the PNF stadium's inaugural match (Italy versus Hungary) was more than just an ordinary international: it was intended 'to strengthen and extend to the southern regions that unification of national sporting activity that makes a notable contribution to the political and spiritual unification of Italy'.[107]

Beyond the *azzurri*'s victory, the regime's real success was achieved off the field of play. As *Lo Sport Fascista* described, the match was an 'organizational success that confounded many unwise prejudices against the southern crowd'.[108] The following year's third play-off to decide the 1929 championship, was also contested in Rome for the first time. Accorded even greater status than an international fixture, special trains brought supporters from all over the country to supplement the majority of spectators from the capital.[109]

The speed and extent of *calcio*'s development in the 1920s was huge, with the game being played in eighty-three of the ninety-four provincial capitals by the end of the decade.[110] Although the football phenomenon was not just restricted to Italy, the Carta di Viareggio undoubtedly redirected the game and gave it a new lease of life. Its consequent explosion in popularity was exactly what the leadership had dreamt of. Domestically and diplomatically it had been manipulated into a perfect, continual photo opportunity for all that the regime wished to purvey. As *Il Bargello* was proud to proclaim in 1931: 'even in sport, Fascism is teaching the old Europe and showing its greatest export.'[111] Yet, the regime's intervention also produced and exacerbated some disagreeable side-effects, most notably in the development and strengthening of local identities.

Sporting *campanilismo* was a relatively if not completely new phenomenon that exposed many contradictions that the regime had difficulty in accommodating. If football was to contribute to the construction of even an imaginary Fascist national community, there could be no place for destructive local rivalries. However, a glance through the Ministry of the Interior's record of 'incidents' gives a clear indication of the widespread nature of disorder at football matches, which usually reflected long-established city-based rivalries. It was such divisive developments that inspired Manlio Morgagni, in *Il Popolo d'Italia*, to call for more discipline in sport in general and particularly football, which he believed caused antagonisms between regions, provinces, cities, quarters and groups, as the competitive animas of the squads extended to the fans themselves.[112]

While not commonplace, local rivalries also stimulated a growth in violence between fan groups, as animosities were intensified by a parochial press and fans' increasing ability and desire to travel and support the team. Incidents of this type were even occurring prior to 1926, such as the fourth match of the previously mentioned Lega Nord play-off, between Genoa and Bologna in 1925, when gunshots were fired during a confrontation between rival fans at the Porta Nuova station in Turin. Set against the background of two drawn matches and the ill-tempered, unjust and arguably corrupt third replay that encouraged the respective cities newspapers to trade words and insults,[113] it was unfortunate that the trains carrying each team's supporters home, left from adjacent platforms. With fans fighting in the station and on the tracks, shots were apparently fired from a carriage carrying the Bologna supporters. Although nobody was injured, the incident provoked much debate about the future of *calcio*.

The FIGC blamed Bologna and ordered the club to pay a 5,000 lire fine. Scaremongering federal governors predicted the game's demise, although the question as to whether people wanted football to become a 'tragic feud between communes' played out on Sundays, was without doubt relevant.[114] Equally predictably, *La Voce Sportiva* blamed the incident on the federal authority's decision to annul Bologna's 'victory' in the previous meeting, the paper declaring the whole incident a serious slight upon the supporters, the club and the city itself.[115]

The FIGC's report claimed that the Bologna fans had not been provoked. Denouncing this as 'false and tendentious' the Bologna President, F.E. Masetti, argued that the 'obscene gestures, foul displays, stone fights [and] revolver shots' had started with the Genoa supporters.[116] Bologna's ire was fuelled by a conviction that the league structure was deliberately skewed to the benefit of the longer established Genoa Football and Cricket Club.[117] One thousand Bologna fans demonstrated in the city against the FIGC's decision, which the Bologna Prefect, Arturo Bocchini, recorded as 'an imposing public assembly' that wanted to take action against the FIGC leadership's 'revolting misuse of power'.[118] In his letter to the minister of the interior, Bocchini declared his absolute solidarity with the fans struggle against the Federation and its 'gross foolishness of obvious partisanship' with which, he argued, it was trying to regain its lost authority by attacking one of Italy's most honourable clubs.[119] Despite the protests, Bologna magnanimously accepted the decision and 'cordially extended a hand to Genoa to renew a faithfully professed friendship'.[120]

Bologna clinched the title at the fifth attempt in a match played behind closed doors. The only fans to see it were Arpinati and his *squadristi* who stood on the side of the pitch with pistols glinting in the sun; potentially the same ones from which the shots had been fired in the station a month or so earlier.[121] Besides a victory for justice, *La Voce Sportiva* declared it a victory for a new style of play: 'a new system and a new method imported from Hungary and wisely applied by passionate and impulsive Italian characters.'[122] Although a mere footnote to this lengthy collection of incidents, the tactical innovation is evidence of Bologna's achievements in the 1930s coming partly courtesy of its exposure to new, foreign ideas and tactics.

Incidents as grave as those during the 1925 finals were both rare and shocking, but they illustrated the extent to which *calcio* had penetrated daily Italian life. Even by the mid 1920s, this strengthening of *campanilismo* had begun to contradict the regime's exploitation of *calcio* to portray and augment its homogeneous nation. Such 'idiotic campanilistic' tendencies were further scorned by Morgagni, in *Il Popolo d'Italia*: 'It is enough to have watched only one of these matches to convince oneself of the ill they produce, provoking hostility between sons of the same motherland living in two opposite districts, to the danger of the harmonious, unitary spirit emanating from the Regime.'[123]

Unfortunately, the Fascist blueprint recommended the merger of many smaller municipal clubs into bigger societies that were capable of representing their cities in the national arena. Although not necessarily compulsory, the creation of a national league encouraged many local Fascist leaders to demand a concentration of resources and a team capable of competing on just such a level, as Arpinati had suggested would happen. More than just material club assets, these resources included the fans themselves that were united behind the one local representative. This proved particularly strong in cities such as Naples and Florence that only had one team, whereas in Milan, Turin and Rome citizens were divided between dual representatives.

As has already been demonstrated and will continue to be seen in the following chapters, the restructuring of *calcio* that was designed to integrate all Italian clubs into the new national league was complemented by international matches being played south of Bologna. This desire to construct an all-inclusive, football nation – Italy United let's say – was disseminated to all areas and regions of the country and not only the south. One northern example was in the Trieste part of the Venezia-Giulia region. Although it had technically become part of post-1918 Italy, the inclusion of Venezia-Giulia's principal clubs (Trieste FC and SBS Ponziana) within the national league was deemed a way of repaying the region for its loyalty to Italy. It also visually, psychologically and effectively assimilated it into the nation. With the formation of a national championship, these clubs that had formerly been restricted to competing in the Veneto league were now able to 'officially enter into the Italian football family',[124] thereby simultaneously affirming their Italian identities and that of the region.

Symbols were also similarly employed, especially upon Italian regional or city flags. Celebrating the inauguration of Club Sportivo 'Olimpia' Fiume's Cantrida stadium in 1925, the club president requested flags from each Italian city to symbolically adorn the new stadium and form a 'dazzling garland of the signs of the beautiful cities of Italy, in this the most recent sister returned to the Nation'.[125] Interestingly, such examples of *calcio*'s exploitation for nationalist propaganda by the Fascist regime, also continued into the years of the democratic republic.

The expression of strong identities through football was no surprise, but there was considerable concern when, rather than act as bonding agents, teams became potentially destructive forces that might attack and atomize the national community. As *Il Bargello* expressed in 1929: 'Every football match between squads of nearby cities or from the same province, has the seeds of an incident waiting to happen . . . Fascism and sport cannot tolerate this . . . In sport one can be an adversary but one does not need to be an enemy. We already have enough of this at the border.'[126]

Despite the regime's desire to unite the nation through *calcio*, the threat of *campanilismo* featured frequently in the press and Ministry of the

Interior communications. In 1929 a number of entries record the exuberance of various fans spilling over into unacceptable acts and demonstrations of provincial and local identity. Such incidents were not just restricted to meetings of the big city clubs but also occurred on a local level, as seen in Forlì in the province of Emilia-Romagna in 1929. Like many football-related incidents in this period it did not appear to be a direct demonstration of opposition activity, but the prefect of Forlì was still obliged to inform the ministry in Rome of the events between the fans of AS Forlì and AC Faenza:

> Disputes of superiority of one over the other, rivalries of another type and an antiquated spirit of campanilismo were the cause of irreducible antagonism between the same squads and the respective supporters; antagonism that . . . degenerated into complete hostility [and] went beyond . . . the character of brotherhood and of chivalrous competition that should mark similar athletic activities, encouraged and sustained, exclusively, for the best physical and moral development of youth.[127]

Earlier in the same year, there was considerable concern about the match between Lazio and Napoli. With Naples possessing one of the most intense and potentially combustible city identities in the country, especially when placed in direct competition with Rome, the *Questura* (provincial police HQ) of Rome condemned the local Neapolitan press for escalating the importance of the match.[128] One example was *Il Piccolo*'s encouragement of Napoli fans to draw together in a symbol of the club and to cheer the team to victory; the voice of the fans again deemed important in achieving the desired result.[129] The potential for conflict between rival sets of supporters was also recognized by *Il Popolo di Roma*, which saw 'the comparison between the two publics [as] no less interesting than that between the two squads.'[130]

The match did not escape the Ministry of the Interior's attention and it communicated that, if necessary, the *Questura* would suspend it for reasons of public order. On the eve of the game, the progress of 2,000 or more travelling Napoli fans was transmitted back to the ministry by the *Questura* in a number of telegrams that conveyed the sense of a military operation.[131] While the crowd was lively the match was played in relative peace, which may have been due to either the 0–0 scoreline that kept tempers from flaring or 'the severest police measures taken and the timely intervention of public force', which gave the impression 'the authorities would not have tolerated any disorderly events'.[132]

On these occasions the rivalry between supporters of respective clubs took precedence over the sporting nature of the contest. Provincial antagonisms were also not unusual and following earlier violence between fans of the Calabrian teams of Catanzaro and Cosenza, the local press led a campaign to promote friendship between the two groups. Somewhat ambiguously, however, *La Giovane Calabria* stated that the 750 'Catanzaresi are not going to provoke. But they are not going to be the sheep in the 'wolves' lair.'[133] Once again, a heavy police presence staved off any trouble.

These few examples among many recorded by the Ministry of the Interior, indicate how the regime was unable to suppress the strong city-based identities that had existed throughout the peninsula for centuries and were being incited by *calcio*. As the *Questura* noted, such incidents exemplified: 'the spirit of campanilismo that . . . should no longer constitute any more than a sad record of the past.'[134]

Such was the interest in the burgeoning numbers of fans and consequent local rivalries that a literature began to emerge, specific to this phenomenon, one anthropological assessment making a strong distinction between the character and nature of fans from the differing metropolitan centres.[135] There were also predictable references to the past by those who believed the new stadia were lowering the masses' critical abilities. Yet, whatever anybody may have said or thought about the numerical explosion of football supporters, it was impossible to ignore the regime's efforts to transform traditional Sunday afternoon rituals into something more secular and arguably more widespread. By 1934, for good or bad, Carlo Levi noted the vast number of Italians following the fortunes of their city's team:

> The stadiums are full every Sunday with enthusiastic crowds, despite the high prices; they spend hours competently discussing the respective merits of this or that player . . . of the papers one reads above all the sports page; on the radio one listens to match reports; on Sunday evenings the crowds anxiously and restlessly wait outside cafes for the results of the day.[136]

The regime's investment in the game had constructed a truly national format that certainly developed a strong sense of identity among the population, if not always in the way intended. While the National League was formed with the specific aim of uniting Italy through the domestic game, it was also designed to raise the technical standards of Italian players with one eye on the potential benefits of a successful international team. While any international achievements would naturally have acted as a societal glue, the regime was also aware of the considerable diplomatic kudos and international prestige to be gained from a national team capable of defeating the best countries in the world.

The Fascist restructuring had imposed profound changes on *calcio*, which now possessed an organizational hierarchy capable of controlling and disciplining its main protagonists. However, this was not achievable through organization alone, as there was also need for financial investment in the sporting infrastructure if mass audiences, the likes of which had not been seen on a regular basis since Roman times, were to be attracted and controlled. With football out of intensive care and recovering well in the Fascist convalescence unit, the regime turned its attention towards restructuring the game's bricks and mortar by encouraging and supervising the development of stadia that were multi-purpose on a number of different levels.

–4–

Building the Future

The PNF in pursuing effective sporting propaganda, which started with the intent of decisively and energetically caring for the physical education of our youth, decided to build a sports ground in every commune of Italy that, responding to the modern needs of the sport, might be easy and inexpensive to produce. PNF, *Campo Sportivo del Littorio*

In terms of its organization, the regime had already invested heavily in *calcio* as a conduit through which it believed an Italian Fascist identity could be stimulated, promoted and diffused among the nation. The key to any such success was the leisure-time mobilization of the masses, which saw the promotion of the fan – as opposed to merely the football follower – and the growth of the mass football crowd. Although not an entirely new phenomenon, the expansion of what had been small interest groups into tens of thousands of supporters stemmed from Fascism's promotion of the game and its construction of stadia throughout the peninsula, which complemented its physical education programme and drive for racial fitness.

Stadia, however, were more than just venues for football. Designed to symbolize Italy's Roman past, Fascist present and promise for the future, they performed an important propaganda function. Yet so eclectic were their sources of inspiration that they failed to conform to any consistent architectural model, as recognized by the architect Giuseppe De Finetti. Commenting on the eight stadia built for the 1934 World Cup tournament, he described them as showing 'a lack of tradition and unitary method; comparing them does not only result in a lack of similarity but some do not even present a symmetrical and closed form'.[1]

While stadia often appeared to be conflicting representations of the past and the future they were also key features in the identity of many Fascist cities, their often diverse architecture a powerful and radical symbol that often reflected the nature of the city's politics. Extending Berezin's argument that the public piazza represented 'the temporary community of fascist feeling, that would define the fascist self or identity',[2] I suggest that stadia and football arenas offered the same potential but with bigger, more attentive audiences that attended more often.

Despite *calcio*'s many positive contributions to society it still had its critics, many of whom were concerned that the new stadia with mass crowds were little more than modern centres of degeneration. Others detected more positive aspects to the expansion of *calcio*, which was quickly transforming from a game into a spectacle.

The work of theatrical writers and actors had traditionally played an important role in developing, establishing and marking new national epochs, and as the novelist, journalist and theatre critic Massimo Bontempelli recognized, there was more to their success than merely the nature and quality of the performance itself. There was also the audience: 'The spectacle is a collaboration. The participation of the public, with its attendance and discussion of the theatre, constitutes a great part of the theatrical life of a given country at a given time.'[3] Bontempelli believed that each new era or epoch defined itself by creating its own myths, which were often expounded through performance art, an idea that Emilio Gentile comprehensively developed in his study of the sacralization of politics under the regime.[4]

As will be seen, Fascism did not oppose theatre by definition, but its bourgeois exclusivity created an ethical dilemma that contradicted the image of the regime's new political and social order. Mussolini's plan to combat this ideological conundrum with the construction of Fascist theatres failed, which, according to Bontempelli, provided an opportunity for *calcio* to become a focal point in the cultural life of the masses. In reality, it already was.

Far from exclusive middle-class venues impacting negatively on society, modern stadia were the mass theatres of the present and the future, novel in their dimensions, style and capacity to accommodate huge audiences that contributed to the spectacle. Describing the experience of supporting a particular team as 'a collective act of abandon, of generosity',[5] Bontempelli identified the growing importance of supporters even if he failed to stress the key role of stadia in the spectacle. More than just training grounds and 'theatres' for the masses, stadia unquestionably served as propaganda vehicles in the regime's attempt to construct a national culture and community. As Tim Benton notes in his study of architecture under the regime: 'at every site where large numbers of people gathered, buildings, sculptures and paintings were enlisted to transform comradeship into tribalism, pride into a sense of superiority, a sense of belonging into hatred of outsiders . . . Buildings played a crucial role in this political process.'[6]

The Level Playing Field

Improving the desperate condition of existing sports facilities had been discussed for many years, with particular reference to the impoverished state of school sport. The few halls and gymnasia that did exist, especially in southern Italy, usually lacked running water and washing facilities, and were insufficiently ventilated, which often contributed to the type of respiratory illnesses and poor growth that physical activity was intended combat.[7] Despite this desperate shortage, the parliamentary deputy De Capitani still found himself ridiculed in the Chamber, in 1919, for daring to raise the need to construct gymnasia throughout Italy.[8]

Among socialists, only Terzino's article in *Sport e Proletariato* in 1923 drew attention to the lack of sports facilities.[9] Even in Rome, those that did exist were owned by private individuals or institutions, such as the army, while outside of the capital stadia such as the Arena in Milan were primarily used for bullfighting, fairs and displays that made little contribution to the well-being of the masses. Terzino's proposed solution had already proven successful in other countries: 'Where they are not already, stadia might become municipal property with the obligation on the behalf of the commune to rent them, at a reasonable price, to associations that might want to hold worthy sporting activities.'[10]

As with their blueprint for the development of mass sport, the socialists had once again pre-empted, inspired or stimulated Fascist plans for a national programme of stadium construction. True as this may have been, it would be wrong to suggest the resulting programme was anything other than a Fascist project. As the architect Paolo Vietti-Violi observed in *Casabella*, the monthly dedicated to international architecture: 'the rebirth of sport and above all the spirit of sport in Italy, as wanted, directed and organized by the Fascist Regime, has itself brought about an impressive renewal of sporting works.'[11]

The completion of the Littoriale complex in Bologna signalled the regime's intent to take sport and stadium building seriously, its commitment becoming law on 21 June 1928.[12] From this point onwards, prefects were expected to familiarize themselves with CONI's technical specifications and the potential financial difficulties that had already been experienced by many communes, prior to approving the construction or modification of sports buildings. To make projects as economically viable as possible, the compulsory specifications for stadia were partially reduced, although the PNF still published a detailed pamphlet that included a variety of designs and specific features and dimensions to which the new *campi sportivi* were expected to conform.[13] While the regime clearly accepted its responsibility if every commune were to have its own sports facilities, equally it did not seek a monopoly and was happy to encourage private initiatives, as *Lo Sport Fascista* made clear:

> It is necessary to fight back against the fatalistic attitude of expecting every-thing from the government or the commune. We think in this case that the communes might have exhausted their noble work when they gave the neces-sary land for the construction of the field . . . The rest, that is the equipment and the management of the field, should be done by an existing in situ sports society, or by a society that could be created for the occasion . . . However, you will not forget that the communal sports field must be 'the field for everybody'.[14]

The Marquis Luigi Ridolfi, president and secretary of the Tuscan Fascist Sports Authority, and the leading Florentine Fascist Alessandro Pavolini, took up the challenge in their region. After conducting a census of sports facilities, they informed the various mayors of the shortage: the 'neces-sity for sports grounds in every centre, including small ones, makes itself more urgent and unavoidable each day. It is absolutely necessary that each commune has its own sports field, where it is possible to train and prepare our youth.'[15] As they continued to stress, large stadia were not always necessary, as moderately sized, more or less rectangular sports fields that could accommodate both track and field athletics and football would serve the purpose.

Others suggested the legislative demand that all football stadia possess a running track was both unfair and potentially unworkable, which had particular relevance for those clubs struggling in the south. As the party secretary Augusto Turati stated in a circular to government officers and sports leaders: 'This initiative needs to be of special advantage for sport in the south, which, due to the absolute lack of facilities, exists with great difficulty and overcomes unheard of problems.'[16]

Motivated by the extreme lack of facilities in their region, Ridolfi and Pavolini, aided by other significant voices such as the Florentine Fascist weekly *Il Bargello*, launched a campaign to address the issue on both the macro and micro levels. Acknowledging the deficiency in sporting facil-ities as a national problem, the magazine publicized the gravity of the situation in Tuscany, where Pisa and Florence contained the only two athletics tracks in the region's nine province.[17] Nonetheless, the generally accepted need to develop athletics facilities in the regions in particular, went unregistered, as the minimal sources of funding continued to be siphoned off by already well established sports.

A local initiative, Pisa's newly completed stadium was used to demon-strate the possibilities throughout the peninsula. Where economic factors prevented communes from contributing to the costs *La Gazzetta* suggested alternative, private forms of patronage,[18] while *Lo Sport Fascista* cited a Bolognese fundraising measure that bound individual acts of generosity into the responsibility of the collective, to request 'spontaneous contributions from the population.'[19]

The regime's desire had not been specifically to develop athletics among the nation so much as to establish a culture of athleticism among the masses.[20] The construction of sports facilities also carried the additional benefit of significantly contributing to the alleviation of unemployment, in addition to improving the health of local citizens.[21] While the economic benefits had yet to show in 1929, *Lo Sport Fascista* noted the improvement in the nation's health: 'Fascism did not create sport, but it knew how to create the mass of sportsmen [and] the athletic conscience in the Italian people. Tomorrow the sporting education of the population will be complete. You will see the communal sports grounds will have a use.'[22]

Frustrated by Tuscan inactivity, *Il Bargello* demanded CONI's forceful intervention 'among the sporting leaders of the provinces of Livorno, Lucca, Arezzo, Massa Carrara, Grosseto, Pisa and Pistoia to make understood, once and for all, that it is a pressing and unavoidable necessity, to give to athletics what has already been given to other sports'.[23] While fully publicizing the dearth of facilities may have embarrassed the authorities into rectifying the problem to some degree, the deficit was also transformed into a political opportunity, the architect Paolo Vietti-Violi locating the source of the problem directly in the liberal era: 'Until a few years ago we still judged foreign stadia, in Germany, France, and especially America . . . as insignificant works.' However, a 'more careful and intelligent education of the sporting mind has recognized the errors of the past',[24] which resulted in new stadia superseding those that had formerly been the yardstick. One of the earliest examples was that of the 'Società anonima Nafta' in Genoa, created by Vietti-Violi himself. A multisport stadium designed to blend in with the city's hills, it accommodated football, athletics and cycling and proved to be one of the first of many such Fascist stadia built with an emphasis upon both practicality and style.

Despite the desperate need for new sports facilities, all construction projects now had to conform to a rigid set of guidelines as provided by the party secretary and the commissioner of CONI.[25] As *Lo Sport Fascista* demanded, it was time to end CONI's consistent inability to impose these guidelines, which had resulted in the earlier approval and construction of new buildings that failed to refer to the 'diverse technical norms that govern each sport.'[26] Irregular-shaped football pitches and running tracks were no longer acceptable if sport was to serve the regime's needs successfully.

Legislating for Good Taste

Fascist sports buildings were not only works of beauty but also expressions of the athletic culture towards which the youth of Italy was being directed.[27] By 1930 over 3,280 new sports grounds of all sizes and descriptions had risen to serve the variety of needy organizations in over 2,000 communes. A stark contrast to the 1870 figure of zero,[28] there were also enough large, showpiece stadia by 1932 for Fascist Italy to make a successful bid to host the World Cup tournament two years later.[29]

Yet, if Italy was to really 'affirm its expertise in the architectural contest',[30] De Finetti believed that the regime needed to impose the demands of the 1928 legislation more thoroughly. In spite of the 3,280 new facilities, local rivalries and self-interest were still resulting in buildings that fell below the established standards:

> Italy, which a few years ago seriously set about sporting competition and met with triumphal success, also needs to affirm its expertise in the architectural contest. Since 1928 Italy has possessed a far-sighted law that imposes a severe technical preventive control on each new sports building. When this law is applied to the full and the stubborn resistance of local autonomies and ambitions gives way to the clear unity of intent that is the law, then the Olympic spirit . . . will also be able to clearly express itself in our architecture.[31]

De Finetti appeared to have exaggerated the extent of the problem, but despite the notable statistics there was still a dramatic disproportion between stadia in the north and south. One comparison was the thirty-nine separate facilities in the small Piedmont town of Vercelli with thirty-eight in the huge metropolis of Naples.[32] This disproportion accepted, De Finetti still demanded quality and quantity that would reflect the aims of the regime.

In 1934 the PNF secretary and CONI president, Achille Starace, appointed a Commissione Impianti Sportivi (CIS) – Commission of Sports Facilities – under the auspices of the 1928 law, to determine and implement the technical and financial considerations necessary for sporting works. The Commission represented an attempt to address the problems that had restricted the 1928 law's quality control, and as the ultimate standards watchdog, the CIS was empowered to:

a) Approve the project, alone, from technical and financial points of view.
b) Approve part of the project and recommend necessary modifications.
c) Order additions, dimensional changes and general orders to be carried out.
d) Approve variations to the project sent after its first approval, or variations to already existing works.
e) Reject a project.
f) Carry out periodic checks, by one of its members, on works on progress. (The costs for each of the inspections are to be met completely by the body responsible for the work).[33]

Theoretically, these powers made it easier for the CIS to impose the construction norms that would guarantee sport's continued vitality and development, plus the regime's commitment to the design or aesthetic aspect of sports buildings. As highlighted in the preface of the CIS's *regolamento* – regulation – Fascism was interested in sports buildings from more than just the perspective of functionality: 'each sporting work, from the most modest to the monumental, is always a potent and efficient method of propaganda. Thus it largely needs to satisfy not only the technical demands of who trains there, to encourage him to persevere in his noble work, but also the needs of the spectator.'[34]

Demonstrating the regime's desire to exploit sport as a means of propaganda this statement emphasized the importance of athletes *and* spectators, which was a clear progression from traditional thinking that had only been able to focus on the apparently degenerative aspects of spectating. Besides ensuring surroundings in which the athletes felt truly 'at home', the *regolamento* also determined that the seats, stairs, entrances, access streets etc, needed to be studied and resolved with care.[35] As large crowds became regular features of football, it indicated the regime's desire to increase its control over them. Although the behaviour of supporters had theoretically become the responsibility of the clubs themselves,[36] this paternalistic concern for supporters' welfare reflected Fascism's desire to protect and defend the well-being of organic society, even if this amounted to protecting it from itself. It also indicated the regime's awareness that it was not only the athletes themselves who could be influenced by, or even contribute to the development sporting propaganda, as the fans had a role too.

Other key considerations in all new proposals, if unnecessary economic and aesthetic excesses were to be avoided, were functionality, practicality and above all thrift.

The norms detailed here have the scope to prevent useless fantasies and superfluous costs and serve, at the same time, to avoid the disadvantages of bad economic designs. For this reason it is established that the lay-out and construction of sports fields needs to be subject to statutory dimensions and systems, already tried by experience, so as not to condemn the athletes that train there, to inferior conditions.[37]

While no necessary equipment for particular sports was to have been sacrificed at the altar of economy, extras received scrupulous attention. A clever semantic argument suggested that in reality they did not exist; they were either necessities or otherwise. This demanded that proposals for new stadia were accompanied by a detailed breakdown of individual pieces of equipment, in a budget that guaranteed the project's financing and completion.[38]

Specific as these guidelines were, given the established norms derived from the experience of already completed projects, rather than imposing homogeneity upon Fascist stadia they allowed considerable room for manoeuvre. As will be seen, the enormous contrasts between the flagship stadia of Bologna and Florence, completed within five years of each other, showed the considerable artistic licence permissible within stadia designed to represent the dynamism of the regime and facilitate athletic endeavour. The considerable and technical norms of the CIS *regolamento* do not demand point by point analysis in this study. However, there are some that shed further light upon the regime's exploitation of sport, in the broadest sense possible, to further its propaganda needs.

The bare minimum established for any sports ground that included a football pitch or athletics track was separate changing rooms for two teams and the referee, plus a spectator area surrounding the ground with direct access from the street. One of the ruling's major concerns was the need for good communication links within the city and effective crowd control, which required an adequate number of ticket offices, entry points, stairs to access the terraces and differentiated seating areas.[39]

No doubt in response to past errors and neglect, training facilities were also made a prerequisite for any successful proposal, thereby reflecting Fascism's dual drive for both excellence and the development of physical exercise among mass society. It was an element deemed especially important for those cities with the worst conditions and the greatest masses,[40] of which the regime wanted to ingratiate as many as possible into sport. To achieve this, while taking account of the continuing growth of urban society, all projects submitted to the Committee had to include a study for their potential, future expansion.

If the commissioning body, be it the commune or otherwise, decided upon a competition among architects and engineers to select the best entry, the CIS also held the right to approve the design brief and competition rules. Yet, while the *regolamento* was specific in what sports buildings and stadia should include and be designed to achieve, its aesthetic demands contained enough ambiguity to encourage creativity: 'The architecture of sporting works does not need to be an end in itself; but it does need to be clear and simple, characterised by the criteria of pure modernity. Every unnecessary decoration is to be avoided and the equivalent sum will be spent on improving the facilities and the field.'[41]

Again, the Commission was in the enviable position of having the full benefit of hindsight at its disposal. By studying already completed stadia, such as Bologna and Florence, it was able to ascertain that with the combination of skill, imagination and modern techniques, architects and engineers could produce dramatically diverse stadia that were functional, economical and aesthetically avant-garde, while remaining comfortably within the regime's bounds of acceptability. In fact, far from compromising Fascism, the apparent paradox of these stadia had already shown how their diverse artistic roots, which embraced both *romanità* and modernism, could combine to form what was championed as its very own distinct style. Neither backward- nor forward-looking it represented the present, thereby responding to Mussolini's earlier call for 'a new art, an art for our times, a Fascist art'.[42] Despite the underlying reasons necessitating the CIS's *regolamento*, it was keen not to repress creativity in sporting architecture: 'The path that this ruling renders obligatory, far from being put together in order to restrict planners, looks to benefit them . . . so that the completed project makes an effective contribution to the propaganda and sporting education for which it was created.'[43]

So long as their work conformed to the guidelines, planners, designers, engineers and architects were more than free. In fact, they were positively encouraged to express their creativity and imagination. First and foremost, however, the rules dictated that stadia had to be bifunctional: not just in the sense that they worked as training grounds for the sporting development of Italian youth, but also that they contained an aesthetic value.

Given the number of large-scale stadia that had already been completed by 1934, the ruling could easily be interpreted as the regime slamming the door long after the horse had bolted. However, the artistic licence it provided suggests that, in fact, the regime neither intended nor desired to further impose itself, as its needs were already being well catered for. Apart from strengthening its grip on the localities, the limited nature of the changes in the 1934 *regolamento*, from the 1928 law, suggest it was more of an opportunity for Fascism to associate itself fully and more visibly with the rarity of a success story. In effect, rather than a radical attempt to Fascistize the sporting landscape, the CIS gave an official stamp of approval to the various ideas, arguments, influences and designs that had been in public circulation for some time and had formed the theoretical foundations upon which almost all stadia were constructed under the regime. Without detracting from the positive sense of direction the ruling intended to impart, it is clear that rather than breaking with tradition, the new set of norms was a synthesis of contemporary thought on how to derive the maximum benefit from all aspects of the explosion of sport and football.

Architecture and Sport

Stimulated by the regime's interest in construction, architects, engineers and journalists began to focus their attention upon the practical and aesthetic demands of modern stadia, thereby raising their level of importance in the process. Content to belong to the Fascist syndicate and work for the party, the new generation of modernists and rationalists proclaimed themselves as the only true architects of the regime, in a pamphlet handed to Mussolini at the beginning of the Second Italian Exhibition of Rationalist Architecture in 1931. 'Old architects are an emblem of impotence that will not do . . . Our movement has no other moral mission than that of serving the Revolution in hard times.'[44]

Naturally, the design and construction of stadia was only one aspect of the general contemporary architectural debate under Fascism that resulted in an expanding number of journals and magazines, one example being *Quadrante*. Formed in 1933 by a group of architects and edited by art critic Pier Maria Bardi, the monthly intended to bring some clarity to Italian architecture, which it believed had become a mass of confusing and often contradictory terms. As part of this process, the magazine's founders declared their intent to develop 'in the heart of European rationalism – a definite, coherent and uncompromising Italian style' founded on rationalism.[45] It would be an affirmation of ' "classicism" and "mediterraneanism" – designed in spirit; and not in form or folklore – in contrast with the "nordism" or "baroquism" or with the "arbitrary romanticism" of the new European architecture'.[46]

While the journal opposed 'foreign tendencies', it did so without excluding the study of foreign trends and ideas, all of which contributed to its construction or reinforcement of national identity through architecture.[47] As the modernist architect Pier Luigi Nervi explained in *Casabella*: 'The works that we carry out are not only the face of our society, but also mirror our spirit and ability: a lasting mirror and face that the future generations will pass judgement on. Thus, how is it possible not to be bothered by it?'[48]

One of Italy's most adventurous architects, Nervi believed it was not so much the quality of the materials that were most significant in a building's construction, but more 'the spirit, the aesthetic idea and static quality with which the elements are composed and proportioned.'[49] While reflecting many of his already significant contributions to the Fascist landscape, most dramatically the Giovanni Berta stadium in Florence, his comments also stressed the important role of architecture in the development and construction of football stadia, if they were to represent the regime adequately. Despite the importance of monumental projects, both big and small stadia featured regularly in almost all architectural magazines and journals of the era, as professionals grappled with the difficulties of accommodating the diverse and sometimes contradictory demands of sport and Fascism.

The Fascist interpretation of sport, which was essentially preoccupied with 'movement and speed', led G. Barbero to proclaim that those who 'are interested in it, even if only from the architectural point of view, have been caught in the mechanism; and in their projects they cannot fail to reflect on the impressive images of the athlete's sprint, the speed of the machine, or of the togetherness of the crowd'.[50] If not exactly new, the relationship between Futurist ideas, sport, speed and athleticism was certainly novel, with Barbero's most interesting observation reserved for the role of the crowd: 'Futurist sporting architecture that is occupied by sport as spectacle, is working for the game and the crowd. When the game becomes a passionate spectacle it is because the public has made it so.'[51]

The regime was not alone in its interest in sport during this period, as the rebirth of the Olympic Games had stimulated other countries and cities to create sports zones, as in Amsterdam and Los Angeles. Although similar to the Littoriale's multisport concept in Bologna, they nonetheless differed due to its Futurist/modernist appreciation of the importance of the crowd. As Barbero observed:

> the development of sports architecture runs parallel to the development of recreation, and the rising passion of the crowd completes it when it reaches that synchronised zenith that assimilates the athletes in the race, the machine, the mass and its cry. From this moment of dynamism rises the creature of the arts, they rise, those constructions that are thought to indulge the sporting impulse . . . Architecture passes from the built stadium to something more intensely planned that ties the sensibilities of the artist-architect to that of the crowd, the sprint of the athlete, the speed of the machine, to the plasticity of the mass.[52]

Despite the growing international interest in sport, nowhere was this interpretation better demonstrated than in Fascist Italy where a number of modern multisport stadia had risen to critical acclaim by the mid 1930s. From the smallest sporting constructions, such as the *Case di Balilla* – youth clubs[53] – to the monumental, all contributed to establishing the Fascist civilization. As Emilio Gentile has demonstrated: 'Fascism entrusted the materialization of its myth to the architectural world.'[54]

More than just trying to engender a love of sport, the construction of big and small stadia helped the government project a positive image of the nation, although not at any cost. As one government memorandum noted, the creation of sports grounds and monumental stadia were useful for national dignity and good for propaganda, but only when they did not weigh too heavily on the already stretched finances and did not encourage exhibitionism.[55] According to Renato Ricci, head of the ONB, these new stadia complemented the type of society that the regime was attempting to construct through the promotion of sport: 'It is a question of developing the physical culture of the collective more precisely, ordering it in a way to get greater efficiency and to form a new mentality . . . that could be precious without being of great financial cost.'[56]

Apart from Bologna and Florence, two of Fascism's most impressive and significant sports construction projects were in Turin and Rome. Work on Turin's Stadio Mussolini began in 1931 and was completed within 'a remarkable 180 days' according to *Casabella*.[57] Conforming to the multisport concept, the stadium provided facilities for football, rugby (*palla ovale*), athletics and swimming. Deliberately built in the city outskirts with good communication links and room for future expansion beyond its 65,000-spectator capacity, its oval-shaped design was said to ensure the best views from whatever part of the ground. Access, organization and safety had been carefully planned, right down to the staircases made from anti-slip stone.[58]

An example of rational modernism, the Stadio Mussolini was completed in time to host the 1933 Italian student games, De Finetti recording the event as showcasing the brilliance of Italian Fascist architecture.[59] Despite the stadium's strict budget, *La Gazzetta* still bragged about 'its great architectural conception and its vivid expression of modernity', which were achieved by combining simplicity and functionality.[60] Built principally in reinforced concrete with its structural elements left deliberately exposed, the stadium was another startling and original example of Italian architectural and engineering progress.

Dominating the principal entrance to the forecourt was the freestanding 40-metre-high, reinforced concrete Marathon Tower, with 'Stadio Mussolini' emblazoned on the front aspect. Similar to the tower in Florence, it also contained a glass façade, which was illuminated by night for the entire city to see. Being named after Mussolini was an honour bestowed upon only the worthiest buildings. Many others, such as the stadium completed in Naples in 1934, that requested permission as an expression of the 'city's profound recognition of the Duce',[61] were not deemed worthy of the 'honour'.[62]

The Turin stadium's resemblance to that of Florence was not so surprising given that the young architect responsible was Raffaello Fagnoni, who had been based in the Florentine Scuola Superiore d'Architettura under the supervision of the famous Giovanni Michelucci. Reflecting the dynamic, modernist style of such stadia in Fascist Italy, *La Gazzetta's* critic observed how Fagnoni had created something intrinsically original by blending local traditions with modern construction and design techniques. 'With this new building that rises in Turin, the architect Fagnoni knew . . . how to make an original work without returning to designs, at the cost of what might amount to an antique or a modern imitation.'[63]

So important was the general stadium-construction programme that it was exported beyond the mainland and into the colonies. Here, it was hoped that stadia might exploit both indigenous and imported cultures of sport to help project Fascist civilization upon the colonial regions, as a method of Italianization. Following the export of football to Tripoli, *La Nazione* reported how the increasing interest of expatriates and locals made the original, adapted sports ground inadequate for 'such a dignified and modern city'.[64]

Stimulated by examples in the motherland, the Tripoli municipal administration ceded an area of land and 500,000 lire to build a new stadium for the athletic and military preparation of the youth and the excitement of the crowd: 'The stadium will be completely equipped for all athletic games, and will be one of the best gyms for the physical education of those youths living in the Colony.'[65] Although giving his skills free of charge, the engineer Bono was still required to design a stadium that possessed 'architecturally strong Roman lines . . . worthy of the new fascist Tripoli', in an obvious effort to affirm and further Italianize the land's new identity.[66]

Differing stadium designs illustrated the contradictions of an eclectic 'ideology' that consistently linked itself with its Roman past while professing the merits of modernity at its most extreme. In this way, stadia were used to project the regime's modern and imperial inspiration, which was an integral part of Fascism's identity.

Roman Stadia in Fascist Cities

Fascism deliberately sought to reconstruct the glory of Imperial Rome and legitimize its rule through mythology connecting the two, but its building programme for large sporting works and stadia also, logically, referred to Ancient Greece.[67] In fact, the modern Italian sporting incarnations drew much inspiration from both the Roman and Greek empires in which ancient sport reached its apogee. As the architect and designer Silvio San Pietro notes, the ancient gymnasia were 'the architectural basis of the later stadia and hippodromes'.[68]

The original stadia in Ancient Greece, as seen in one of the greatest sporting cities Olympia, possessed only one stand/colonnade for spectators. Positioned parallel to the length of the field and running track to protect spectators' eyes from the direct sun, the design endured for the first thirteen ancient Olympic tournaments. Eventually it was superseded by a larger playing field and running track with two straights and one curve, three-quarters of what we would nowadays associate with an athletics track. Ensuring the best views of the action for all spectators,[69] it was replicated in the Athens 'Panathenaea' stadium, built in 1896 to celebrate the first modern Olympic Games.

Founded in 776 BC the one-day Olympian Games were repeated every four years, relatively unchanged, until 472 BC when the contest was expanded to include more events over five days. Many aspects of the ancient games and stadia were still found in Fascist sport, although ancient Greek sport's association with paganism was frowned upon by some Fascists as too narcissistic. Despite these pagan links, religion and sport were not necessarily rivals and one of the most interesting features of the Greek structural landscape was the way in which stadia and sports facilities often resided in close proximity to buildings dedicated to spiritual pursuits.[70]

So popular was spectator sport that ancient stadia also needed to be able to cope with vast crowds, which was probably the single most important stimulus in their continual development and evolution. Entrances and exits for spectators, which were originally limited to a single point, were increased to accommodate the crowds going to Rome's Circo Massimo, which was styled upon the Greek hippodrome. Once sporting events began to change from races into physical contests, the Romans abandoned the old rectangular-styled stadium and blended it with that of the Greek theatre, to produce an intrinsically Roman venue: the circular arena or amphitheatre. As San Pietro explained: 'Today's stadia vary little in design from their original classical counterparts. In many cases, the modern stadium derives directly from the classical Greek arrangement on two parallel sections squared off at one end and linked by a curved section at the other ... Others draw on the elliptical shape of Roman amphitheatres, or even the circular form.'[71]

With terraces surrounding the central field of play, it was gladiatorial spectacles that were contested rather than athletic competition. While some believed the ensuing battles between both man and man, and man and beast, demonstrated the strength of Rome, others argued the opposite. In fact, the crowd's hunger for such spectacles and the ensuing 'collective madness' fuelled the belief that such gladiatorial contests had contributed to the Empire's decadence and decline.

While ancient Greek stadia were always built next to the big cities, the Romans located them in the most beautiful parts of central localities, to enable easy access for citizens and create a strong bond between the arena and the city. However, in time, practicalities rather than preference restricted them to the suburbs where, as De Finetti explained, they could still become an integral part of city life:

> it is only as a prominent building in a settled urban landscape that the stadium becomes that 'secular assembly' that the ancients undoubtedly wanted and that we contemporaries would justly want to create; there it can become a focus of life no less than the theatres and the buildings dedicated to the arts. Only a mental apathy can be hostile to the urban idea of the ancients.[72]

The strong relationships that developed between the cities, citizens and arenas/stadia of ancient Rome and Verona, were something that 1930s contemporary planners were keen to replicate in the new wave of Fascist construction.

As 'masters of spherical design [and] severely rationalist architects', De Finetti observed the Romans optimum methods of crowd control through the use of multiple entry points, internal staircases and graduated terracing.[73] Rome's Flaminio and PNF stadia, opened in 1911 and 1928, Bologna's Littoriale, in 1927, and the 1933 Stadio Mussolini in Turin, all demonstrated the diverse ways in which the architecture of the Imperial past was adapted and revived in the Fascist present.

In addition to these stadia, Farnesina and the Foro Mussolini in Rome formed one of the most high profile examples of a sports facility that blended Imperial tradition and Fascist modernity. Launched following a land-reclamation programme, in 1928, to rid the banks of the Tiber of perpetual stagnant water at the foot of the Monte Mario, it was a perfect example of the Fascist concept of *bonifica* (reclamation), which could refer to the restoration of swampland to constructive use or the more alle-gorical regeneration of society, whereby bad weeds were torn up and the soil revitalized.[74] Besides *bonifica*, the project also showed Fascism's intent on transforming the city and Italy as a whole by juxtaposing Roman classicism with its own revolutionary beliefs, thereby creating an identity of its own. As Vittorio Orazi perfectly described in *La Citta Nuova*: 'After Caesar's Rome, Papal Rome, here is Rome of Fascist Italy.'[75]

The complex's position alone was dramatic enough, but this was augmented by a tall, white marble obelisk, dedicated to Mussolini, which confronted visitors as they crossed the Tiber. It marked the entry to the forum that began at the via Piazzale dell'Impero, a marble walkway decorated with Roman-style mosaics of sporting scenes and huge tablets of stone engraved with Fascist mottoes celebrating the principal moments in the history of Italy and the movement. Later integrated into the Foro Mussolini, the Farnesina complex included the Stadio dei Cipressi – Cypress stadium – indoor and outdoor swimming pools, tennis courts, a dance theatre and the open-air training centre known as the Stadio dei Marmi – Marble Stadium. Intended to form the foundation of Italy's bid for the 1944 Olympic Games, the area did provide a vast number of facilities for the Rome Olympics of 1960.

One of the many architects who worked on the project was Enrico Del Debbio, whose design for the Academy and the Marble stadium was another unsubtle juxtaposition of modernity and antiquity, which San Pietro has succinctly described (Figure 1):

> The architecture of the completed complex is charged with moral values and rhetorical content that are expressed by a successful synthesis of the modern and the classical . . . Del Debbio manages to give a relatively small structure a certain degree of balanced monumentality. Along the top of the marble terraces . . . there are sixty white *Hercules* that were donated by various Italian provinces. These veritable *mute athletes* today serve as a sculptural crown to the arena, but at the time they were also seen as a direct metaphor of virility and strength, educational emblems for the Regime's young sportsmen.[76]

Despite the indulgent statues, the stadium's aesthetics were still restricted to a decorative minimum, while its marriage of the old and new further indicated the regime's comfort with unavoidably strong Greek influences. Recognizing this, the contemporary architect and designer of the PNF Stadium Marcello Piacentini, defined the whole complex as: 'a modern version of the ancient *gimnasium* [. . .] a great stage for upright growth [. . .] (a synthesis) of all the characteristics of what is perennially Roman [. . .] (which can also) offer an example of Greek beauty in its chastely

Figure 1 A Fascist gladiator. Catanzaro's contribution to the Stadio dei Marmi.
© Simon Martin, 2004.

naked buildings.'[77] As a description of the Stadio dei Marmi's sculptures
and many of the stadia constructed under Fascism – such as the fully
exposed skeletons of the supermodels of Turin and Florence, which broke
provocatively with tradition – 'chaste nudity' perfectly encapsulated the
blend of the classical past and the daring future that produced the immacu-
late conception of the Fascist present.

As *La Gazzetta* proudly noted at the time, the stadium was 'inspired by
the artistic principles of ancient Rome' and showed 'its opulence in the
abundance of the marble',[78] which also represented more than just the
self-indulgence of a spendthrift architect. Cut from the Tuscan mountains

at Carrara, it demonstrated the regime's autarchic preference for building with nationally and, if possible, locally produced materials. Besides stamping an Italian identity on stadia, it also assisted their rapid integration into local communities by stimulating their economies. In the case of the Stadio dei Marmi, marble was also deliberately chosen to make an impact on the eye that was impossible to ignore. As *La Gazzetta* boasted, in the full rays of the sun the literally blinding stadium was a 'triumph of the most classical simplicity' that resulted from 'the materials used and the essential elements that compose it: the terraces, the great curve, the statues, and the marble'.[79]

Blinding whiteness was a prominent feature of stadia and Fascist architecture in general, even if it was not always economically viable or aesthetically desirable to reproduce this effect with marble. In fact, many new stadia, as will be seen in the case of the Giovanni Berta in Florence, were built entirely from reinforced concrete that, in strong daylight, appeared to be white, almost of marble. This 'whiteness' was a consistent feature of the myth of the new vitality of Fascist life, which architecture was intended to symbolize.

One of the most important architectural contributions to the creation of such Fascist mythology was to have been the Universal Exhibition (EUR 42), which should have opened in Rome in 1942. As one of the regime's largest and most ambitious building projects intended to physically record the era for future centuries,[80] EUR's most distinctive feature was the use of lighting to project the new Fascist civilization. As Emilio Gentile argued: 'white architecture symbolised the triumph of the Mediterranean sun, [and] was intended to represent fascism's victory over fate in future centuries'.[81]

It was an architectural style that featured among many of the new stadia, which were honing and inspiring the future generations. In the Giovanni Berta the prominent Marathon Tower was illuminated at night, while in the Stadio dei Marmi broad daylight provided more than enough energy to radiate its message. Despite being a relatively modest-sized arena, the connection between the past, present and the future was made more through the intensity of the stadium's design and its statues than anything monolithic, which proved to be more the exception than the rule. Driven by the modernist architectural movement, monumental buildings quickly became an imposing feature of Mussolini's cityscapes. In Fascist Italy size certainly did matter and as the popularity of *calcio* continued to grow, so stadia needed to expand if the masses were to be comfortably accommodated and efficiently organized.

Despite the regime's clear affection for its imperial roots, every aspect of its investment in sport was to develop and impose an identity of its own, albeit one that often referred to its Roman heritage. Nonetheless, however practical and well-designed ancient sporting facilities might have been, their mere adaptation was not enough to represent the new regime adequately. New stadia and sports facilities had to contain ground-breaking features displaying Fascism's ancient roots and futuristic influences, while reflecting the regenerative and vibrant role of cities in the life of the urban mass.

This opened the window of opportunity to primarily modernist architects who preferred to concentrate on the present and the future, rather than the past. The importance of modern, urban, city centres resulted in a vast number of competitions and projects throughout the Fascist period. Although only a minority ever progressed beyond the planner's dream, they usually reflected the regime's desire to correct the errors of the past while stamping its own identity on the present. According to an editorial in *La Città Nuova*, while there were still 'too many people in Italy that had not understood the importance of architecture and art', they contrasted directly with 'those young and capable artists that [we]re willingly providing Fascist Italy with works worthy of the time'.[82]

Apparently uninspired by the aesthetic, it was these artists' responses to the nation's radically renovated spirit that would finally overcome 'neo-classicism and all the horrible false modernities that deface cities today'.[83] As Pippo Oriani argued, such futuristic ideals were a direct response to previous styles of architecture and city organization that had produced isolated buildings lacking 'the rapport of continuity or organic unity' with the rest of the city.[84] More than just castigating many of liberal Italy's building projects, his remark outlined the new, community-focused Fascist vision for modern cities. To ensure cities were restructured in accordance with this, they were instructed to draw up redevelopment plans, as Oriani explained:

> The regulatory plans provide for the demolition of the complicated and intricate old road layouts and, with the opening of new arteries adapted to the present day's traffic, they will stipulate the reconstruction according to the concept of the mass (totalitarian vision) and never the single building (fragmented vision). The totalitarian vision of the city thus held, is of a living organizm for which the districts represent the living cells.[85]

His interpretation of the idealized, modern, Fascist city complemented the regime's organic vision of society, whereby individuals constituted the living cells of the greater being. Modern city centres were to contain the general buildings for public life, such as banks and offices, in addition to the entertainment/party centres of the *Case Littorie* and the *Case di*

Balilla, which De Finetti claimed were among 'the most valuable creations of the new Italy. The organization of these young energies not only creates the athletes of tomorrow, but it also creates that popular spirit that will be seen in the stadia . . . as used to be seen in the theatres of yesterday.'[86] In these city centres that had been subjected to the greatest 'horrors' of the past, buildings completely unsuited to the harmony of the modern era were targeted for demolition to make way for more modernistic structures that reflected the new political age. One such attempt was Via Roma in Turin; however, its failure, apparently due to 'invalid re-designs, public adversity [plus] clear and intelligent attacks by critics and artists', was considered a grave threat to the future of Fascist civilization.[87] A similar plan for Bologna's Via Roma also failed to mature.[88]

If the city centres were to house public buildings, the peripheries would contain the more practical and productive needs, such as accommodating the industrial districts and the associated mass workforce. For this reason, the suburbs were a natural and practical site for the Dopolavoro gymnasia, sports fields, stadia, etc.

Despite the desperate need for sports buildings, whether privately or publicly funded they still represented a spiritual and political expression of the country, which had to be reflected in their design. Consequently, Pippo Oriani believed it was no longer appropriate, even absurd, to imitate previous eras in contemporary structures that had a completely different function to those of the past: 'Fortunately in Italy the renovating gust of aesthetic architecture, spiritually tied to our political system, has made itself felt with achievements of great importance. Sports stadia and youth clubs are at the avant-garde of all other constructions.'[89]

So politically important were buildings that simple progress alone was not enough for more intransigent critics who demanded they become an integrated part of Fascist Italy's urban renewal programme. Unfortunately, as Oriani illustrated, local dynamics and desires continued, on occasion, to produce structures that appeared to refer back to the democratic past:

> It is absurd that the modernity of a construction might often depend upon the taste of a local leader and not on the rationale of constructive continuity. Hence, you see stations, post offices, youth clubs, potent futurist creations, open to the most innovative winds of change – and you see public administration buildings that seem to have risen to the monumental memory of democracy. A stylistic discipline in construction is urgent and necessary . . .[90]

La Città Nuova continued its rage against reactionary architecture by attacking existing buildings that even showed some promise, but were 'stupidly diminished by nineteenth-century and neo-classical pictures, and sculptures of an idiotic and anti-virile primitivism. It is time for the architects to understand that only the futurist model is coherent with new buildings.'[91] One example of decorative misuse were the 'outdated' offices of the big banks that were adorned by ornamental motifs promoting their institutions, which offended contemporary political sensibilities.

Decoration was not entirely discouraged, however, as the regime also exploited symbols to construct and impose its identity and authority. Besides the intrinsic political value of widespread images of Fascism, their reproduction was encouraged to help paper over the past. Even for sports facilities, symbols, art and the aesthetic were clearly acceptable as instruments of domestic and foreign propaganda. In fact, so keen was CONI to give a good representation of the regime at the Berlin Olympics that it launched a competition encouraging artists and sculptors to turn their attention 'towards the actors and the spectacles of the modern sporting activity'.[92]

The politicization of the aesthetic towards Fascist needs did not prevent architectural polemics from continuing to rage, as in the wake of Marcel Breuer's discussion of the relationship between politics and architecture in *Casabella*. Arguing that the architect's political background, whether he was a member of the Fascist syndicate or not, for example, was less important than his development of the best possible solutions to construction problems, Breuer suggested that: 'a Fascist can build the palace of Soviets in Moscow, a communist the Mole Littoria in Rome, just as the car manufacturer sells his vehicles without a care for the political colour of his client.'[93]

Describing his ideas as brilliant for their 'absence of sane political sense', Giuseppe Pagano believed that Breuer's many critics in *Regime Fascista* had similarly failed to understand the relationship between politics and architecture, placing too much importance on the political. A balance needed to be struck between the two as neither could resolve artistic problems alone. What counted, in Pagano's opinion, was 'the work and the artistic sensibility' and not just the political leanings of the creator, as 'Membership of the Fascist Syndicate or the Moscow Soviet of architects does not have the magic to transform a violinist into a genius'.[94] Thus, membership of the Fascist syndicate alone could not bludgeon an architect into producing aesthetically and politically acceptable buildings.

If membership of the syndicate did not guarantee the creation of an acceptable work of art, the role of buildings as visual representations of the regime equally reduced the importance of an individual's membership of the official architectural body in relation to their work. In the same way that self-censorship meant that control of the press was less severe than in other dictatorships, so architects' sensitivities and responses to the demands of Fascism reduced the need for a more intense scrutiny of their work. As Berghaus has observed: 'An official attitude of loyalty was the most they were asked to demonstrate; whatever they thought and said in private was of little interest to the functionaries.'[95]

Yet even among Fascist deputies, ferocious debates continued as to what exactly the needs of the regime were and if they might be better served by modernistic tendencies from outside of Italy, or by the example of the Roman past. One such debate in the Chamber of Deputies focused on the proposals for the new railway station in Florence and the *Casa Littoria*, the intended home of Fascism to be built in Rome. In protest at what he saw as 'Teutonic tendencies', the Roman MP Francesco Giunta suggested that: 'To build the Casa Littoria well, it should be enough for us to look at our heart. (vivacious applause) In certain cases membership of the Party does not say anything. We do not need to import anything from other people too distant from us in origin, spirit or tradition.'[96] However, the openly aggressive attack against modern architecture, as led by the former party secretary Roberto Farinacci, only provoked Mussolini into slightly clarifying his position.

On 10 June 1934, within two weeks of the Chamber's discussion, Mussolini demonstrated his satisfaction with the progeny of politics and art by inviting a number of young architects to Rome. According to *Casabella* the reception, which included the group of designers for the new and lauded Florence station, was intended to express the 'pleasure and applause, that he [Mussolini] wanted to extend to the young that seek to realise in architecture and other fields, an art responsive to the sensibility and the needs of our fascist century'.[97] Deliberately disseminated throughout the national press for the benefit of prefects, mayors and local dignitaries, his words were supposed to finally clarify the matter.

Under the headline 'Mussolini saves Italian architecture' (*Mussolini salva l'architettura Italiana*), Pagano triumphantly proclaimed the modernist victory: 'Modern architecture has now become State art . . . modern architects have been officially invested with a great, historic responsibility.'[98] For the regime that fully exploited the potential of the visual image to recreate the past and project visions of the future in the present, artists of all descriptions were expected to contribute to the establishment and maintenance of its identity and authority.

Despite Pagano's belief that Mussolini had handed this responsibility to modern architects, the Duce's statement was far from conclusive and the regime never subscribed to any specific style in its entirety. Fascism was too practical for this. While there was a clear preference for modernism, Mussolini was astute enough not to confine the regime to restrictive artistic norms. In reality, he was more interested in seeing works of art that best represented Fascism, whatever their origins and inspiration. As Ruth Ben-Ghiatt identified within Fascist culture as whole, this not only encouraged inspirational competition among intellectuals seeking legitimacy in their work, it also 'allowed those that did not openly identify themselves as fascists to participate in the public initiatives of the regime'.[99]

Although clearly absorbed by past influences on stadium design, De Finetti was one modernist whose ideas reflected the way the ancient and futuristic could be merged into a radical representation of the present. Uninterested in merely extolling the virtues of Fascist Italy's Roman ancestry, he was keen to learn from positive and negative past experiences so as to avoid repeating previous errors; such as football and sports grounds with no practice facilities. As part of a framework ensuring that new stadia met modern needs, Paolo Vietti-Violi stressed the importance of first defining 'the different aims, the technical and sporting characteristics and even the eventual secondary needs that might initially seem to be of little importance, but later have their own real value'.[100]

No doubt with one eye on Fascism's Roman heritage, an overriding theme of Vietti-Violi's general appraisal of the complete planning process for new stadia was order and control among spectators, while ensuring they became physically and perhaps psychologically integrated into the city. His plan was not specifically designed to control the amorphous masses of modernity that Fascism feared and fed off in equal measure, but there can be no doubt that modern stadia with an enhanced capacity to control crowds would have appealed to the regime.

In fact, the concepts of Vietti-Violi and his contemporaries who had already expressed similar ideas were the result of good sense and forethought for which Italian football still owes a debt of gratitude. To improve crowd control they focused their attention on the physical location of stadia, arguing that they were best suited to city extremities. Not only effective at the time, it also facilitated their redevelopment to accommodate the demands of the modern game with far greater ease than many built in the industrial centres of England. Consequently, if they were to be suburban but not isolated from the masses and the city centres, infrastructure was a key issue. This accounted for the crucial attention paid to public transport and the improvement of access roads for any successful project. Modernity also demanded parking facilities to accommodate the increasing amount of private vehicles that Vietti-Violi suggested would be best controlled by a one-way system around the ground. Within the stadia, he proposed large and clearly signed entry points with turnstiles corresponding to the different sections of the ground to assist the efficient control of ticketing and the movement of spectators; all of which reinforced and reflected the regime's culture of collective discipline.[101]

A logical application of Roman planning to modern needs, Vietti-Violi's simple ideas drew attention to the way in which the needs of sports facilities had begun to extend beyond the event itself. As the number of spectators grew, so did their importance to the regime, which was reflected in the nature of the stadium-construction programme that went beyond just providing facilities for athletes and spectators alike. In fact, there is a convincing argument that the regime saw an opportunity in the massive growth of spectator sport to provide more than simply comfort, safety and style. There was also the chance to control and direct the masses absorbed by the football fever.

Crowds, Masses and the Collective Mind

Both Hitler and Mussolini believed that 'the road to power lay through the mastery of collective psychology, the manipulation of mass passions'.[102] The Duce particularly subscribed to Gustave Le Bon's thesis – *The Crowd – A Study of the Popular Mind* – that 'he applied and developed with unquestionable ability', according to the historian Alberto Asor Rosa.[103] The essence of Le Bon's argument was that by understanding the inherently violent, destructive nature of crowds, politicians in particular could become the mentors of the masses.

In the 1940s Emil Lederer argued that it was just such an amorphous mass, dislocated from traditional Italian society by the catastrophic forces of war and modernity that ultimately turned to Fascism.[104] It is a persuasive if far from conclusive theory. However, despite failing to acknowledge other contributory factors in the collapse of Italian democracy, the argument was appreciated among the PNF and its intellectual supporters.

As the chief synthesizer of all that had thus far constituted research into crowd behaviour, Le Bon defined one, in the ordinary sense of the word, as a gathering of individuals, irrespective of nationality, profession, sex, or the circumstances that brought them together. His psychological definition was quite different, for under certain conditions he believed that individuals within the collective would modify their behaviours. Their ideas and sentiments would become one and the same, thereby overpowering their conscious, individual personalities.[105] This core tenet of his argument suggested that once in a large group, people ceased to behave as individuals capable of exercising their own rational judgement and became subject to the 'law of the mental unity of the crowd'. Irrespective of their occupation, character or intelligence, individuals would assume the collective mind and begin to feel, think and act completely differently.[106] Having lost their powers of reasoning, individuals gained a sense of strength from the anonymity of submersion within the mass.

Le Bon also believed that contagion and suggestibility further defined the behaviour of mass groups. Classifying it as a hypnotic order, he suggested the crowd's every sentiment and act was 'contagious to such a degree that every individual readily sacrifices his personal interest to the collective interest'.[107] As Robert Nye proposes in his study of Le Bon, this all made the crowd 'open by nature to 'suggestions' from the leader hypnotist'[108] and there can be little doubt that Mussolini qualified as this. According to Le Bon, in the hands of a skilled operator an individual that had been divested of his conscious personality within the crowd could be encouraged to obey the suggestions of the leader, thereby committing acts that were contradictory to his normal personality and beliefs.

Van Ginneken's study of Le Bon's theory identifies a distinctly religious aspect to crowds, as they worshipped an apparently superior being. Fearing its power, the crowd blindly submits to its commands and is unable to discuss the leader's dogmas without wishing to spread them; while making enemies of those who did not accept them.[109] Such atavistic, barbarous groups with little power of self-reasoning were thus open to the exploitation of a skilled political elite or individual. As Le Bon argued, the crowd was 'a servile flock . . . incapable of ever doing without a master', which often came from 'the ranks of those morbidly nervous, excitable, half deranged persons who are bordering on madness.'[110] In addition to being irrational themselves, crowds best responded to leaders that were equally on the threshold of madness.

Despite appearing applicable to Fascism, Le Bon's thesis predated the rise of the extreme interwar European right and was directed against the earlier force of socialism. Having witnessed the power of the socialist mass during the Paris Commune, Le Bon believed that 'a knowledge of the psychology of crowds is to-day the last resource of the statesman who wishes not to govern them – that is becoming a very difficult matter – but at any rate not to be governed too much by them'.[111] Although far more detailed and complex than need be enlarged upon here, controlling the socialist mass was Le Bon's key objective.

His confident assertion that 'to know the art of impressing the imagination of crowds . . . is to know as well the art of governing them',[112] was exactly what Mussolini attempted to do. Beyond merely subverting socialism, Le Bon's theory of crowd psychology was synthesized into something that, one could argue, Mussolini and the Fascist regime employed to maintain and strengthen their respective positions of power and authority. The cult of the leader was nurtured alongside that of the party, both of which were reinforced and legitimized by the development of myths, the use of symbols and the exploitation of leisure time.

While it may be debatable to what extent Mussolini was a disciple of Le Bon, there is no doubt that the mass mobilization of society was a key tenet of Fascism, which made the crowds attending mass cultural spectaculars such as football, hugely important. Yet it would be wrong to portray such cultural events as purely crude propaganda, for Mussolini's vision that arguably derived from his interest in crowd theory, was far subtler. As Jeffrey Schnapp argued in his study of Fascist mass theatre, Mussolini wanted to create an art that would educate on a deeper spiritual level than normal and 'conjoin an elemental form of "realism" with something more: magic, mystery, myth and a sense of secular, but nonetheless sacred, rituality'.[113]

Although this interpretation of Fascist art was specifically directed towards theatre, all of the elements contained in the above formula were to be found within the world of *calcio*. The exalted art that contributed to the processes of education and persuasion was visible in the dramatic and symbolic stadia that rose throughout Italy, and the way *calcio* was played. There was also the image and identity of teams to consider; what and whom they represented. These aspects all aided the creation of sacred, secular rituals and myths that ingratiated the regime into the leisure time of the masses.

In fact, it was the massed ranks of *calcio* supporters that partly inspired Fascism's, albeit unsuccessful, promotion of mass theatre. Giovacchino Forzano, an OND official, recounted the experience of his first football match in 1927. Observing the crowd's passion, when sat alongside Giuseppe Bottai and party secretary Augusto Turati, Forzano exclaimed: 'If only they would get so enthused at open-air theater performances!'[114] Turati's response was to make him responsible for a mobile theatre project charged with exposing provincial audiences to Italian high culture. In the process, it would extend the regime's 'spiritual and intellectual reclamation' of Italy and propagate Italian 'in those areas where dialects still hold our marvelous language in the thrall of deformity'.[115]

In this case, it was football that made the PNF leadership appreciate how mass cultural spectaculars could be an effective medium for the development and imposition of national identity throughout the nation. Despite numerous attempts to promote theatre, many of the ideas were arguably better applied to *calcio*. One example was the Istituto Nazionale del Dramma Antico – National Institute of Ancient Drama – that was intended:

> to gather the people together at classical celebrations that point to the [people's] past and unveil anew the beauty of our simple and serene art; and to summon the new intellectual classes to collaborate in this work of regeneration, making them look backward, so that when they look forward, the vision of the past greatness of our race will infuse with greater amplitude and, therefore, dignity their vision of our artistic and political tomorrow.[116]

As will be seen in the following chapters, the fundamentals of this eloquent description of the desired role for theatre that emphasized Fascism's somewhat dichotomous relationship with the past and future, more or less contained the key aims of Fascist football.

Despite the lofty ambitions to create a new theatrical art, by 1933 the genre more or less remained a preserve of the middle classes. This prompted Mussolini to demand that members of the Italian Society of Authors and Publishers (SIAE) interpret the era's collective passions and prepare a 'theater of masses, a theatre that can contain 15,000 or 20,000 persons.'[117] The demand was intended to attack theatre's bourgeois exclusivity that he believed resulted from venues with limited seats at high prices that excluded the masses as much as they included the affluent.[118]

Although lacking specific detail, Mussolini's speech, along with the well-documented writings of Massimo Bontempelli, who Schnapp credits with setting 'the intellectual tone for the entire era',[119] stimulated a number of projects and ideas. Among these was the industrial engineer Gaetano Ciocca's proposal to construct democratic stadium-sized theatres that would give a greater number of people the best possible spectacle at the minimum expense. In the theatre of masses, the 'heart' of the problem was mathematical: combining 'the maximum number of spectators with the best visibility and sound'.[120] Yet, even if it were easier to attract more people who could only afford to pay less, this still did not solve all of the problems as there was also the aesthetic dynamic to contend with, if the passions of the masses were to be sufficiently raised. To address this, Ciocca proposed a theatre for the masses that was both monumental in size and scale of production, which required an enormous stage to accommodate thousands of actors in the show that would be 'the synthesis of the work of the collective, the glorification of popular struggles . . . the expression of the passions of the nation.'[121]

Ciocca's proposal replicated many of the advances already found in the new football stadia that had blended the Fascist present with the tradition of the Roman past. His interpretation of the amphitheatre made the stage the focal point by moving it to the centre of the arena, thereby replacing the old hierarchical seating plan with one that better reflected the apparent social realities of the new era.[122] As De Finetti noted:

> A modern stadium needs to be made for everybody, not for the various privileged classes of spectators: and already the Romans with their highest amphitheatres . . . had also reached the objective to offer everybody seats of practically the same level of visibility. No differently, we need to aim to make ours modern and not only for positive 'social aesthetic' reasons . . . but also for obvious reasons of practical economy. The motto has to be this: "we do not spend even a penny, we do not waste a bit of steel or a sack of cement to make those seats that the public do not love.[123]

Mussolini's dream for mass theatre only reached fruition on 29 April 1934, and the reviews of '18BL' were mixed at best. Despite the general consensus of opinion that the project had failed, *La Nazione* argued that 'the ferment of thoughts and constructive energies are testimony to the combative and constructive spirit of the new generation'.[124] Perhaps the most damning criticism however, was the widespread accusation that it had failed both as a spectacle and as a true representation of the struggles and tragedies of the war and the Fascist rise to power.[125]

Despite the impressive sound amplification many members of the audience, especially those in the cheaper popular seats, were still alienated from the action by distance, thereby repeating theatre's age-old problem. They were also apparently alienated by the script and an inherent difficulty in both associating and empathizing with a truck as the hero. The architect and cultural nationalist Ugo Ojetti uncompromisingly highlighted the inappropriateness of the protagonist: 'Art is man. Machines without men are soulless wood and metal.' His suggestion was supported by the theatre critic Giuseppe Longo who similarly defended the essential human element: 'There is always a danger when one places an inanimate being at the center of a heroic action . . . For temperamental reasons we Latins are not prone to exalting machinery.'[126]

Whatever the reason, despite considerable planning, expense and a cast of over 2,000 performers, the theatre of masses for the masses was unable to produce a spectacle capable of electrifying and mobilizing 20,000 spectators. Theoretically, it was an ideal Fascist cultural project that broke down some, if not all, of the liberal bourgeois barriers that had maintained theatre's exclusivity. In practice, however, the reality could not match the theory.

The failure of '18BL' was persuasive evidence in support of Bontempelli's suggestion that, in fact, football was the medium through which Italy's cultural modernity could best be expressed and the masses mobilized. Directly contrasting with this theatrical one-off spectacular, *calcio* was already electrifying and mobilizing well in excess of 20,000 spectators every weekend, for the best part of forty weeks a year. More to the point, it did so not just at one venue but in stadia throughout the country. Arguably inspired by *calcio*, the theatre of masses for masses was unable even to approach the levels of performance, drama and mobilization that were found in the modern football arena where collective struggle, joy and tragedy were integral parts of every show. Modern stadia with steep terracing ensured that spectators were never alienated from the action, either visually or aurally, while their contributions to the spectacle were also increasingly recognized by clubs like Bologna that began to offer subsidized travel, such was their potential impact on matches.

With crowds of 20,000 to 50,000-plus not uncommon, spectators had more than just a voyeuristic role in an event in which the central protagonists were not only human but often ordinary, if albeit specially gifted members of society capable of inspiring the nation. As *Il Bargello* demanded: 'We want a generation that has strengthened itself in everything that is competitive, that is struggle; and even when one cannot be a player it is still good to participate directly, because beyond muscles it is necessary to toughen the spirits.'[127] Unlike the soulless machines of '18BL', *calcio*'s main characters, the players themselves, represented a Fascist mass society that was ordered, passionate, organic and nationalistic. While mass theatre did not necessarily require the involvement of huge audiences, sport in general and *calcio* in particular was a far more obvious opportunity to attract and manipulate huge crowds, as the Duce recognized: 'It is always necessary to further interest the masses in all categories of sport . . . It is necessary to produce sport practiced by the growing mass of Italians with its undoubted use from the fascist, moral and physical point of view.'[128]

Apart from war, football was the most obvious metaphorical battlefield where heroic individual acts were carried out for the benefit of the collective. Moreover, while '18BL' was criticized for its confused joint scriptwriting process, which included no less than eight Fascist critics, playwrights and directors, responsibility for success and failure in football stopped with the coach. Not only did *calcio* reflect the Fascist vision of organic society in which the needs of the individual were subsumed beneath those of the collective, it also reaffirmed the leadership principle.

Despite *calcio*'s impressive credentials, becoming *the* mass cultural medium through which mass society was to be reached and mobilized required more stadia fitting the bill. Designed to accommodate more than just football, these stadia were open to the general public in addition to hosting mass political rallies and choreographed displays. This ensured their regular utilization and integration into the social fabric of the local community, which was helped by their role in *calcio*'s regular spectaculars, replete with images and symbols that were more often associated with official Fascist events. It was this deliberate display of symbols and imagery that was intended to mobilize the masses subtly during their leisure time, and perhaps there was no better example than the aesthetically contrasting, cutting-edge arenas of the Giovanni Berta stadium in Florence and the Littoriale stadium in Bologna.

Despite the regime's tolerance of diversity in all cultural forms, including art and architecture, creators could not ignore their patrons, as Marla Stone has shown.[129] In the case of virtually all sports stadia built under the regime the patron was the local party, and despite the room for artistic licence provided by the national PNF, the localities were a different matter. Although the two arenas of Florence and Bologna were completely opposite in their design, they strongly reflected the well-defined, proud, individual identities of their respective city leaders and local party hierarchs, while equally conforming to the exacting demands of the game and the regime. By exemplifying the room for individual creativity, they represented the philosophical contradictions of the regime's cultural influences that enabled it to market a modern, futuristic, revolutionary, if somewhat reactionary society, while extolling the virtues of its Roman past. Outside of the capital, nowhere was the regime more connected to its imperial past than Bologna, with its Romanesque Littoriale stadium. Just across the Apennines in Florence, the modernistic and revolutionary Giovanni Berta stadium could not have provided a sharper comparison. As will be seen in the following two chapters, the contrast between the experiences of both cities said much about the regime's view of nation that appears to have manifested itself in a fluid interpretation of local identity that somehow served all needs.

–5–

Arpinati, Bologna, *Calcio*:
The ABC to Success

One day, when considering the wonderful sporting rebirth of the nation and of the infinite good that is guiding youth to the healthy disciplines of sport and physical recreation, Arpinati planned to build in Bologna, this effective rail centre of Italy, a technically perfect arena, capable of hosting enthusiasts of all athletic sports and more than fifty thousand spectators. All of the city helped and encouraged the pioneer of such a bold idea and in the shortest of time the project, set on a solid financial base and with no speculative ends, rather with noble intentions, began to be realised. *L'Assalto*, 'Il Littoriale: ideato, voluto, costruito da Leandro Arpinati'

Celebrating the Littoriale stadium's official opening the Bologna Fascist Federation's weekly publication, *L'Assalto*, ensured that Leandro Arpinati was remembered as the creator of one of Italy's greatest modern constructions. The idea to build a great stadium in Bologna came to him while visiting the Baths of Caracalla in Rome and was said to have been rooted in his profound conviction 'that sport might be the best way to give our youth a healthy, moral and national education beyond the physical'.[1] Besides improving the health of the nation, a stadium of international repute would put Bologna firmly on the map and help Italy attract the major sporting events that would serve its quest for domestic and international respectability.

'The first amphitheatre of the Fascist Revolution'[2] was an apt description of the Littoriale, by Arpinati's biographer, that deliberately linked the imperial past with Fascist modernity.[3] By combining traditional and modern architecture, building materials and techniques, the Roman amphitheatre was adapted to the needs of the Fascist era. The result was the most modern stadium in Europe that Gallian believed 'signalled the muscular prestige of the race: the Littoriale is worthy of the Colosseum, for its significance as a building and as the first true monument of the new epoch'.[4]

From 1924, a close relationship developed between the stadium, the regime and the city of Bologna,[5] which was the first in Italy to come under

Fascist control. Yet almost as soon as the gates opened on the new sports ground for the people they were slammed shut on democracy, following an assassination attempt upon the Duce in Bologna, on 31 October 1926. The consequent abolition of all remaining constitutional freedoms signalled the beginning of dictatorship, strengthening the case for those who argued that sport was little more than a diversionary activity.

The Littoriale's construction illustrated the regime's awareness of the potential of sport and football in particular, to improve the health of the young and mobilize the masses to a level that had previously proved unattainable. For this reason, the arena's managers were charged with designing a programme of affordable events to benefit the nation and the physical education of its youth.[6] The Littoriale's success story was also embellished by the achievements of its main occupant, Bologna Football Club (BFC), which the commune did everything to maintain at the pinnacle of the Italian game. However, its success only further exposed it to many foreign ideas, through regular forays in the Coppa d'Europa and the influence of six Central European coaches from 1921 to 1942.[7]

Bologna's experience can be seen as a microcosm of *calcio* in general under the regime, providing a crude, working example of Gramsci's theory of hegemony in which the combination of culture and the state maintained the status quo, as the ruling elite made concessions in order to seek new alliances and maintain its dominance.

The Littoriale served both local and national ambitions that were not always complementary. Far from exemplifying shared interests, the monument highlighted the inevitable contradictions that arose from the regime's promotion of local sports initiatives for the good of the national whole. A huge achievement for the nation's self-belief and international reputation, it also intensified provincial sentiments of *campanilismo* as Bologna and its football club rose to the pinnacle of Italian sport.

Arpinati: Mayor of Bologna and Man of Sport

Born into a socialist household in Civitella di Romagna on 29 February 1892, Leandro Arpinati was a dishwasher before training as an electrician and working on the state railways. As the leader of a local anarchist group he met Mussolini, the socialist, for the first time in 1910. Although differing in political philosophies, their immediate affinity was apparently built upon a common desire to establish a new form of society. Employed in a reserved occupation Arpinati avoided the Great War,[8] but its aftermath still had a profound effect. Post-1918 Italy was in chaos with over 600,000 soldiers dead and over 500,000 having returned mutilated. In addition to the economic burdens of the conflict, there was also the psychological damage of failed irredentist ambitions to contend with, all of which contributed to the creation of a political vacuum that was exploited by the ex-combatants association, the *Fasci di Combattimento*, from which the PNF drew much support.[9]

Emerging in the Po Valley, Tuscany and Emilia-Romagna, the Fascist squads used violence to break up socialist meetings and impede the work of the new agricultural wage labourers' unions. A founder member of the Bologna *fascio*, on 10 April 1919, Arpinati became its leader the following year. Dominated by students, his frustration with the *fascio*'s inactivity during the summer months precipitated its radical restructuring in October 1920, after which, according to Adrian Lyttelton, it '*merged* with older patriotic organizations' to suddenly become 'a force of major political importance'.[10] Arpinati established a personalized rule over the squads, meting out summary justice to those members who indulged in the vendettas of the winter and spring of 1920–1 that terrorised socialists and their local institutions.[11] Reflecting Arpinati's pragmatic leadership as much as any suggested sense of justice and fair play, the *fascio*'s destabilization of the local political culture only reinforced his growing authority.

The *fascio* showed its new teeth on 21 November 1920, when Arpinati led an assault on Bologna's civic centre, the *Palazzo d'Accursio*, in an attempt to prevent the communal Socialist administration from taking office. Demonstrating the radical nature of both the city *fascio* and its leader, who developed a reputation as a man of action, the exact events of the incident are vague and vary according to the source, although the battle did leave ten dead socialists[12] and one martyred nationalist, Giulio Giordani. Eight years later *Lo Sport Fascista* recorded its version of events in an article dedicated to Arpinati:

> He was committed to the battle . . . head of a squad of one hundred friends that in a few hours, on his orders, struck down the socialism that held the glorious city like a conquered land, reviving the population and restoring order. From that day it was the start of a methodical struggle against the socialist tyranny that extended from the city to the countryside rooting out the bad antinational plant wherever.[13]

In January 1921, Arpinati was arrested for illegally possessing firearms. According to one recent biographer, this 'was the first Arpinati, daring and impetuous, an instrument of the regime and of capitalism, son of that common fascism, far from those power games that came to be built around him'.[14] Among the many failures to appraise his career impartially, his daughter Giancarla Cantamessa Arpinati has likewise tried to defend his reputation.[15] Yet, despite his high position within the PNF Arpinati left few writings, which only increases the difficulty in sifting the myth from the mire.

There can be little doubt, however, that his views were often unconventional and he did not always toe the party line. This was evident in his opposition to corporatism and his spirited attempt to defend institutions of local government when under attack from the Fascist federations. Arguably reflecting his idealism and political pragmatism, although more likely *Lo Sport Fascista*'s preferred portrayal of the new head of the FIGC, Arpinati was said to have been everybody's friend, which might have surprised some Bolognese socialists: 'Arpinati was never hated. In Bologna and in the entire province, he never had and does not have enemies. Liberals, democrats, socialists, masons speak of him with respect, often with fondness, with admiration; with no little affection and gratitude.'[16]

Apparently committed to a new political and social order, Arpinati was a pragmatist too, although it was his idealism and fairness that Vittorio Pozzo later recalled. As coach of the Italian national team for almost the entire Fascist era, he had an especially close working relationship with Arpinati, who he believed: 'was a morally straight man. With him you could have frank and sincere meetings, without paying so many complements . . . The man, in himself, I liked, and I was not wrong:[17] he died for his ideas that were, to a certain extent, anti-fascist.'[17] Again, socialists and Arpinati's political opponents in general may have thought differently.

Following Mussolini's rise to power Arpinati became secretary of the Provincial Fascist Federations in Bologna, head of the entire province, *ras* of all the *ras*. Committed to the construction of a new Fascist society, it has been suggested that he began to explore alternative means of establishing and maintaining consensus in this period. One non-violent option was through his control of Bologna's daily newspaper *Il Resto del Carlino*.

As part of a complicated deal involving the 'Poligrafici Riuniti' group,[18] Arpinati became proprietor of the newspaper on 4 March 1927 when Senator Edoardo Agnelli transferred 7,100 shares to him at a cost of 2,000,000 lire. How and if he actually paid for the shares is an issue of great speculation, despite the Agnelli family's conviction that the donation had been to Bolognese Fascism rather than its leader.[19] Arpinati's daughter has since argued that the shares were a gift to her father rather than the commune or the regime.[20]

The definitive reason for the transaction remains unknown, following the seizure and apparent destruction of documents pertaining to the deal. One historian of *Il Resto del Carlino* has suggested that the good of the local and national party was the Agnelli family's main motivation,[21] although appearing to serve party interests while tending those of the family may be closer to the truth. Besides intimidation, legislative controls and agreements with newspaper proprietors, the regime also sought to expand its press control by establishing deals with groups of financiers to purchase newspapers on its behalf. Somewhere within these potential explanations probably rests the truth, but it is the confusion surrounding these shares that Arpinati's daughter has argued implicated him in the financial scandal that ultimately ended his career in 1934.[22]

Despite its declining readership, Arpinati's complete acquisition of *Il Resto del Carlino*[23] unquestionably assisted his control of the city. In Bologna, as in the rest of Italy, journalists were forced to join the Fascist syndicate if they wished to continue working. Those who had been employed by the anti-Fascist press were struck off the professional list,[24] while from 1927–8 the syndicate actively attempted to purge papers of non-Fascists and appoint sympathetic members to editorial positions.[25]

Arpinati could also count on other supporters among the Bolognese press, such as *Vita Nuova*, the weekly publication of the provincial Fascist Party that was a forum for the expression of new political and cultural ideas, plus his two personal creations, *L'Assalto* and *Il Littoriale*. The latter, a daily dedicated to national and specifically local sporting life that became the official mouthpiece of CONI,[26] apparently wooed over one-million *Il Resto del Carlino* readers.[27] Through these organs, with the support of some national papers and journals, the publicity surrounding the entire stadium project raised Arpinati's profile and embossed his reputation as 'the man of sport'.

Apparently in recognition of his efforts within the city, Arpinati was made *podestà* (Fascist mayor) on 31 December 1926, following the abolition of the old *sindaco* system. In his final press communication the departing *sindaco* (mayor) and Fascist, Umberto Puppini, outlined the reasons for the choice of his successor: 'Such reasons – it might be in the brave work of Leandro Arpinati as head of the revolutionary Bologna squad . . . the successive tests of organization and construction . . . his actual rise to first Magistrate of the city – have been carved in the mind and intimately felt in the heart of all.'[28]

In the traditions of a movement that glorified death as much as life, Puppini also gave Arpinati's appointment the posthumous approval of Giulio Giordani, the nationalist martyred in 1921: 'The spirit of Giulio Giordani . . . has returned to the chamber that was a shrine for the tragic sacrifice. He is here among us, gentlemen; we are sure that he is pleased.'[29] He concluded by entrusting Arpinati with the responsibility of safeguarding the city's reputation and best interests.[30]

His faith was not misplaced as Arpinati continued developing the city's prestige and importance in a variety of ways, none more so than through Bologna FC and the Littoriale stadium. Having also been made vice-secretary of the national party, Arpinati's workload expanded beyond just city affairs. Yet, such was his apparent influence over the locality and its institutions that his biographer proclaimed his dominance in all areas of the province, although this may have been a deliberate attempt to create the illusion of great authority. 'Perhaps it is already felt in many areas of Italian political life, certainly in all the sporting areas reawakened, organized and revalued by him for Fascist Italy . . . Italian sport needs Arpinati.'[31]

Despite his apparently unique role in reawakening Italian athleticism, Arpinati became known as more than just 'the man of sport'. If Mussolini was credited with the inspiration and vision to improve the nation's fitness, Arpinati was quickly established as the interpreter and practitioner of the Duce's wishes. According to Gallian, once Mussolini had shown 'the qualities of our race, the attributes of our land: Arpinati, alone, signalled what will need to be the great battles of the championships and the Olympics'.[32] To achieve this goal he was given a national responsibility in what was perhaps his most demanding and arguably most successful role. Having been vice-president of the *Federazione Italiana di Atletica Leggera* (FIDAL) – the Italian Athletics Association – since 1925, Ferretti asked him to assume the presidency of the FIGC and oversee the implementation of the Carta di Viareggio.

Arpinati added the CONI presidency to his portfolio in 1931, which he held until 1933 when his dismissal from the Interior Ministry signalled his political decline that culminated with internal exile. In fact, *calcio* was allegedly at the root of the rivalry/feud with Achille Starace that ultimately led to his removal from office. Refusing the party secretary and his guests entry to an international match, Arpinati directed them to the ticket office along with everybody else.[33] Generating animosity between the two, the incident also contrasted Arpinati, the apparent Fascist ideologue, with Starace whose career could be said to have been more pragmatic. The incident was also an early indication of the regime's use of ticketing for such mass popular events as an opportunity to portray itself as the enforcer of law and order, as it did during the 1934 World Cup.[34] Arpinati also acquired friends during his time as FIGC president, his dismissal provoking letters of support from the Hungarian and Japanese federations. Edoardo Agnelli, President of Juventus FC, was one of the many within Italy who was said to have expressed real gratitude for his work within the sporting sphere.[35]

Despite his former secretary, Mario Lolli, arguing to the contrary, *calcio* was unquestionably reordered under Fascist terms during

Arpinati's tenure at the FIGC.[36] Given that subservience to the needs of the regime was a principal reason for the Fascistization of the Federation and *calcio* as a whole, Lolli's protestation rang somewhat hollow. In fact, even the early years of Arpinati's presidency saw a considerable centralization of the game. Dismissed from the FIGC on the eve of success, he failed to oversee Italy's most significant international victories. However, he was undoubtedly responsible for succesfully implementing a long-term development plan that ensured *calcio*'s future rude good health.

In 1928, long before the successes could have been predicted, Gallian made a startlingly prescient, if baseless, assessment of the quality of the seeds sown by 'the man of sport' and the crop they would yield. At the time, the reality of what the future held was less important than the contemporary image he was constructing:

> Arpinati introduced that sense of athletic responsibility that had not previously existed in Italy; he is the man of preparation, because he understood that in Italy, in that field, it was all to do, everything to prepare: only in some years time will the fruits be seen and they will be the most beautiful ever known.[37]

By 1934 the accuracy of Gallian's prediction and the fruits of Arpinati's labour were evident for all to see, including the new FIGC President, General Vaccaro, as the *azzurri* embarked on an unprecedented period of world domination. Not only had Arpinati's Littoriale provided the best facilities for Italian athletes it had, according to Gallian, also inspired a tenacity and desire to succeed among all athletes:

> that is what counts the most . . . to hear from their mouths the intentions and desires for tomorrow; to run into the stadium with the *fascio littorio* on their chest: and fight. I have often been stunned or amazed, when I have had the opportunity to admire them all, nourished by Leandro Arpinati: in Rome and outside, their minds often turn to the Littoriale as the first sign of the new falange of Italian sport.[38]

Arpinati was unquestionably the driving force behind the conception and the construction of what De Finetti hailed as 'the first great post-war sports facility to be built by public enterprise'.[39] It was a suitably vague assessment of the Littoriale's financial backing, which, as will be demonstrated, stretched far beyond the public purse and will. Undeterred by murky accounting processes, Gallian declared the project a shini' example of the shared intent of the regime and Arpinati to put the na' firmly on the route to recovery. His appraisal of the Littoriale's merit' revealed how the regime could only define itself and forge a se' identity through comparison with the outsider, rather than any positive sense of self:

> the amphitheatre of Arpinati's, the Bologna stadium, is really the opposite, the reaction, the vendetta, against modern Paris, the authority of old literature and of old decadent types: it is the reaction against a lifestyle that loved hypocrisy and covert force, against simplicity, the clarity of cold steel: it is the life of the sun against the life of the night . . . it is health against illness.[40]

Perhaps aware of Arpinati's meteoric rise within the party, his clients, supporters and colleagues were all keen to recognize publicly his contribution to the city's regeneration. As Lando Ferretti noted in *L'Assalto* in 1926: 'He celebrated the anniversary of the March on Rome, in 1923, with the opening of the Casa del Fascio; the second with the inauguration of the Fascist University; the third with the start of the works for the 'Littoriale' that need to be completed, in twelve tireless months, by the 29th October this year.'[41]

In Fascist eyes, Arpinati, the Littoriale and Bologna were rising together.

A National Stadium for a Provincial City

Despite his violent early career, once the Fascist takeover was more or less complete Arpinati envisaged a less aggressive role for the local party, as the 'hub, the central motor of every political, cultural or sporting activity in Bologna'.[42] Rather than any radical change in his ruthless political outlook, this apparent conversion to non-violent politics seems to reflect how the party took itself directly to the people, once the regime was secure. As part of this process the construction of the Littoriale was presented as the initiative and property of the *fascio* and not that of the commune, although technically it was owned by the Società Pro Casa del Fascio. Although directly controlled by Arpinati, this was an autonomous body created within the Casa del Fascio for the purpose of receiving the public finance necessary to build the Littoriale.[43] Theoretically neither the *fascio* nor the commune could interfere in its business,[44] but the reality was quite different as both parties meddled at almost every given opportunity.

What is beyond dispute is Arpinati's role in championing the idea of the new sports complex, which he justified in a detailed representation to the city mayor in March 1925. Stressing the importance of the stadium for fans across the region and Italy, he argued it would improve the nation's health by encouraging a love of sport and distracting young

Italians from bars and other vices. To achieve this the complex needed 'a field for team games and another for all the Olympic events, a running track, a big swimming pool for exercises and competitions, a covered gymnasium and a series of service rooms for the athletes or the public that pour in on competition days.'[45]

His case was strengthened by the *fascio* having already obtained 60,000 square metres of land in the Melloncello district, one-and-a-half kilometres to the southwest of the city walls. Arpinati asked the commune to contribute 3 per cent of the costs on the interest of the capital, estimated in the region of four million lire, for a period of fifteen years, during which time the Pro Casa del Fascio would reduce the debt.[46] The building was a perfect venue for the new Higher Teaching Institute for Physical Education, which, as part of Bologna University, would be unique in the country. However, his trump card was the prestige the stadium would bestow upon the city: 'Allow me to point out . . . that the intervention of the commune would speed up the works, enabling them to finish in the current year and bypass the other cities in Italy that already have projects of this type and might finish before Bologna.'[47]

On 20 July 1925, the commune's Executive Committee recommended awarding 150,000 lire per annum to the body acting as proprietor of the stadium. This was conditional on the building being made available free of charge to the Higher Institute of Physical Education and Bologna University students during the fifteen years in which the commune was repaying the loan, after which the municipality would become the proprietor.[48]

Among the majority of councillors that supported the plan one of the most vocal was the soon be mayor, Councillor Manaresi, who applauded the proposal's response 'to the modern concept of physical education of the masses' that had become so important in the most advanced nations of the world.[49] Highlighting the Czechoslovak minister for sport's position as second in the government hierarchy, he suggested this showed how many European politicians and thinkers had begun to envisage a new role for sport, linking nationalism with racial fitness:

> Sport is also education of the spirit and we, who intend to rejuvenate our race need to encourage all of the initiatives that serve to diffuse the love of sport even further among our people. The success of our athletes in foreign lands . . . constitutes the best Italian propaganda abroad. Justifiably, Mussolini has said that beyond representing a heartening physical progress of the race, our champions are our best foreign ambassadors.
>
> The national government understood the highest function of sport and, consequently, encouraged every initiative in this field. Therefore, I do not

hesitate to believe that the initiative so courageously undertaken by Arpinati and so efficiently encouraged by the communal administration is the most appropriate . . . (Applause) [50]

Councillor Ballarini added to Manaresi's sentiments by stressing how the proposal would help to preserve the leading position in Italian and European education that Bologna had held for centuries. As Manaresi summed up: the administration was 'always improving a works programme that again reaffirms the primacy of our city . . . that time will not be able to cancel and nobody will ever be able to ignore (Applause)'.[51]

All thirty-one members unanimously approved the plan that allocated an annual contribution of 150,000 lire, for fifteen years, to the Campo Polisportivo's (Multisport Ground) proprietorial body. The commune's financial commitment to constructing the new stadium was based on more than just providing a stylish, eye-catching display window for the city's football team, as it was the concessions towards the existing institutions for physical education and the provision of free sporting opportunity that ultimately secured the local authority's backing.

In 1927, to exploit the Littoriale's multisport potential and satisfy Arpinati's desire for a nationally important sports society in the city, Bologna FC became a federated member of the newly constituted multisport association 'Bologna Sportiva'. Besides pooling resources, the new structure was intended to help member clubs and societies achieve even more national success and recognition by channelling all of the city's young talents through it. As the *fascio's* publication *L'Assalto* explained: "Bologna Sportiva', different from many other sister companies, has not looked to buy up champion celebrities, but rather, by the will of Leandro Arpinati, has dedicated almost all of its activities to raising the mass of youths that serve in its ranks and from which great champions will inevitably emerge.'[52]

By 1932, with almost 1,500 members in the various sports clubs, of which 279 were footballers,[53] 'Bologna Sportiva' had contributed to making Emilia-Romagna one of the strongest sporting regions in Italy. As the journalist A.M. Perbellini argued in *Calcio Illustrato*, Arpinati did more than just create the Littoriale in Bologna:

He aroused the collective ardour for physical discipline, he created a Bolognese sporting conscience. And not that conscience which forces people to watch matches, to know the champions and the tables, to fight over an offside or a penalty decision, but that higher atmosphere that forces the individual and the collective to follow and admire the sporting spectacle as an incitement to action.[54]

To honour Bologna's sporting progress another local sports newspaper was launched. *La Sberla Sportiva*'s aim was to further support and encourage the city's athletes without becoming 'a flag of outdated regionalism, but ... being the sporting mouthpiece of our region that has a capital importance in the framing of Italian sport'.[55] As local pride and the city's identity intensified with every victory, local opinion formers demanded the placement of Bologna's sporting progress within the context of the nation, in order to dampen any excessive *campanilismo.*

Symbolizing Fascism's commitment to Bologna's regeneration through grass roots sport, the Littoriale was also an integral part of the city's expansion towards the suburbs. This included an innovative trade fair district, horticulture centre, hospital, schools, houses, an airport at Borgo Panigale and the new Hippodrome for trotting, all of which Arpinati hoped would make it the most important city in the north and centre of Italy.[56] Besides developing Bologna's national profile, this construction programme enabled the local party to stamp its identity on the city, while erasing those of former leftist administrations.

Arpinati's quest to make Bologna one of the most important cities in Italy was helped by its strategic position at the hub of the Italian national rail network. Following the construction of the new direct train line to Florence that cut through the Apennine Mountains via a series of tunnels, Bologna became the principal interchange for almost all passengers travelling north or south. From Turin and Milan, whether going towards Bari or Rome, passengers had to either pass through or change at Bologna. It was a key factor in Arpinati's justification of the Littoriale: the 'geographical and rail position of our city made me think about the possibility of creating in Bologna ... an important national centre for sporting displays of every type'.[57] His belief was confirmed in the programme notes for the 1927 European swimming, diving and water polo championships: 'The fortunate geographical position of Bologna today gives it a great strategic and commercial importance. It controls the two principal routes that cross the Apennines and lead to Florence ... One can judge the importance of Bologna as a commercial centre since it is the principal transit point between southern and central Italy.'[58]

Bologna was rediscovering or reinventing itself under Fascism and the Littoriale was helping to develop its economy by demonstrating its geographical and institutional advantages. In the space beneath the stadium's seats and terracing were a number of rooms and salons to accommodate a variety of shows and conventions to promote and develop the city's industrial, commercial and agricultural sectors, as described in the commune's monthly publication:

Alluding to the advantage and the prestige that Bologna will derive from this, we were thinking implicitly of the initiatives that will take place, which, up until now, could not even be discussed due to the lack of a venue adapted to them.

It is clear that one talks of shows and expositions of every type . . . All of Italian labour, from agriculture to industry, must find the most practical and well-mannered hospitality in the Campo Polisportivo.[59]

Besides the many shows, expositions and fairs that it was hoped the Littoriale would attract, the booming spectator sport of *calcio* proved very lucrative for smaller commercial enterprises. Those sceptics who questioned both the wisdom of the money spent on the Littoriale and the economic merits of *calcio* were silenced by the dramatic impact of the inaugural international between Italy and Spain, in 1927.

The combination of the rail network, Bologna's geographical position and the growing phenomenon of sports tourism, resulted in a huge influx of fans for the game, which, as *Il Resto del Carlino* stated, made an extraordinary impact upon city businesses: 'When sport becomes a necessity for people to enjoy themselves at spectaculars and large contests capable of including tens of thousands of people, it benefits commerce and industry perfectly and directly.'[60] Although it was Arpinati's own paper that was endorsing the commercial wisdom of 'his' construction, the alleged impact of a crowd of 60,000 plus upon such a small city, was persuasive.

It is impossible to assess exactly how many fans came from outside of Bologna, but on the day of the match the city's hotels were said to have been completely full and turning away customers in their droves. Restaurants ordered three times the normal amount of provisions in antic-ipation of the rise in trade, and still ran out, while some bars were forced to close having exhausted their supplies of coffee, sugar and beer. Public services, such as taxis and carriages, also came under assault from the huge volume of spectators trying to reach the stadium from the city centre, one driver apparently making the journey over sixteen times in the space of two hours. The rest of the crowd, more than half in all probability, arrived by foot and public transport that was stretched to the limit.[61] This mass of people caused further chaos in the stadium, thereby questioning one journalist's recollection of the day's organizational perfection: 'this formidable march of people was able to flow to the stadium without even the minimum of incident, it occupied without congestion the allocated seats . . . The merit of a simply perfect organization, completely worthy of the event.'[62] Chaotic or not, Bologna's traders and small businessmen appreciated the inherent value of the Littoriale to the city's economy.

While it was hoped that staging large events and international tournaments would improve both the city's and the regime's chances of hosting even higher profile events, the Littoriale's facilities were primarily intended to develop sporting opportunity and health and fitness within Bologna. However, despite its early promise, the complex was rarely a hive of activity as many considered its position in the city suburbs too far to travel. So deserted was the 1927 trade fair that it was moved back to the town centre the following year, where it remained until 1935 when the stadium was used again, this time with the accompaniment of a number of sporting activities to entice the public. The athletics, tennis and swimming facilities were equally underused and a competition was launched, in 1934, to design a poster to attract more bathers. The 500 lire prize money went to the sculptor Bruno Boari for his submission 'Maggio 1934' (May 1934), after which the commune distributed 1,000 bill posters, 3,000 posters and 10,000 postcards throughout the city.[63]

The apparent antipathy of the Bolognesi seemed to extend to the stadium itself. After the enthusiasm of the first international, when it was crammed beyond capacity, the Littoriale was rarely sold out for football matches, even during Bologna FC's golden era from 1925 onwards. Although transport issues were cited as a disincentive, Bologna was a city of only around 200,000 inhabitants. Requiring one-quarter of the population to fill it, this statistic brings us closer to the true, political purpose of the Littoriale's construction. Unless the architect failed to consider the size of the potential market, which was limited to the city population due to age-old animosities between the Bolognesi and the countryside's Romagnoli, it was clearly too big, irrespective of the team's achievements. Therefore, it seems reasonable to suggest that the monumental scale of the Littoriale was, first and foremost, intended to serve a visible propaganda role rather than respond to the needs and desires of Bologna's citizens; thereby reflecting Arpinati's true vision of the stadium as a national rather than local arena.

Bologna's Excellence, Fascistically Funded

While there was significant government and public funding for the Littoriale, the role of the local savings bank (Cassa di Risparmio di Bologna) has rarely been mentioned. Besides revealing the unscrupulous capabilities of the local party when trying to fund a project it could ill afford, its bank loan undermines De Finetti's reference to the stadium as the first built solely from public enterprise.[64] The commune's commitment to financing a large percentage of the stadium's costs[65] included a clause in which it renounced all responsibility for any debts the bank might contest against the Società Pro Casa del Fascio, should it default on its repayments.[66]

The commune sent an agreed annual sum to the Pro Casa del Fascio, which used it to repay the initial loan to the bank. With these instalments not commencing until 1927, a central government payment of 1,000,000 lire met the immediate construction costs[67] and 'encouraged' local agencies not to renege on their financial commitments, thereafter. On behalf of the commune *podestà* Arpinati promised to follow the national government's example by 'contributing adequately to the construction costs of the "Littoriale"'.[68] It is perhaps this that convinced De Finetti the stadium had been publicly funded.

In 1931, with the Littoriale long completed and the annual loan repayments being made without hitch, the commune guaranteed another loan for the Società Pro Casa del Fascio from the National Insurance Institute (Istituto Nazionale delle Assicurazione). The sum of 14,000,000 lire was intended to rationalize the Society's debts deriving from the construction costs of the Casa del Fascio and the Littoriale. If it defaulted on its repayments, the Littoriale and its assets would become the *de jure* property of the commune, all of which was said to have been 'extraneous from the Savings Bank'.[69]

Despite this loan, the Pro Casa del Fascio began to experience serious financial problems in 1933 that resulted in its liquidation by December that year,[70] after which ownership of the Littoriale passed directly to the commune,[71] which denied any responsibility for repaying the original loan. Two weeks later the bank made its first formal demand to Mayor Manaresi for the outstanding payment that was now six-months overdue, thereby beginning a lengthy, complicated legal wrangle. Manaresi's legal office maintained that the commune's only obligation was to ensure the free use of the Littoriale for schoolchildren during the term of the repayments.[72] Thus, once the stadium became the property of the commune the terms of the original agreement were invalidated along with the obligations of both bodies, thereby enabling the municipality to discharge any financial commitment.[73]

The issue remained unresolved in 1938 and following a final desperate plea from the bank[74] there are no further records, which makes it impossible to determine how, or even if, the impasse was resolved. However, given the commune's complex legal arguments[75] and the bank's continuing demand for the repayments some four years after they had ceased, it seems reasonable to assume that the local authority had no intention of discussing the issue. With the onset of war one could surmise that the issue fell below more pressing matters and may well have been swept under the carpet. With ten annual repayments outstanding, the Casa di

Risparmio di Bologna contributed the significant sum of 1,500,000 lire to the Littoriale's costs. Yet, even added to the central government's contribution, this does not account for the stadium's entire budget as the commune again pushed its begging bowl into the faces of local citizens and the city's banking institutions.

Only weeks before the Littoriale's opening ceremony in the presence of Mussolini, Arpinati launched a 'buy a brick' appeal in *Il Resto del Carlino* asking readers to contribute as much or as little as they could afford. Raising a total of 857,175 lire,[76] it was another example of the local party taking itself directly to the people in an effort to create a shared experience around the new stadium, even if 'contributions' were not always voluntary. Small businesses were expected to give at least 1,000 lire. Those that refused apparently had big problems, with contributions from some of the 'red' cooperatives that were still in existence indicating the scheme's compulsory nature. Besides creating a breeding and training ground for the future generations, prospective contributors were reminded of the other benefits for the city, the most important being its new position at the centre of Italian sporting life.[77]

'Subscribers' received a receipt displaying a brick and a 1,000 lire note, with some of the lucky ones having their names and donations published in *Il Carlino*'s daily, if incomplete, list. To 'inspire' the entire city to dig deep, there could only have been one person at the top of the list on day one: 'the name of the first subscriber, Benito Mussolini, is a warning and an encouragement.'[78] Portraying the fundraising exercise as an organic 'community action' representing loyalty and consensus to the regime and the city, was intended to encourage further public contributions.

> The appeal launched to the city by Bolognese fascism through the voice of Leandro Arpinati, for the purpose of presenting to the Duce . . . a complete and magnificent show of the constructive strengths of our civic pride, is collecting the largest consensus it has ever been able to . . . The second list that . . . is another testament of that loyalty to fascism, of that accordance to the fruitful works of fascism that the greater part of our citizens declare today like yesterday, as always, knowing that only by the chosen road will Italy soon reach the widest horizons promised by destiny.[79]

Besides its national significance, the Littoriale's local importance was a crucial factor in the appeal, day three emphasizing its role in maintaining the city's historical position as a centre of Italian learning, thinking, culture, arts and civil progress that *Il Resto del Carlino* suggested had been reduced to the level of all other Italian cities by the Liberal State.[80]

The Littoriale was also significant as, for the first time, it gave equal weight to the importance of sport and more traditional forms of culture in Bologna's regeneration. Situating sport at the vanguard of the city's restoration, was intended to include and associate the masses of Bolognese society with the project. As *Il Carlino* confirmed:

> Bologna foresees the future and it has given itself to 'sport' with a renewed clamour, with an intelligent and exclusive passion. Sport will be the key for the future society, because no moral progress, no intellectual fortune can await a people that might abandon itself to the weakness of vices or idleness. Sport is the only thing that can preserve a people from moral tiredness, from social neurosis, from apathy: the only thing that can warn against luxury and its desertions.[81]

Besides symbolizing Bologna's renaissance, the Littoriale also heralded the sporting regeneration of Fascist society as a whole: from the smallest playing fields to the largest stadia, from amateur participants to professional competitors. As the novelist and *Il Resto del Carlino* journalist Guglielmo Bonuzzi argued in a publicity pamphlet, the stadium was the largest, most daring and convincing demonstration of the regime's utmost commitment to the use of sport for the physical, mental and moral development of the nation:

> It has been justly and repeatedly observed that *sport* needs to be valued as a school of discipline, as a gymnasium of courage and strength: two convergent elements, productive for individual and collective fruits, because forming and preparing the spirit and the muscles of the young, contributes to giving the motherland a generation of robust and courageous citizens. The Littoriale of Bologna – that perfectly fits into the dynamic of contemporary social life – responds to this precise goal.[82]

For these local and national reasons *Il Carlino* readers were encouraged to contribute as much as possible on a daily basis, for almost one month.[83]

Given the financial demands of such an ambitious work and the complex, arguably deceitful means by which the funds were obtained, it is hardly surprising that the building's final cost was never definitely ascertained. One source has put it in the region of 16,600,000 lire[84] in contrast to Arpinati's claim of 12,000,000 lire,[85] although accounts to prove this were never provided despite frequent requests.[86] It was a similar story with the the Casa del Fascio, both of which partly account for the question marks that punctuated his name particularly after his fall from grace.[87] Nonetheless, whether by hook or by crook, without

Arpinati's enthusiasm and fundraising scams the Littoriale would most certainly never have been built, for which Bologna, the regime and the Duce had good reason to be grateful.

Myths, Legends and *Lo Stadio*

King Vittorio Emanuele III laid the Littoriale's first brick on 12 June 1925, with the work intended to be completed in time for the fourth anniversary of the Fascist takeover, in October the following year. According to *L'Assalto*, the tight timescale and especially harsh winter and spring of 1925–6 resulted in a fine example of organic Fascist society, as workers laboured 'with order, discipline . . . [and] . . . admirable industry'.[88] By 31 October 1926 the stadium was ready for the opening ceremony, although it was two years before it was finally completed. It was still a highly impressive achievement and a credit to the efforts and energies of those 300–1,000 workers employed;[89] an illustration of the stadium-building programme's impact upon national unemployment.

Officially, the design and build process was a collaboration between Arpinati and the engineer Umberto Costanzini, head of the technical office of the Casa del Fascio. However, the more experienced Giulio Ulisse Arata, who agreed not to appear on the official documentation, was the real architect.[90] As the first major sports project commissioned by the regime and the yardstick against which future stadia were measured, it was a huge career opportunity for Costanzini.

Supplementing the stadium arena were two swimming pools of international standard, one indoor length of thirty-three metres and the other outdoor length of fifty metres – the first of its type in Italy – four tennis courts and a gymnasium, in addition to the Institute for Physical Education. The stadium was capable of holding more than 50,000 spectators and contained a football pitch conforming to CIS regulations. Suitable for international matches, the commune's own publication stated how: this 'characteristic is of special interest for a city like ours that occupies first place in the national football competition'.[91] Already possessing a football club famous throughout Europe, it was hoped the Littoriale would further spread the city's name by hosting international matches.

Providing facilities for track and field athletics based the stadium's design around the old Greek U-shaped model, which was enlarged and grafted onto a semi-amphitheatre to produce a hybrid, blending modernity and antiquity. Further connections with the past also became evident once the work began in 1925, when excavations for the swimming pools unearthed nine Etruscan tombs that had unfortunately been destroyed by the works, plus six stele from the end of the fifth to the sixth centuries

BC. The discovery was connected to the late-nineteenth century excavation of hundreds of the same tombs in the Certosa area.[92]

Combined with the stadium's Roman style, these links further reasserted the regime's claim to have been the spiritual heir of earlier civilizations, which Mussolini drew attention to in 1929. Singling out the Littoriale as the best demonstration of a Fascist stadium, worthy of ancient Rome, he declared it: 'a shining example of what can be done with the will and tenacity of Fascism, as personified in Bologna by Leandro Arpinati.'[93] The myth of Rome was intended to legitimize the regime's rule by rooting its identity in that of the past while connecting this with promises for the new civilization. As Tracy Koon notes: 'Mussolini's infatuation with things Roman was the central and pivotal point in his view of politics as spectacle.'[94]

Despite repeated connections between the Littoriale and antiquity, there was still a desire to distinguish it from the old Roman amphitheatres and their decadent associations. As Arpinati stated in *Lo Sport Fascista*: 'the Littoriale is not a circus act only for spectacles, but it is a centre of vitality, a school, a gymnasium [where] every necessary method is offered to the young who want and need to grow in the virile school of Fascism.'[95]

The Littoriale's façade also possessed a strong medieval influence, which was very in keeping with the city. Although its terracing was completely constructed in reinforced concrete, unlike the stadia of Florence and Turin where this was left deliberately exposed, the Littoriale's was shrouded behind a façade of brickwork. In the words of Silvio San Pietro: 'the powerful, unbroken facade is articulated by a series of dual openings with superimposed arches which are divided by a regular rhythm of cornices, pilaster strips, window openings, entrances and slight projections – the entire wall surface being in bare brick, the traditional building material of Emilia Romagna.'[96]

While creating an aesthetic harmony with the rest of the city, using over eight million locally produced bricks also had considerable economic benefits.[97] Unlike the marble obelisk erected at the entrance of the Foro Mussolini in Rome, which had to be sailed down the coast from Carrara, the bricks minimized costs while boosting this part of the city's economy. Consequently, the red brick façade, which had virtually no structural importance, must be seen as a political and aesthetic construction designed to integrate the stadium within the city and its populace.

Most importantly and most visibly, this harmonization was achieved through the Littoriale's position beside the four-kilometre, 660-arch portico running from the Certosa cemetery in Melloncello up to the gates of the shrine of the Madonna of San Luca, visible on the Guardia hill above.[98] Although rendering covers the portico's brickwork, the arches and windows of the Littoriale's façade blend perfectly. In addition to physically linking the stadium to the shrine above, the portico also connected it to Bologna's fourteen-kilometre network of covered walkways that brought pedestrians to and from the centre. Emphasizing the importance of these renowned porticoes with an organic analogy, more than just structurally and even psychologically connecting the Littoriale to the city, those of the main thoroughfares of vias Saragozza and Sant'Isaia acted as the arteries and veins that carried the stadium's lifeblood to and from the city.

The physical connection of the stadium to the city's portico network was completed by the construction of the monolithic, six-storey, 42-metre Marathon Tower, which mediated the slight gap between the stadium's perimeter wall and the San Luca portico. Designed by Arata, it was commissioned by Arpinati immediately after the stadium's opening ceremony in October 1926. Towers in general were striking symbolic features of Fascist architecture, which, according to Tim Benton, represented 'a combination of the medieval civic tower and an abstract symbol of authority'.[99] Even the most modest municipal buildings possessed a *torre del Littorio*, while Marathon towers were an unavoidable feature of many stadia built in this period. In his non-technical vision of the Fascist city, the journalist and romantic novelist Ridolfo Mazzucconi similarly stressed the important role of towers: It 'will be a city of towers and of high palaces . . . the tower expresses in a sublime mode the divine audacity of man' (Figure 2).[100]

The Marathon Tower's central arch was also positioned precisely above a plaque on the portico wall commemorating the execution of Father Ugo Bassi, by an Austrian firing squad on 8 August 1849. Reaffirming the nationalist and regenerationist connection, *L'Assalto* hoped that Bassi's spirit might have been released during the stadium's inauguration: 'I love to think that on 29 May the patriotic spirit of the Barnabite might have floated, finally placated, blessing it!!'[101] From the internal perspective, the Tower's propaganda role was further served by a large arch opposite the covered stand for dignitaries, which contained a huge bronze statue of the Duce in heroic pose, on horseback.

The stadium's aesthetic further stimulated the debate as to what actually constituted Fascist art and architecture. Fascism was too eclectic to be restricted to any particular style or genre and many intellectuals agreed with Giorgio Pini, the director of *L'Assalto* and one of the leading figures in the Bolognese Fascist Syndicate of Journalists, that 'a new art, strictly tied to the fascist rebirth, undoubtedly needs to affirm itself'.[102] Naturally, as one of Fascist Italy's biggest and most high profile structures, the

Figure 2 Arata's neo-Roman, monolithic masterpiece that perfectly mediated Fascism's eclectic influences with Bologna's medieval heritage. © Simon Martin, 2001.

Littoriale became a central protagonist in the debate. Some argued that it contradicted itself as Fascist work by reflecting the splendour of Roman amphitheatres, while others drew attention to its inherent Futurist influences. Somewhere in between was the third way option whereby establishing what was not intrinsically Fascist appears to have been the key to deciding what actually was.

As Pini further argued: 'the "Littoriale" does not represent a Roman return neither a preface to the coming architectural futurism. One is talking of a perfect work of actual fascist art, a document of our era, an affirmation of a civilization and style that stands alone, a classic expression of a classic regime.'[103] His albeit personal and subjective classification of it as 'a monument that future generations will remember as the titanic force of Fascist Italy',[104] was still prescient. His bold statement, without actually defining the nature of Fascist art, exemplified how the lumpy contradictions of such opposite schools of thought as *romanità*, futurism and modernism, were often pushed through the regime's cultural processor and blended to a satisfactory consistency, without actually resulting in the emergence of anything particularly new. As Ivo Bonuzzi explained, the truth about the Littoriale: 'reveals itself, to who thinks about it, as a typically fascist work . . . the clearest of lines appear as a sign of our times, which is an achievement that reflects, synthesises, expresses the force, the beauty and the greatness of a victorious Regime, through the constant testimony of its most significant monuments.'[105]

Irrespective of its architectural and aesthetic merits, if the stadium was to truly reflect the genius of the regime and the greatness of the era it needed a suitable name, but this proved equally polemical. From its conception, the Littoriale had generally been referred to as the Campo Polisportivo or, occasionally, as la Mole Arpinatiana, with respect to both its huge size and the role of Arpinati. To establish a more permanent name, Arpinati turned for inspiration to Professor Baldoni, a Latinist. Despite its Roman and Fascist connotations, 'Littoriale', his first proposal after two months contemplation, left the Bologna hierarchy completely underwhelmed. Although acceptable to Arpinati the name was deemed too broad for something with such a specific purpose, even though the brief had apparently referred to the potential themes of *fascio* and *littorio*.

Returning to basics, Baldoni questioned the stadium's purpose, its essence? His answer was: 'the place where one develops and tempers the nobility of the spirit and body of the new race, which is the fascist race.'[106] From this, he formed what he considered to be the perfect solution. Deriving from a mixture of Greek and Latin – like the stadium's architecture – while sounding Roman, he proposed the single word of 'Eugenéo', supporting it with an almost algebraic formula: '"eu" = good, and "genes" = stock, progeny, descent, race. And the composed word "eugenés" acquires the significance: "of good stock", "of noble race." Thus when we say *"Eugenéo"*, we signify precisely, and with exact literal sense, *"the place* (implicit) *of the good stock, of the noble race"*.'[107]

His proposal interpreted the essence of what Fascism was trying to achieve through sport: that being the creation of a strong race in facilities that reflected the regime's modern vision and ancient cultural heritage. Furthermore, 'Eugenéo' was intended specifically to encompass the stadium's eclectic identity by expressing its strong connections with the imperial past and the Fascist present in Bologna. However, his formulaic proposal was rejected as too erudite for the masses for which the stadium had been constructed, reflecting the regime's desire to avoid anything remotely elitist in its effort to reach mass society.

Arpinati eventually settled for the original suggestion of 'Littoriale' as it blended the past with the present. Referring to the Roman *littori* (legal officers) whose symbol of power was the same bundle of rods bound up with an axe that had been abducted by the Fascist Party, 'Littoriale' proved so apt, inspirational, or perhaps just safe, that it became a popular name for many Fascist stadia. Either way, Arpinati's creation had a name and it was time to put it to work.

Putting Bologna on the Map

The regime's desire to restructure and reorder Italian cities along Fascist lines influenced the design of all new stadia, one of the greatest concerns being the efficient control of the increasingly large crowds that were attending football matches. With significant attention having been paid to the arrival, entry and exit of supporters, *L'Assalto* claimed the Littoriale had resolved many of the old problems and, indeed, it appeared to have done so.[108] Built in the suburban southwest of Bologna where there was the space to accommodate the stadium and its anticipated crowds, quick access to and from the city centre for football supporters and attendees of the many fairs and shows that it was expected to host was a primary planning consideration. Two new tram lines were laid along vias Saragozza and Sant'Isaia, 3,000 vehicle parking spaces created around the stadium, in addition to 222,216 lire being spent on road improvements.[109]

The first significant test was the stadium's inauguration on 31 October 1926, to mark the fourth anniversary of the Fascist rise to power. Attended by Mussolini, the event provoked 'heart-felt jubilation in all of the city', according to *Il Resto del Carlino*.[110] It also tested the Littoriale's ability to cope with major events, while demonstrating its capacity to bestow domestic and international prestige upon the party, the city and the regime. However, the Duce's twenty-four hours in Bologna were more memorable for the assassination attempt that launched the beginning of dictatorship.

After entering the stadium on horseback, Mussolini was saluted with a display of waved handkerchiefs by the various male and female Fascist groups, avanguardisti (ONB members aged 15–18), balilla, syndicate members and general public from all over Italy. In its account of the day, *L'Assalto* recalled the Roman Empire before alluding to how the stadium had further united Italy:

> When . . . we saw the mighty Duce enter like a conductor of people, bathed in the light of the sun that had finally driven away the clouds, greeted by a mass that only eternal Rome will have seen paying tribute to the 'triumph' and a victorious Consul, we truly thought that the hearts of all Italians must have been beating with his.[111]

Despite this grand recollection Mussolini's stay was brief. Although reserving only a few words for the waiting crowd, they were enough for *L'Assalto* to state that: 'whoever participated in that mystic, warlike, poetic and solemn inaugural ritual, as no other fascist ceremony has ever been, cannot forget the emotion of that moment.'[112] It typified the type of 'cultural fantasy'[113] employed by the press to record and rewrite historical events according to the regime's needs.

After awarding some medals, Mussolini led the crowd on horseback to piazza Vittorio Emanuele, in the heart of the city. As he departed along the via Indipendenza towards the station, pistol shots were fired at his car. A 13–year-old in avanguardista (youth group) uniform, Anteo Zamboni, was apprehended and attacked by the crowd before being lynched in the street: 'his body, full of revolver bullets and knife wounds, was torn to pieces, and his arms and legs were carried around the city in triumph by the Fascists.'[114] *L'Assalto* declared the crowd's reaction a proud moment that reflected the city's strong sense of identity and values: 'To our credit for this reason, the summary and immediate execution of the attacker paints and outlines our impetuous and straight character that knows to reward virtue and inexorably punishes cowardice and guilt.'[115] The exact details of the incident remain unclear and there is little hard evidence to justify Zamboni's summary execution, besides an inconclusive note that he apparently wrote the night before.[116]

The suspicion remains that he was the unfortunate victim of a faked assassination attempt that provided the regime with an opportunity to crack down hard on dissent, but nobody in government seemed interested in ascertaining the facts. Turati had already decided that those complicit in the attack against Italy, more than just Mussolini, would be punished. This did not necessarily just involve the Bolognese, as *L'Assalto* identified the complicit as those in general opposition to the regime: 'We need to strenuously defend ourselves and our Head against them: because today he signifies Italy, possessing all of its virtues and interpreting all of its needs.'[117]

Ad hoc retribution was immediately taken throughout the country. Socialist and other opposition party offices were burnt in Milan, while in Rome, Genoa, Naples and Cagliari, socialist and liberal houses were broken into and their occupants threatened. 'Legal' retribution followed within the week, the Council of Ministers passing a number of decrees creating special powers to suppress subversive anti-fascist activity. The net result was the closure of socialist and opposition press, the expulsion of socialist deputies from the Chamber, the internment of suspected anti-Fascists and the restoration of the death penalty for any would-be assassins of the monarch or the head of government. Perhaps it was all an unfortunate coincidence, but the juxtaposition of the opening ceremony for one of Fascism's greatest creations for the people with the repressive legislation that followed is indicative of a regime that demanded the utmost loyalty in return for material improvements and leisure-time opportunities.

As leader of the Bologna *fascio* that organized the day, Arpinati might have expected bleak career prospects but quite the opposite was the case, adding further weight to the conspiracy theory. On behalf of Bolognese Fascism, the Duce sent him a message to confirm that the incident had not soured a memorable event:

> I want to renew my joy and applause for the unforgettable display of yester-day; Bolognese Fascism was, as ever, at the height of its glorious tradition, of its completed works, of future power . . . it is truly the architrave of Italian Fascism.
>
> I will never forget the spectacle of the Littoriale, I believe there was never such a perfect adhesion between the Regime and the people in the history of Italy; never was there a more formidable collection of people in spirit . . .
>
> The criminal episode of the last minute does not darken the glory of the day.
>
> I send you the *fascia mauriziana* lacerated by the bullet: you should conserve it among the relics of Bolognese Fascism.[118]

More than just a national monument, the Littoriale had assumed an unenviable role in Fascist history.

As if the pomp and grandeur of the stadium's inauguration had not been enough, there was also the first international football match to celebrate on 29 May 1927. Played against Spain in the presence of the heir to the Spanish throne, Prince Don Alfonso, his two-and-a-half day visit included a number of events, dinners and receptions during which he was shown the improvements of Italian life under Fascism. With Bologna decorated in both countries' national colours, the Italian king gave Alfonso the keys of the city that, according to Bonuzzi, confirmed the warmth of his welcome and the 'affinity of temperament that exists between the two peoples, sons of Rome'.[119] As an opportunity for the regime to stress the apparent bonds of race and friendship between the two nations, *calcio* assumed significance as both a diplomatic barometer of Fascist Italy's foreign relations and a medium through which the regime hoped to build and reinforce friendships.

In the pre-match information published in *L'Assalto*, the FIGC invited citizens to come and help 'solemnise the welcome to the illustrious guests that wanted to honour with their presence the celebration of a ritual, the ritual of our blood and of our race that renews itself eternally'.[120] This somewhat Futurist belief in the regenerative qualities of Fascist society would have been more suited to the Littoriale's earlier and more secular inauguration when, in the presence of the Duce, guests were officially invited to 'Fascistically consecrate' the new stadium that was decorated with a vast amount of Fascist iconography.[121] Perhaps reflecting the presence of the Spanish, Catholic heir, there was a more religious aspect to the first international match; the Cardinal Archbishop blessing the pitch and sprinkling it with lustral water before the kick-off.

Figures for the number of spectators varied from 50,000 to 70,000. Although it is difficult to verify these, the Littoriale's capacity was almost certainly exceeded, as overcrowding forced thousands of fans that were unable to reach their seats to remain in the walkway beneath the stands.[122] Reality proved that controlling and manipulating such huge, amorphous masses was not as easy as the theorists and architects had suggested.

The event did show the stadium's significant contribution to the local economy and its arrival as a venue of international importance that put the city, nation and regime in the limelight. It also brought the emerging Italian team to international attention, its victory justifiably interpreted as a sign of *calcio*'s significant improvement. Yet, as Ivo Luminasi appreciated: 'We have still not reached the final and most significant target. And it is for this that the *azzurri* . . . point decisively, in the not too distant future, to a higher goal and a most sought-after victory: that of the Olympics.'[123]

The Littoriale, Bologna and Fascist Italy all basked in the glory of the match, *L'Assalto* going so far as to suggest that even the sun was Italian that day. Most importantly, the *azzurri* had 'shown the world how "Mussolini's Italians" also know how to vie in "constructive power" with their antecedents, Caesar's Romans . . . Could Italian unity have had a more symbolic consecration?' it asked rhetorically.[124]

Understandably keen to maximize the day's significance, domestic publications such as *L'Assalto, Il Resto del Carlino* and *La Gazzetta* all included reportedly positive foreign reaction. One example was the apparently respected German journalist Walter Bandermann who vouched for the quality of the *azzurri*'s play and the spectacular nature of the event itself that, in his opinion, eclipsed the 1924 Olympic football final in Paris.[125] The Barcelona daily *Vanguardia* was also said to have praised the achievements of Italian sport in general but especially Bologna, for having given the nation the biggest and grandest stadium in Europe:

Bologna . . . has the glory of being one of the toughest ramparts of the Italian fascist movement and the pride of having provided the norms to shape the fascist belief in a construction programme . . . The Littoriale is a symbol of the ideal of physically improving a nation that fascism made itself, deciding that sport needs to be valued as a school of discipline and a gymnasium of courage and strength, two converging elements, fertile for individual and collective fruits.[126]

The sporting attitude of the Italian fans was also apparently recognized by the Spanish press,[127] which was used as evidence of Fascism's successful campaign to educate the masses spiritually and morally. Certainly the regime was always keen that its representatives portrayed an image of fair play, even if, when necessary, this contradicted reality.

Fascism's image abroad was important and the Littoriale was responsible for illustrating the energy and progress of the new era. Soon after its completion, other communes and countries interested in replicating it began to request information. Allesandria, Padua and Genoa soon formulated plans to develop their own versions, Turin used it to help design the Stadio Mussolini,[128] while the Portuguese Football Federation asked the Italian Consulate for photographs and details to show the authorities what was possible.[129]

After winning the right to host the 1934 World Cup tournament, the Littoriale became one of the jewels in the regime's publicity campaign. As recognized by the Italian Consulate in Vigo, it was a golden opportunity to highlight the country's progress under Fascism:

Certainly one of the elimination matches will be played at Bologna, in the Littoriale. For this I ask [the Mayor] to send me some photographs of the Stadium, of the swimming pool etc with information and details of all services for the press and players, the capacity of the Littoriale etc – all of the publicity material necessary for the purpose.[130]

Foreign interest was not ephemeral and some eight years after its construction, in March 1935, the mayor of Madrid requested photographs and copies of the stadium plans as part of a study into building a similar venue in the Spanish capital.[131] Crucial to its enduring appeal was the Littoriale's multisport design, which enabled it to host a variety of international sporting events. These included the previously mentioned 1927 European swimming championships that further spread the reputations of Arpinati, the city and the regime. As the programme stated:

The multiports stadium built in two years . . . by Leandro Arpinati, deputy of Bologna, is the superb expression of the active vigour of Bolognese fascism and of the new impulse given to athletic sports in Italy . . .

Bologna and Italy owe much recognition to Mr. Arpinati ... who knew how to carry out the work with tenacity ... reuniting the majesty of the monumental Roman tradition and impetus towards a renewed physical and spiritual dynamism.[132]

In this way, international events were exploited as propaganda opportunities both at home and abroad, the domestic market again being reminded of how the regime's restoration of Roman greatness was strengthening Fascist Italy's reputation abroad. As *Vita Nuova* further illustrated:

> through the centuries of ups and downs and pain, the great Latin imperial spirit that built the Colosseum survived in the descendant craftsmen of the Littoriale ...
>
> Italian sport, especially now, following its many sporting and organizational successes ... has acquired great credit abroad ...
>
> The fruit of this credit is the concession to organize sporting contests of the highest international value.[133]

Due to competition from other countries with longer sporting histories and a general, chauvinistic, belief that one of the world's lesser sporting nations was incapable of organizing prestigious events, Italy had great difficulty acquiring the rights to host international tournaments. Consequently, the swimming championships were an opportunity for the regime to publicize the quality of its athletes and its commitment to sport, while reassuring those who doubted its organizational skills. If anybody remained unconvinced, *Vita Nuova* reassured them of the 'facts':

> Italy has organized the contest that was conceded to Bologna, and Bologna has passed the test in such a brilliant way as to draw admiration from the most expert and demanding foreigners that watched the tournament ... The main thing is that they all admired without limitation the enormous work of Arpinati, that graces Bologna, Fascism and Italy; that they might have returned to their countries with a better memory of Italian hospitality, taking with them prizes upon which the sign of the Littorio has been embossed.[134]

Hosting international sporting events was not the only way for the regime to publicize its progress. In addition to Bologna Sportiva's important development work within the local community, its football section became an international flagship for both the city and the regime. So important was it that, besides playing home matches in the Littoriale, the club also received generous grants and tax breaks from the commune. Exploiting its first *scudetto* in 1925, the club's initial request for financial help to overcome problems partly connected to an unpaid bill for communal rates in 1922–3, referred to its strong role in Bologna's local identity:

> As you know Bologna FC, holding the Italian Football Championship, lifts the name of Bologna, and to continue its victories in the name of its city, finds itself in a very needy economic condition, not only due to the enormous daily costs that each football squad meets, but also due to the burdens of holding the greatest honorary title in sport.[135]

Describing how many communes encouraged their local squads with fiscal exemptions or financial aid, BFC requested a grant to help continue its 'educational and patriotic work' to hold 'the name of Bologna high in the field of sport.'[136] Hoping for a loan that would 'allow it to confront, with the least amount of worry, the tough struggle to hold onto the greatest title of champions of Italy',[137] the commune's response was a disappointing 2,000 lire. Unabashed, the president requested more money the following year when the club's financial position failed to improve.

In the intervening period Arpinati had become *podestà* and this time the administration stretched to 5,000 lire.[138] Buoyed by the change in leadership or perhaps genuinely in need, the president requested further assistance six months later, if the club was to fulfil its ambassadorial role:

> Reasons of healthy local pride force us to ask for the commune's support for the football Society of 'BOLOGNA' that with many sacrifices, competing in vigorous sporting battles . . . had the prize of an extremely gratifying success in the name of our city . . .
>
> While the Fascist Government has encouraged and provided for sporting events as elements of propaganda and for the physical improvement of the Italian people . . . we dare to hope that our appeal will be successful and that our city will respond adequately to common expectations.[139]

Despite the club's appeal and the *podestà*'s affiliation, budgetary restrictions prevented Arpinati from committing the commune to a further grant, although he did promise to consider the issue at the next budget talks.[140] He was as good as his word, justifying the club's case by its importance to the city:

> such a figure is inadequate not only for the needs of the said Society, but also for the importance that its activities and its performances have acquired in the city's sporting life.
>
> It is also held, by news of various other communes, that the development of local sporting institutions in general and football in particular is encouraged differently elsewhere, which is not so much by considering the material

impetus from city commerce as favouring the healthy training of youth in the same interests of the nation.[141]

His impassioned plea saw the grant increased to 20,000 lire, thereby indicating either Arpinati's great influence within the commune, or its commitment to the team's continued success. The truth may rest somewhere in between the two, but the club president was clearly aware of its bargaining power and used this to beg funds regularly; always citing its contribution to Bologna's cultural and economic life in the process: '[The] squad that defends the city's colours, makes a notable contribution to tourism and, consequently, to commercial consumption on matchdays when a crowd of fans that consume and spend, flock from the neighbouring centres and exceptionally also from notable distance (Figure 3).'[142]

1930 saw the commune's final payment of 10,000 lire to stimulate more activity and prosperity at the underused Littoriale,[143] after which the municipality's own financial difficulties ended all subsidies to charitable and cultural institutions.[144] Bologna FC's main financial drain was the cost of maintaining an outstanding squad, with considerable sums of money spent on players' wages and 'expenses' that ranged from 300 to 3,000 lire per month at an annual sum of around 450,000 lire, excluding

Figure 3 A rare full-house at the Littoriale, circa 1928. Note Giuseppe Graziosi's bronze statue of Mussolini on horseback, in the Tower's arch, which was later melted down and remodelled into two partisan figures. © Fondazione del Museo del Calcio.

team win bonuses of 70,000 lire.[145] Despite the commercial benefits of success, there was still the heavy expense of attracting the best players. In 1931 to 1932, this accounted for 858,465 lire of the club's spending that was set against 271,000 lire recouped in sales; a net loss of almost 600,000 lire.[146]

Naturally a successful team attracted more spectators and bigger gate receipts, which increased four years out of five, from 1927 to 1932. However, the financial rewards were related to not insignificant costs that amounted to 377,000 lire spent on new players alone, from 1930 to 1932. Even such expenditure did not guarantee success, although Bologna's 1932 Central European Cup win did add 500,000 lire to the coffers.[147] Although apparently good business, takings were notoriously too fickle to be relied upon as bad weather and bad performances often had drastic effects. Moreover, even an increase in income was a double-edged sword, with over 31 per cent lost to opposition teams, taxation and the league.[148]

After investigating Bologna's plight, the commune agreed the club was in financial difficulty. Having made an annual profit only twice in the previous six seasons it was running a debt of 562,000 lire, of which 300,000 lire was owed to the Bank of Rome.[149] Recognizing the club's albeit 'modest' contribution to the city's tourist industry, the commune set the rent for its use of the Stadio Littoriale at one lira per year, for the next one to two years.[150] Irrespective of the unquantifiable financial benefits for the city, the commune's support was justified by a team that made regular repayments in kind and prestige. After Bologna's first championship victory in 1925, the titles, accolades and prestige continued to amount, as in 1929 at the PNF stadium in Rome, when the club secured its second *scudetto* with a 1–0 victory over Torino in front of the Duce.[151]

Reduced to nine players, Bologna's impressive stamina was testimony to the work of the coach Dr. Fellsner, whose modern training techniques and attitude reflected the core ethics of Fascist sport: the desire to win and the refusal to concede defeat. Most interestingly, Leone Boccali argued in *Lo Sport Fascista* that Bologna's achievement showed how representing one's city could be intense without necessarily increasing sentiments of *campanilismo*:

> Bologna won worthily, because when the final turned completely against it, the team found a ruthless will to win. But to speak of will is to say little: one is talking of conscience, of spirit of body, of a healthy love for the home town . . . Salaries and victory prizes are all important for the red and blue players, but they never lost sight of . . . the moral value of the Title they wanted to win.[152]

Even Arpinati, the supposedly neutral head of the FIGC, was not immune to local pride and went straight to the Bologna dressing room to exchange affectionate embraces with the players. Impartial or otherwise, his joy was understandable given his commitment to *calcio* in Bologna. According to Boccali, the team's achievements were key factors in Bologna regaining its position among the most important cities of Italy: "Bologna Sportiva' is a great family that understands all of the city, of which the football eleven, with the recent victory, has renewed the prestige of an already great reputation.'[153]

At a banquet organized for the players by Bologna supporters, even Arpinati accepted that *campanilismo* was an acceptable motivational force, so long as it did not become destructive. Citing his own 'neutrality', he argued that his two year federal leadership had: 'already given the Italian public the impression that something had changed, soon all will need to be convinced that there is no club of the heart for the federal president . . . At this moment it is not the honourable Arpinati who is talking to you, but the rigid applicator of the federal rule.'[154]

Of course, *Il Littoriale* had no interest in portraying anything other than his impartiality, which *Calcio Illustrato* also reaffirmed: Arpinati 'has never in fact hidden his passion for Bologna; but he has always known how to put a formidable barrier between his intimate passion and his role as chief arbiter'.[155] His apparently healthy and committed support for his team was held up as an example to all.

In a number of diverse ways, the phenomenon of *calcio* in Bologna came to reflect the regime's domestic and international politicization and exploitation of the game, the full extent of the team's impact abroad being considered in a following chapter. Clearly Arpinati was the driving force behind *calcio* in Bologna and, despite allegedly honourable motives, he certainly appreciated the national benefits that both he and the city would gain from success. As one of the regime's most publicized architectural projects, the Littoriale stadium represented not only the beginning of Fascism's investment in sporting infrastructure, but also the architectural politics of the era, which becomes even more evident when compared with the new stadium built in Florence only six years later.

Despite the monumental size of the Littoriale, the attempt to augment the city's status in the national arena through *calcio* still required a team worthy of the stadium. For this reason the commune, often under Arpinati's influence, offered Bologna FC as much financial support as possible. In turn, this strengthened the local identity and sentiments of *campanilismo* as the team became one of the best in Italy. Ironically, it was exactly what the regime had been trying to avoid, despite using Bologna's 1929 championship victory to show how it was possible to love both one's city and country. Of course, the reality was different. As will be seen, Bologna's international achievements were so significant that however strong its local identity, the club was unable to avoid having its name, status and reputation hijacked by the regime.

In these ways Bologna FC, the city and the stadium further exemplified the natural dilemmas and contradictions that confronted the regime following its investment in *calcio*, which is reinforced by comparison with Florence. Whereas the local party's involvement in grass roots politics through the medium of sport resulted in the construction of a Romanesque stadium inspired by the regime's self-professed imperial roots, Florence did the opposite. Not only did this represent the radical nature of *its* local party, but it also showed how within Fascist society there was room for individuality, even if the regime did not quite know how to deal with it.

–6–

Radical Florence: The Cradle of *Calcio*

Unlike many other European languages, no literal or phonetic translation of the English word football exists in Italian, which reflects *calcio's* strong local traditions and its particular Italian identity deriving from the medieval game of *calcio fiorentino*. Played in Florence from the sixteenth century, some have argued that this was in fact the original format of the modern game. Others dispute this and attribute the import of association football, at the end of the nineteenth century, to Swiss, Austrian and German engineers, technicians or merchants.[1]

Whichever of these theories is accepted, there can be no questioning the long-term Florentine fascination with the medieval and modern game, which both blossomed under Fascism. Thanks to the local Fascist leaders *calcio fiorentino* was rediscovered and Florence acquired a football team to compete in the new national league in an architecturally radical stadium that reflected the city's proud connection with the game and its avant-garde local party.

Strangely enough for a city that claims to have been the cradle of *calcio*, AC Fiorentina was a late arrival, in 1926. The date is nonetheless very significant as it relates to the reorganization of both the local Fascist Party and *calcio*, as part of the national 'normalization' campaign. There were football teams in Florence prior to this point, but none were capable of uniting the entire city. The formation of Fiorentina from a merger of the two principal Florentine clubs achieved this and soon sparked demands for a stadium worthy of the team and the city. The place of worship for Fiorentina fans, this new construction had to reflect the city's strong independent identity that was being revitalized by Fascism, which derived from its central role in the renaissance. The resulting stadium put Fiorentina and Florence on the Italian sporting map, while the international prestige from its innovative design spread the reputation of radical Florentine Fascism throughout Europe. Neither was the stark modernism of the Giovanni Berta a one-off, as it reflected the type of avant-garde architecture that the Florence-based 'Tuscan group' was becoming renowned for. Representing the type of independence that Florentines had expressed for hundreds of years, the stadium further intensified the city's already strong sense of identity. Combined with the team, this contributed to the formation of a Florentine Fiorentina family that waved the city's fleur-de-lis banner with greater vigour than ever before.

Ridolfi Realizes the Dream

The driving force behind the merger and the rejuvenation of Florentine sport was the Marquis Luigi Ridolfi Vay da Verazzano, the youngest member of an old, noble Tuscan family who became Fiorentina's first president. Despite his aristocratic local roots that extended as far back as Lorenzo the Magnificent, Ridolfi involved himself in Florentine sport to benefit popular ends and equip the city to rival those of the north. Many of his ideas were stimulated by his connections within emerging Florentine Futurist groups, among which he befriended the artist and intellectual Ardegno Soffici and the movement's leader Filippo Tommaso Marinetti. It was through such contacts that he discovered a strong passion for movement and speed that complemented his interest in sport and influenced many of his ideas, some of which were so imaginative that they only came to fruition during the last ten years of the twentieth century.

Ridolfi's first sporting passion was athletics and as leader of the Florentine ASSI Giglio Rosso club he guided it to renowned national and international successes. It was his prototype for AC Fiorentina. Like Bologna FC's president Renato dall'Ara, Ridolfi's work spanned both the Fascist and the post-war democratic eras, careers that are arguably examples of what Ruth Ben-Ghiat has termed the 'collective complicity' that 'made it difficult to defascistize Italian culture after the Second World War'.[2]

Having been president of both Fiorentina and the Florentine Provincial Fascist Federation (1926–9), Ridolfi's post-Fascist career was particularly interesting. As Fiorentina's head, he worked closely with leading PNF cultural figures and the city mayors, Giuseppe Della Gherardesca and Alessandro Pavolini, to promote and develop the club alongside other Florentine sports associations. According to Andrea Galluzzo, he was 'one of the rare, truly enlightened personalities, who, during the twenty years of fascism and . . . also in more recent and brighter times of the free republic, was blessed by that indispensable political power that allowed only him to realise the most ambitious projects.'[3] Not surprisingly, with high profile supporters of the club, Fiorentina was closely linked to the local Fascist Party. On transferring its offices to the local Casa del Fascio in 1929, all society members received free membership and reductions in certain bars and restaurants in town.[4]

Ridolfi's principal skill was as a mediator capable of bridging the gap that had so often resulted in strong local personalities defending their own interests rather than uniting in the city's interests. It was a prominent skill in many of his achievements that was most likely facilitated by his unusual blend of noble origins and Fascist Party membership. Florentine disunity had preoccupied local and national Fascist leaders since Tullio Tamburini's rise to prominence launched inter-party conflict between radical intransigent Fascists and the more conservative integrationalist revisionists.[5] It was a serious dispute that reflected a crisis of support for the regime at the local level, which Adrian Lyttelton interpreted as 'a cleavage between "elite Fascism" and "mass Fascism"'.[6]

Such revisionist/revolutionary disputes that essentially concerned the nature of the party and its future role in society, often erupted in the most radical Fascist towns and cities. One such Florentine manifestation was the virulent anti-Masonic campaign[7] of 1924 that, according to Lyttelton, demonstrated the presence of the 'totalitarian dynamic of 'permanent revolution' or at least permanent terror; new enemies were found to replace the old'.[8] The attacks by the local *squadristi* that preceded a reign of terror upon Florence and the surrounding area in early October, were not solely against the Florentine Freemasons but also against independent anti-Fascist elements of the bourgeoisie, such as members of the University of Florence and magistrates who were thought to protect masons. An opportunity for the squads to indulge themselves and for the *ras* to entrench their local positions of power further, Lyttelton suggests they showed the radical nature of those in the Florentine *fascio* that 'had taken on the air of guardians of the revolution'.[9]

When Roberto Farinacci failed to adequately impose order on the locality Italo Balbo was sent to bring the local party back under control, although it was 1926 before the *fascio*'s subservience was imposed again and the crisis of the party ended. After Mussolini demanded an end to the destructive force of *squadrismo*,[10] the local party's weekly publication *Battaglie fasciste*[11] demanded that local factions unite around the regime. With the internal battles concluded by the Fascist Grand Council's secret dissolution of the squads, the *fascio* announced the Duce's order for its reconstitution that was intended to unite the city: 'Greater than the necessity for struggle and for avant-garde politics, what looms today are works of civil and educational action.'[12]

It was at this point that Ridolfi became secretary of the Federation of Florentine *fasci*. Already well known among local Fascists, having been second in command of the II Florentine Legion during the March on Rome, he was one of the few members of the Italian aristocracy to reach such a position within the party, in a major city. As the PNF secretary Turati explained, Ridolfi was specifically appointed to 'end the factions within Florentine Fascism',[13] and he set to work during his investiture when he appealed for unity and an end to local recriminations and polemics.

> From today, rancour, discord and factions need no longer exist in the city and the province. Leaders and followers will hear that with the new Party Statutes it wants to open a new style and a concept of duties, of the needs of the individual and the collective that is more adherent to the actual requirements of Fascism, which are vaster and more complex than those past times of glorious political struggles and bloody battles.[14]

Preferring sport over politics, the formation of AC Fiorentina in the same year handed Ridolfi a gilt-edged opportunity. Besides addressing Turati's specific brief to relaunch Fascism in the localities after the early years of crisis, Fiorentina was a chance to build a mass popular Florentine institution with no direct history of factional infighting, which was capable of providing the social glue that central government believed was lacking.

Football within the city had been keenly contested since 1870 by the well-known clubs of Palestra Ginnastica Libertas and Club Sportivo di Firenze. Fierce rivals, their animosity reflected the city's ancient Guelf and Ghibelline divisions that had prevented its representatives from uniting to make a national impact, thereby slowing the development of the local game and the city's sporting reputation. In fact, as Arpinati had both intended and predicted following the Carta di Viareggio, it was Libertas's promotion to the first division of the restructured national championship in 1926 that brought the city to its senses, forcing the rationalization of Florentine football and the merger of Libertas and Sportivo into AC Fiorentina. Finally, the city had a single representative with the necessary resources to compete on the national stage.

Yet, even the prospect of competing in the national league did not prevent these rivalries from threatening the merger that was far from a foregone conclusion. According to Galluzzo, the eventual unification of these two previously warring factions came only 'thanks to the rigorous censorship exercised by Luigi Ridolfi who suffocated the interminable vitriolic polemics among the old members of Libertas and Club Sportivo'.[15] So strong were these rivalries that one month after the merger's official conclusion, the new club was still combating general apathy among supporters. As *Il Nuovo Giornale* made clear, the negativity surrounding Florentine football was serious: 'Florence, that was the cradle of the noble game . . . needs to respond enthusiastically to the appeal of the former two societies that, in sacrificing all of their traditions, were affirming something that is truly an enhancement of Italian and Florentine sport.'[16]

While Ridolfi proved a talented negotiator and builder of Florentine unity, his success was undoubtedly related to his extensive connections within local society and his genuine belief in the merits of a single club capable of putting the city on the national arena. However, his most important skill was the ability to convey the merits of the merger to the supporters, as one of the more committed Fiorentina fans, Rigoletto Fantappiè, explained in 1927:

> Luigi Ridolfi was a man of faith and remained struck by the feeling that for us boys Fiorentina was a faith. The viola squad was an ideal that he shared with us. In that era the fan did not carry much weight, but he showed an exceptional willingness towards us. For him categories did not exist: he spoke with everybody.[17]

With such a competitive history between the two teams it is hardly surprising that the unification process did not lack its polemical moments. However, aware of the direction in which the game was moving and the city's recent past, pragmatism prevailed and the two clubs merged on 19 August 1926. AC Fiorentina's club colours were originally a mix of Libertas's red and Club Sportivo's white, with the city's fleur-de-lis adopted as its motif. A further demonstration of Fiorentina's manufactured unity was the board of directors, which comprised of five members from each team. In the light of age-old antagonisms within the city, the new unity, as represented by Fiorentina, was promoted to the point of enforcement, as an attempt was made to construct a bond between the club and the Florentine public. This was perhaps at its strongest and most necessary at the beginning of the 1928/9 season when Fiorentina, competing in group B of the national league, was striving to finish in the top eight in order to qualify for the first, single national division the following season. As a key promoter of the club, the Florentine daily *La Nazione* extended its demand for support from almost every member and institution of local society:

> The squad will bear with itself the name of Florence and, accordingly, all of Florence needs to feel the beauty of the responsibility given to the players. However, it is not out of place to repeat . . . the necessity for public city organizations in general to financially help the local club. It is a requirement of all sportsmen and, we add, of good citizens that truly love the city.[18]

Florentine Fascism: A Radical Party in a Radical City

Besides illustrating the importance of the team's presence in Serie A, *La Nazione*'s statement was indicative of Florentine pride. Although the *fascio* possessed a strong identity, its support for the regime was unstinting, as Marco Palla points out: 'in the years 1927–8 even in Florence the PNF chose the route of subordination to the State, by means of a direction that conformed with bureaucratic zeal . . . to detailed addresses from the Prefect and other local centres of power.'[19]

Reflecting the *fascio*'s, nonetheless, undiminished strength of identity, Pavolini's non-conformist avant-garde weekly *Il Bargello*, defended its new and radical Fascist orthodoxy, while promoting all that was great about Fascist Florence. As the first editorial explained: 'Il Bargello wants to be a Florentine paper; not an American magazine. Good wine, and above all, our wine.'[20] Further evidence of Pavolini's radical thinking was the inclusion of the arts, if not women until 1938,[21] in the University Littoriali sporting contests, to form a cultural Olympics that Arrigo Petacco has described as: 'a gymnasium of ideas and new forms, even unorthodox, where there was the space to debate and even to doubt.'[22] This encouragement of fresh cultural ideas while orienting local policy towards the general concepts of central government gave Fascist Florence and the local party a distinctive radical character.

Reflecting this apparent desire for the city to return to its radical roots, Pavolini was nominated as federal secretary of the Florentine *fascio* on 10 April 1929, at only 25 years of age. Although incredibly young for such a responsible position, he possessed an extraordinary curriculum vitae, which included participation in the March on Rome, as he had been in the capital by chance. As a talented tennis player, a prolific and respected journalist, and an intellectual with degrees in both law and political science from the University of Florence, he was physically and intellectually equipped for the job.

In Palla's opinion Pavolini's succession from Ridolfi, who had been imposed by the party to unite and subordinate the city, was a sign of the local *fascio* retaking the path of activism from which it had been diverted back in 1926.[23] Ridolfi's support for Pavolini's nomination tends to support this, while also reflecting Petacco's suggestion that it was more of a 'technical succession' than any sort of a coup.[24]

However, faced with a fait accompli Ridolfi may also have been wisely securing the new *podestà*'s support for his future plans, having already become preoccupied by the task of developing Florentine sport. By 1930, so considerable had Ridolfi's portfolio of duties become that Turati pressured him to renounce his sporting interests and responsibilities in favour of a full-time political career. He did the opposite and left party activism for good,[25] after which he remained the central figure in Florentine sport until 1942 when he became president of the FIGC, a position he held until his death in 1957.

In the context of the earlier suppression of the local party's extremism, the suggestion that Pavolini's appointment might have been designed to re-radicalize the *fascio*, may seem strange. However, even Turati was realistic enough to appreciate the potential impossibility and almost certain impracticality of imposing a set of generic norms to which all localities were expected to conform. As he stated in a published address to the Florentine Fascists: 'contrast was inevitable in life: we cannot all be the same, like a column of chanting monks. But we are talking about not losing too much time criticising without curing anything else. It is a matter of not losing ourselves in factional struggle until we destroy the chance to build anything.'[26] It further indicated the realization within the PNF that there may indeed have been different routes to Fascism, which allowed the localities to express their identities through acceptable, individual means.

Pavolini had clearly been identified as the best qualified person to rejuvenate the Florentine *fascio*, according to PNF and local needs. As Lyttelton has noted, sport was one of the principal methods by which he could achieve this:

After the great purges of 1925–6, it [Florence] recovered, under Alessandro Pavolini, something of its old aggressive, populist image, especially among youth. Politics was not the only way of raising the temperature and avoiding apathy. Fascism had early and successfully identified itself with sport; the racing driver and the football star were endlessly exalted as the proper models for youth, bold, amoral and anti-intellectual. The astute and energetic leader could win a genuine popularity by patronage of his local team.[27]

With both Pavolini and Ridolfi equally keen on promoting and developing Florentine sport, their working relationship that was a keystone in the restructure of the local party was no surprise. As Turati suggested, had it not been for the definite style of cultural politics that their shared sporting interest provided, Pavolini's attempt to discipline Florentine Fascism might well have failed. The party:

reconquered part of the antique vitality . . . through the internal restructure and propaganda activism of a restoration programme of the material and intellectual supremacy of the city of Florence that was not lacking the support of long myths and traditions, and that was able to consolidate real exigencies, channel ambitions, strengthen a wider class solidarity and give an outlet to that provincial role, summed up in the formula of 'fiorentinismo'.[28]

Regenerating the city enabled the *fascio* to impose its identity upon Florence, and constructing public buildings was a significant part of this. Prior to Fascist enthusiasm for development, Florence had remained more or less structurally unchanged since its sixteenth-century heyday. However, by the end of the 1800s its restrictive walls, narrow streets, increasing population and poor hygiene in certain quarters were forcing its expansion. Development was also stimulated by Florence's, albeit brief, period as the capital of Italy, which demanded the construction of adequate accommodation for the government and its functionaries. Agreed in the Convention of September, signed as part of the unification process, Denis Mack Smith has suggested that the relocation from Turin was 'an indication that Rome was no longer on the agenda',[29] although others believe it was merely a pragmatic move until Rome could finally be acquired.[30] Space within the old city walls was no longer adequate, making it necessary to 'build houses, expropriate buildings, clear roads, widen the city boundaries, improvise extraordinary works . . . to alter in brief the economy, to change the habits of the entire city and impose new ones on it'.[31]

In 1865, Giuseppe Poggi drew up a city Regulatory Plan that disposed of the old fourteenth-century walls and replaced them with public promenades that united the streets inside and out of the old city centre and somewhat brutally, removed the former spatial limitations. Further encouraged by the 1920 Roads and Highways Department plan that opened the space between the old city and the surrounding hills to development, the northern end of Florence was primed for change.[32]

Poggi's original expansion plan included the Campo di Marte, just outside the old city walls. The area of agricultural land that was transformed into a sport zone bridged the gap between medieval and modern Florence, thereby further encouraging its peripheral development. The first plan to establish an Olympic-sized stadium on the site that remained connected to the military was proposed in 1915,[33] although the exigencies of the war years made this impractical. The years of relative economic and political stability in the mid 1920s also saw limited Italian construction and, ironically, it was the international financial crisis of 1929 that stimulated the biggest programme of building works in Italy, as the government sought to alleviate unemployment with public works schemes.

The public works programme complemented Mussolini's Ascension Day speech when, railing against the impact of urban overcrowding upon the health of society, he proposed the clearance of the diseased city centres that threatened to sterilize the nation.[34] *Il Popolo d'Italia* developed the argument, in 1928, when demanding urban regeneration by whatever means possible. Its 'cry' was to 'make the exodus from the city centres happen by any means, even coercive – if necessary; hampering with any means, also coercive, the flight from the country; to oppose the wave of immigration into the cities'.[35]

As a statement of the regime's intent to bring life and facilities to Florence's periphery, the Giovanni Berta stadium had significance beyond the mere facilities that it offered. Like Bologna's Littoriale, which had a clear international and domestic propaganda role, the Giovanni Berta signified all elements of the city's physical, psychological, moral and cultural rebirth that it was hoped would begin to restore Florence to its Renaissance position of intellectual and cultural primacy in Italy, while also commanding international interest.

Ridolfo Mazzucconi's vision of Fascist urban life also complemented many of the organic, regenerative and almost democratic concepts of the modern city as a social body that required looking after for the good of the national whole: 'The Fascist city will be maternal and hospitable to everybody; even for the workers and the poor, who will need good, pleasant houses that do not make them crave the street or the bar. It will have stadia, theatres, schools, baths and poorhouses.'[36] His vision reflecting Fascism's organic view of the city was complemented by Pavolini's surgical analogy justifying the need for a new Regulatory Plan:

> Thus, to the loving citizen comes the nightmare of the great engineers and famous architects, who, armed with scalpels are ready to carve large, terribly practical cuts in the flesh of this mysterious and delicate creature that is the city . . . the terror that comes . . . by following the abstract and scientific fantasy of the rationalised city kills the spirit of our urban ' little motherland'. But in reality . . . such a weapon is absolutely necessary to destroy the microbes and cauterise the infections of a chaotic increase.[37]

Immediately on becoming *podestà*, Pavolini began work on his vision for Florence, blending its ancient traditions and monuments with modernist creations that reflected the new socio-political order and the radical nature of Florentine Fascism. Two of the most distinctive buildings were the Santa Maria Novella railway station and the Giovanni Berta stadium, although some critics opposed the construction of such big edifices of propaganda that failed to tackle the chronic housing shortage.

The first agreement between the railway authorities and the commune had been brokered in 1910, however the war and, primarily, intellectual debate prevented work from beginning in earnest before 1932. The arguments surrounded the rationalist/traditionalist polemic that had been raging within intellectual circles over the construction of ornate, monumental buildings. Essentially, rationalist art and architecture was a new style through which Fascism was identifying and imposing itself. Yet while the regime was undoubtedly modernist and keen not to recreate the imperial-type buildings of the past, it never cut all ties with this heritage. Citing the Colosseum as an example, Pier Maria Bardi argued that rationalism possessed both Italian and even Roman roots, thereby redefining modern rationalist architects as traditionalists with no servitude to the past.[38]

Concurring with Bardi, Pavolini rejected Angiolo Mazzoni's original, grandiose plan[39] for the station, which only needed to be functional. To find an acceptable solution he launched a national competition, inviting planners and architects to submit their proposals for the scheme. Among the many rationalist submissions was that of the Tuscan group, from the Florence Higher School of Architecture, which had already constructed a number of stylistically and aesthetically significant buildings in the city. Under Fascism, Florence had become a veritable architectural capital of Italy. Yet, while the majority of these buildings that rose during the 1930s served the regime, they did not necessarily conform to some Fascist mono-style, as aesthetic diversity was a feature of the city's changing skyline.

A committee was assigned to select the winning proposal with supreme authority resting with Marcello Piacentini one of Italy's most influential and respected architects, who favoured the Tuscan group's proposal. Although traditional in his approach, Piacentini was open to new ideas and invited several young architects onto the editorial board of the Fascist syndicate's journal *L'Architettura*, to help redesign and modernize it. More than just indicating the shifting trend in Italian architecture, according to Tim Benton, it showed how from this point onwards 'the attempt to win favour with Mussolini depended on delicate alliances with the architects in power, and especially with Piacentini'.[40]

Despite its collective inspiration, the station project was commonly associated with Giovanni Michelucci; the city's most high profile architectural figure. The rationalist group renowned for its stylistic sense of adventure proposed a station that courted controversy, with criticisms in the national press objecting to both its design and juxtaposition beside the church of Santa Maria Novella. Even *La Nazione*, the official daily mouthpiece of Florentine Fascism, was unable to defend the project unequivocally, although the majority of the local press were supportive.

In March 1933 the local Fascist arts and literature periodical *L'Universale* entered the fray, supporting the project in the editorial of an issue dedicated to rational architecture. Defending the style on the basis of eleven different points published prominently on its front page, it was number nine that apparently applied to the station: 'In rational architecture, and only in it, the young recognize the features of the modern Fascist civilization, rational in politics, economics and agriculture, the civility of reclaimed stadia and assemblies, a straightforward civilization that is Imperial.'[41] It was interesting and novel to equate rationalist modernism with the era of empire, but nonetheless an approach that mediated the argument between the two.

The polemic continued in the following issue where, in the process of discussing the station's qualities, *L'Universale* identified all that rationalist, Fascist architecture was about: 'Above all it pleases us because it responds to our spirit, because it is synchronised with what we feel is the spirit of the present time; because it seems like a building of another type, for example a monumental station, heavy, scenographic, with one foot in the modern and the other in the antique.'[42]

Committed to ensuring that Michelucci's project went ahead, *L'Universale* declared it: 'one of the most vigorous features and elements of Italian and Fascist civilization'.[43] Further supporting the proposal the periodical reprinted Giuseppe Pagano's defence of the outstanding and intrinsically Italian nature of Michelucci's design, which had already been published in his own architectural magazine *Casabella* and supported by a large number of prominent architects.[44]

In the meantime, Pavolini prudently awaited Mussolini's thoughts before wholeheartedly supporting the project. The Duce's approval eventually arrived, although it seems he was more convinced by its architectural merits from the aerial perspective where it appeared to form a giant *fascio littorio* that the designers maintained was pure accident.[45] However, as Benton has noted: Most 'Italian cities still have a fascist railway station and post office; the efficient modern style of these buildings, together with their more or less discreet iconography of fasces, shrines to Fascist martyrs and Italian or Latin inscriptions, entrenched the claims of state propaganda.'[46]

The reception held for the architects at the Palazzo Venezia in 1934 indicated more than just Mussolini's approval of the project and the work of the Tuscan group in general. It was also interpreted as a sign that modern architecture had been accepted as the official Fascist style and a public opportunity to defend the architects from ageing members of the Chamber of Deputies, led by Farinacci. The Duce's official communication, published in *Il Bargello*, 'expressed his satisfaction and applause that he wanted to extend to the young who sought in architecture and other fields to realise an art responding to the sensibilities and needs of our Fascist century'.[47] However, this still failed categorically to resolve the architectural debate surrounding rationalism, modernism and Fascism. As *Il Bargello* clarified: 'He did not intend to defend one tendency and one school against another. But he clearly said that his sympathies and applause go to who endeavours to create in architecture and other fields, an art responding to the needs of our century.'[48] It was an endorsement, if not an emphatic one, that ensured all roads remained open to further exploration, thereby enabling the accommodation of such apparently contradictory stadia as the Littoriale and the Giovanni Berta. As *Il Bargello* concluded, while rational modernism may not have been perfect, Mussolini's declaration was now:

> stimulating and inducing the artists to new roads, making them walk alone without the props of the past in the rarified air of the Revolution . . . Because walking alone in the new air of Italy touched by the high Fascist tension can be signified by a true artist putting into work like the Stadio Berta, pride and honour for Fascist Florence.[49]

One of the first truly rationalist projects, the station symbolized the Fascist national project by embracing new technology to literally unite the nation through improved transport infrastructure.

The station's Tuscan identity was strengthened by the use of local stone and marble to supplement its reinforced concrete shell. Similar to the reasons why Bolognese brick had been used to construct the Littoriale, this type of local stone was both economical and visible in many of the city's landmark buildings. The terminus's interior was a mixture of marble from Carrara, Catelpoggio, Levanto and Amiata, decorated in a style that mimicked the Duomo and many of the city's other significant ancient buildings.[50] Despite its radical design, the station comfortably blended into the city environment.

It was another example of Fascism presenting itself as a mixture of the past and the present through distinctly stylized political architecture in public works projects that were intended subtly to stimulate consent. As Edoardo Detti noted in his study of the city, the station showed how Fascism used buildings to demonstrate the strength of the regime by producing domineering monumental works that were intended to compensate for the loss of local communal powers.[51] If Detti's theory is accepted, then there really could be no better example of a public edifice built in the name of consensus than the Giovanni Berta.

Myths, Legends and *Lo Stadio*

Since 1922 the stadium in Via Bellini had been the home of Libertas, but the formation of Fiorentina and the consequent increase in spectators soon prompted the campaign for a new stadium. Yet there was more to the demand for a new arena than simply the growing size and status of the club and the safety of the increasing number of supporters. As the local sports weekly *Lo Stadio* pointed out, Florentine pride also had to be considered: 'Fiorentina's ground has now been exceeded. The enthusiasm and the passion that animates our crowd make it seem claustrophobic, as it really is. The necessity however . . . is to equip Florence with a stadium that can admit the masses and be a theatre of sporting displays of exceptional importance.'[52]

Situated on the city periphery, less than one-and-a-half kilometres from the centre and close to the nearby railway station, the Campo di Marte area had already been identified as the perfect site with enough space to enable future development. Able to meet this CIS regulation, the arena's position was also intended to stimulate the city's expansion, which, as the Littoriale had already shown, demanded attention to local infrastructure. The first significant improvements were seen in 1930, when the dusty roads were covered in bitumen and a tram service extended specifically to cater for those going to the stadium.

The idea for the arena was conceived following the local Fascist Giovanni Berta group's request for a concession of land to build a sports ground in the nearby Le Cure district, in November 1929. An ex-naval serviceman who saw action in the Adriatic campaign in 1915–18, Giovanni Berta was a fierce anti-socialist and joined the local *fascio di combattimento* in 1920, after which he was involved in the Fascist assault on Bologna, during which the nationalist Giulio Giordani was martyred. It was a portent of things to come for Berta who was also martyred the following year, when he was allegedly murdered by a group of demonstrators during a socialist strike. Having been attacked, he was apparently thrown from the Ponte Sospeso but clung to a rail, at which point his hand was severed and he fell to his death in the Arno. His body was taken to the family chapel in one of the city's famous landmarks, the San Miniato al Monte church set on the hill above the Boboli gardens, where the following epitaph was inscribed on his tombstone:

> For Giovanni Berta
> Soldier of Italy
> Here lies the body . . .
> that
> the new Red barbarians
> drowned in the Arno
> throwing him from the bridge
> trampling and stamping
> on his hands that were hanging on
> beating his head
> while the innocent screamed:
> Mamma.
> And the Arno is testimony
> to our good and bad people
> that shouted their horrifying curse
> that you still hear echoing
> in the silence
> at the place of the infamy.[53]

Recollecting Berta's fate, Carlo Nannotti, the Fascist fiduciary of the Le Cure district, drew consolation from the mystical regenerative effects that he believed the martyr's death would have upon the city and its populace: 'The blood that flowed from the hands of Giovanni Berta, has not stayed in the water of the Arno, every drop has penetrated the veins of the new youth, that youth that will live healthily in the air purified by the Fascist Revolution.'[54] As ever, the true facts of the event are hard to ascertain, but this is the myth of martyred Fascism that was deliberately attached to the new stadium through its name. It was both a memorial and a symbol of the sporting rebirth of the city, region and nation under Fascism, as *Lo Stadio* proudly proclaimed:

> We can completely verify in our region the tangible sign of national sporting progress. The 'Giovanni Berta' stadium, the most modern and beautiful in Europe, has worthily completed the artistic face of Florence, whereas Pisa, Signa, Piombino, Montevarchi, Pontedera and soon Livorno, Pistoia, Siena, have and will have complete and rich grounds, perfectly equipped for every type of sporting activity.[55]

The local group's modest plan became more grandiose following the intervention of Ridolfi, the *podestà* and Giuseppe Corbari, the secretary-general of CONI. With Fiorentina competing in Serie A for the first time and Via Bellini no longer able to serve the club's needs, the original plans were dropped in favour of a larger stadium, which would serve Fiorentina and allow future international matches to be played in Florence. As Dr Nannotti stated in a letter to the *podestà*, the concession of land at the Campo di Marte finally and definitely resolved 'the nagging question that has been debated for a long time, thus giving to this pre-eminently sporting district a great development for the physical education of our youth'.[56] Like the Littoriale, the Giovanni Berta was dedicated to the development of sport for the local masses while performing an international propaganda role for the regime.

At the time, the architect cum engineer Pier Luigi Nervi had recently completed a covered stand for the Giglio Rosso athletics club, where Ridolfi was also president. How Nervi was commissioned to build the first stage of the Giovanni Berta stadium is disputed, some saying he was appointed while others have argued that he won a tender or competition.[57] If any competition or tendering process did take place, it seems that a lack of publicity left Nervi as the only entrant,[58] although such was his local reputation based upon his previously completed projects that there was no serious reason for any opposition to his appointment. However he was commissioned, the most important factor in the design was the patron of the scheme; that being the commune. As with work for private patrons, Nervi, who was an influential member of the Florence Higher School of Architecture, had to respect the funder's demands that included a number of technical specifications laid down by the commune.[59]

While the city's aesthetic and architectural merits interested some Florentines, for the masses the more important debate was just why it had taken so long to build a stadium worthy of Serie A, and how it could now be constructed in the shortest time possible. The wait was justified as soon as the stadium's architectural merits were visible. According to Michelucci, these said much about the city and the regime: 'Florence, with this stadium of pure modern character, has produced a work that superbly represents the reawakening of Italian energies and the concern that the regime has rightly also given to the physical education of youth.'[60]

The mayor and the commune authorized the construction of the covered stand on 17 July 1930, allocating 700,000 lire for the job.[61] Ironically, having taken so long to get this far, time was now in short supply and Nervi had to commence work no more than ten days after signing the contract, under the threat of a 500 lire fine for every day the project went beyond the 180 working days it had been agreed it would take.[62]

Nervi's company took in the region of 60 per cent of the fees, but he was also compelled to recruit the workforce of over 1,000 employees direct from the *Ufficio Provinciale di Collocamento* – Provincial

Recruitment Office – with a number of other smaller Tuscan firms accounting for the remaining 40 per cent. For such a huge and prestigious project, it is quite remarkable that Nervi was only allowed to recruit a limited number of colleagues with whom he had previously worked outside of the city.[63] It demonstrated how the commune attempted to use low cost public works programmes to stave off the cumulative effects of the devalued Lira and the world economic crisis. In accordance with the mayor's wishes, the project's economic burden upon the commune was kept to a minimum by constructing the stadium principally out of reinforced concrete,[64] a modern building fabric with which Nervi had already made his name.

The Florentine commune seemed to employ a similar accounting system to that of Bologna, which presents the same difficulties when trying to determine the exact construction costs; two estimates in the same publication putting each seat within the region of 55 to 150 lire.[65] The costs of the project are generally considered to have been the responsibility of the commune, which covered them with two significant loans. The first came from the Istituto Nazionale delle Assicurazioni – National Insurance Institute – in 1928. The sum of 70,000,000 lire[66] was to be repaid over twenty years, and was to include a number of extaordinary, necessary and urgent works in the city.[67] The second came from the Cassa di Risparmio di Firenze – Savings Bank of Florence – for 2,300,000 lire, to construct the two end terraces and complete unfinished works to the inside of the stadium. In addition to the commune's financial support, Galluzzo states how Ridolfi also made a considerable personal contribution of around 2,000,000 lire, to complete the second stage of the building process and acquire all of the necessary lighting and sound equipment.[68]

Initially only awarded the contract for the covered stand, Nervi went on to complete all four sides of the stadium in two principal phases from October 1930 to November 1931 and July to December 1932. The finished product had a capacity of 35,000 spectators, 6,000 of whom sat beneath the daring roof, which had been constructed out of a specific type of concrete and steel, only available from Italian producers.[69] Most strikingly, in accordance with the mayor's demand for unobstructed views from the stand, the roof was almost cantilevered to eliminate the central pillars or supports as much as possible.[70]

The mayor's considerable demands warranted the full application of Nervi's talents to reach a solution that was structurally, economically and aesthetically satisfactory, while covering over twenty metres of seating with unobstructed views.[71] Independent of the terracing, the roof rested on supports that, according to Simon Inglis's more recent study of the stadium, were 'inclined so far back and so high up in the stand that unless one is looking side on, the slender concrete canopy appears to be miraculously cantilevered.'[72] So daring and radical was the plan to remove the supporting trusses that had previously impaired the view in all other stadia, many doubted the structure would survive the necessary engineering tests, let alone those of time. As the architect Giovanni Koenig later described, before it could be opened to the public:

> One of the greatest living experts on reinforced concrete . . . who was called by the City Council to inspect the work on site, was openly sceptical about the stability of the cantilever roof. His opinion became widely known, so it was taken for sure the roof would collapse. The day the supporting scaffolding was to be removed, poor Nervi found the work site deserted. With the help of a few assistants who believed in him, he set about hammering out the wedges that had been placed between the reinforcing supports.[73]

Built in a mere 120 days, Nervi's roof was so innovative, impressive and functional that it was admired and replicated throughout Europe and South America. According to Koenig, who made a number of detailed studies of the stadium, Nervi had 'created a collective space in which a huge public was contemporaneously the actor and spectator. For centuries in Italy, no similar popular spectacle had been seen.'[74] His assessment reflected exactly what Fascist stadium policy had been trying to achieve; not only were the rising stadia propaganda objects, they were also integral parts in creating and developing a mass popular, collective spectacle. Those who sat in the new stand looked down upon an unusual 500-metre athletics track with a 220-metre straight that forced the terracing beyond either end of the cantilevered roof, at a cost of the stadium's symmetry. Only half elliptical, it was now D-shaped, causing many locals to suggest it had been deliberately built so in honour of the Duce.

The city council commissioned the engineer Alessandro Giuntoli to design a rich figurative decoration for the stadium's principal entrance. Completed with modernist columns that connected the rational modernity of the regime with its more grandiose imperial past, Silvio San Pietro declared it a complete misunderstanding of the modernist nature of Nervi's stadium.[75] While the façade of the main entrance was generally less acclaimed than Nervi's work, it could also be interpreted as a perfect example of how Fascism accepted and accommodated the coexistence of monumental tradition with rational modernism. Whether deliberate or not, the end result was the same.

The next stage of the project was the uncovered stand, Marathon Tower and entry stairways on the opposite side of the ground, the plans for which were approved by the mayor in July 1931.[76] The augmentation of the stadium was warranted by Ridolfi's acquisition of top quality players, which were propelling Fiorentina towards Serie A, thereby increasing the need for extra capacity. Although exposed to the elements, the stand was equally dashing and innovative in its own way, the drama provided by the 55-metre modernist Marathon Tower and its revolutionary helicoid entrance stairway.

There were three such stairways in total, their design a response to the commune's demand for 'the easy flow of spectators, taking into account their anticipated number'.[77] This innovative feature, which was only facilitated by the use of reinforced concrete, enabled Nervi to overcome traditional problems of overcrowding at ground level entry points by immediately shepherding supporters to the highest seats, from where they could disperse. As De Finetti appreciated at the time:

> The flow of the public comes in a manner that I believe is absolutely original, like I have never discovered in any other stadium neither ancient or modern: the crowd goes up by means of external stairs to the apex of the stand and from here distributes itself in the best manner, from the immediate view that one has of the seats available.[78]

More than just a practical stroke of genius, the stairway positioned at the centre of the stand possessed unique aesthetic grace, conceived as it was, in Bardi's opinion, 'out of abstract inventiveness and perfected through calculation'.[79]

Structurally, the tower was less complex but certainly no less impressive. A complete contrast to the Marathon Tower in Bologna, the Florentine version was equally monumental and domineering, adorned by the *fasces*. Taller, thinner, much sleeker, it was and remains a supermodel. Fitted with a lift that ascended to a radio transmitter and a small box for the public announcer at the top, its base possessed an *arengario* (balcony) from which mass rallies could be harangued. The tower also had a curved glass window along its rectangular front. Illuminated at night, it marked the city's extended periphery and was a clear reference point for Florentines (Figure 4).

In the sense that towers punctured the skyline of Fascist Italy in general, the Giovanni Berta's version was not extraordinary. Where it differed though was in the sleekness of its design and the construction material used, the likes of which had never been seen before.

With the stadium in use, it became apparent that its two open ends exposed the pitch to the full force of the wind. For this practical reason, which met the demands of the CIS *regolamento* on stadia, Nervi

Figure 4 Nervi's interpretation of the Marathon Tower. Unabashed Fascist modernism, perfect for haranguing crowds. © Simon Martin, 2001.

completely enclosed the Giovanni Berta with terracing at either end. Besides protecting the pitch from the wind that frequently disrupted play, the two *curve* (curves) augmented the stadium to a capacity capable of hosting international fixtures. This had been Ridolfi's ultimate dream and something that the commune, with some regret, had been unable to demand, as the following communication with the *podestà* explained:

> Furthermore the actual number of seats in the stands already built are insufficient, both because international matches are only assigned to those cities that have stadia with capacities for at least 30,000 and because independent of that, this season, in four or five championship matches, there have been 8–9,000 more fans than the 12,000 the stands can actually hold.[80]

Perhaps the most interesting aspect of Nervi's design was his deliberate exposure of the stadium's structural elements. Firmly embracing modernism he made the reinforced concrete structure its main feature, rather than disguising it. It was a complete contrast to Bologna where the brickwork façade was specifically designed to do the opposite. Simplicity and efficiency were Nervi's aims and this was the most striking difference between the Littoriale in Bologna, built only five years earlier yet seemingly from a different era. Despite their stark differences, both served equally important international propaganda roles for the regime while satisfying local needs. Whereas the Littoriale was an application of Roman stadium design to the modern era with modern materials, Nervi quite simply broke the mould, as observed in *La Città Nuova*'s article on sports buildings that found: 'sincerity and architectural originality . . . in the Berta stadium of Florence, a truly fundamental work for our sporting architecture'.[81]

When finally completed in 1932, the stadium was fully equipped to undertake its local, national and international propaganda duties. As Koenig later noted: 'Everybody understood that after many years of darkness, Florence finally had a collective work worthy of the times and of its architectural tradition . . . thus it found for itself, almost gift-wrapped and certainly unexpectedly, one of the rare masterpieces of modern architecture.'[82] One of the first examples of modern construction techniques used to break decisively with the traditions of the past, it still provides one of the most compelling examples of Fascist architecture for the Fascist era. As Inglis has succinctly summarized: Nervi 'had the audacity to demonstrate that modern stadia did not have to resemble Roman temples, pseudo-classical palaces, nor even disguise their function behind curtains of brick or stone'.[83]

With the *curve* awaiting construction, the stadium was inaugurated with a match against the European stars Admira of Vienna, on the 13 September 1931. Immediately before the kick-off an aircraft flew over the stadium from which the pilot, war hero Vasco Magrini, launched the match ball before performing some aerobatics.[84] Connected to the Campo di Marte's former use as a local airfield, the display once again juxtaposed the stadium with another form of modernity embraced by the regime, thereby visually displaying its technical progress. In front of a crowd of 12,000, Fiorentina won the match 1–0 with a goal from the phenomenal Uruguayan import Pedro 'Artillero' Petrone. Most importantly, *Il Bargello* was delighted to report how the new stadium had finally brought the national standing of Florence up to the levels of Bologna, Milan and Turin, thanks to the work of the *podestà* Della Gherardesca, Ridolfi and Pavolini.[85]

Famous throughout the peninsula, the Giovanni Berta appeared in a number of specialist magazines at home and abroad. One such Italian publication was *Casabella* whose editor, the renowned polemicist Pier Maria Bardi, lauded its beauty throughout the world: 'In Moscow, I felt the need to speak of it as a masterpiece.'[86] He also acquired a degree of notoriety for the stadium by describing it as the first example of Fascist architecture.[87] Indisputably, it was a shining example of modernity, which had superseded the Littoriale and taken stadium design to a new level.

Given its radical appearance and growing reputation, there is little surprise that the Giovanni Berta earned the regime considerable domestic and diplomatic capital. The source of great admiration throughout Europe, many requests were made for information regarding its design, such as the Hungarian Athletics Association's desire to replicate it in an 80,000-capacity version of its own.[88] It was not the only request, with Sweden, France, Austria and the Soviet Union showing similar interest, while a model of the stadium was also put on display in the Italian pavilion at the 1936 Berlin Olympic Games.[89] As Francesca Agostinelli argued more recently, the Giovanni Berta not only signalled the official entry of sporting buildings into national architecture, it also broke the dichotomy between construction and architecture that had been created in the sphere of culture.[90] It was only after the Berta's arrival that sports buildings began seriously to interest the architectural press, as seen in the huge amount of publicity for the 1933 Stadio Mussolini in Turin.[91]

Although the stadium's design was very much admired throughout Europe, it really came to prominence through the many competitions that it hosted, the first international event being an important football match against Czechoslovakia in the Coppa Internazionale Europea – International European Cup – in 1933. The choice of Florence itself was significant, as barring five matches in Rome, one in Padua and another in Naples, the national team had never played outside of the northern power bases of Turin, Milan, Genoa and Bologna (Figure 5).

A day of great pride for the city and the regime, *Il Calcio Illustrato* dedicated its front page to the event, informing its readers of the 'magnificent construction that honours Fascist Italy, perhaps more for its architectural style than its technical perfection [that] is finally hosting an international match'.[92] While the lack of an adequate stadium accounted for the *azzurri* having never previously played in Florence, the choice of the city showed how the regime and the FIGC were attempting to foster an interest in the national team throughout Italy. On a wet day, the ground was full to capacity. Ridolfi was surrounded by local and national dignitaries in the tribune of honour and the Italian team was packed with the

Figure 5 'A screaming monster of thousands and thousands of mouths' (see p. 188). With the digatories dry under Nervi's dashing roof, Florentines roared the *azzurri* on to victory in the 1934 World Cup. © Fondazione del Museo del Calcio.

best players in the country, although it was local boy Mario Pizziolo who commanded the Florentines' attention.

With the *azzurri*'s victory the stadium passed its first test, laying the foundations of a lucky reputation that would serve the Italian team in the near future. The following November it staged another Coppa Internazionale match against Switzerland, in which Italy again ran out worthy winners. The game was preparation for the following year's World Cup tournament, when the Giovanni Berta formed a principal role in the regime's propaganda campaign. As De Finetti pointed out, the stadium was 'the most beautiful for its structural audacity and elegance, the work of one of the clearest creators and calculators of reinforced concrete that might be among us'.[93] With two matches scheduled for Florence, the Italian Consulate in Vigo requested photographs of the stadium and other sporting works in the city, plus details of what facilities would be available to the Spanish players, press and public, who would be coming to support their team: it was 'a good opportunity to show the results, benefits and progress of our Fascist Regime not only for sport, but for all aspects of Italian life'.[94]

The second of the two scheduled matches, a quarter-final between Italy and Spain. One of the most violent games in the tournament's history, it required a replay the following day, which attracted an even bigger crowd. The match was arguably the most perfect synthesis of the stadium, the crowd and the sportsman, united in serving the regime. More than just a victory, Italy's defeat of the strongly fancied Spanish team was interpreted as the ultimate sign of the emergence of the *Italiano nuovo*, the new Fascist man that never conceded defeat and thus always succeeded in winning.

Fiorentina: Fascist Sport in a Fascist City

Besides hosting high profile fixtures, in the true spirit of the 'era of stadia' the arena was very much a part of the Florentine community, open to local sports clubs, schools, Balilla and Dopolavoro groups that had also been reorganized by Ridolfi. From 1929 onwards he restructured Florentine sport by focusing on existing resources as opposed to making any dramatic changes. Reflecting CONI's new norms, a single, large society remained at the centre of each sport around which a number of smaller, local groups operated. The activities of these *Gruppi Rionali Fascisti* – local groups – were still important as they were expected to concentrate on training students and those competitors aspiring to greater things, before transferring them on to the principal society of the region or city.[95] An example of this structure in action was the Giglio Rosso athletics club that was linked to a number of satellite groups within the city, all of which belonged to the Italian Athletics Federation.

Despite being encouraged to develop, smaller societies were unable to progress beyond their given place in the sporting hierarchy, as participants in national competitions could now only be selected from the large central club and not the *gruppi rionali*. Ensuring that the elite athletes competing in the city's name benefited from the best facilities available, it also reaffirmed the Fascist hierarchy that ran through all aspects of society. Besides the Giglio Rosso athletics club, the Club Sportivo Firenze for cyclists, the Palestra Ginnastica Fiorentina Libertas for boxers and gymnasts, and a rowing club, the jewel in Ridolfi's crown was the AC Fiorentina. Aware of the bigger picture, his drive to improve local sporting prestige was felt at grass roots level where he established and improved smaller sports grounds for these new *gruppi rionali*. Acquiring land, resurfacing running tracks and constructing small covered terraces was funded by a number of grant applications made to the commune in excess of 2,600,000 lire.[96]

Equally keen to develop sporting opportunity throughout the entire province, he communicated the chronic shortage of facilities in a letter to the mayor on behalf of the sports branch of the local party: 'The necessity for a sports ground in every centre, even small, becomes greater and more unavoidable each day. It is absolutely necessary that each commune has its own sports field, where it can train and prepare our youth.'[97] Ridolfi's motivation was very much local, first and foremost, although, in accordance with Fascism's organic view of the nation, curing and caring for this composite cell would contribute to the greater good of all. With only twenty-two sports grounds in the province and four under construction, he was joined by *Il Bargello*'s Giovanni Buratti in imploring the best local minds to tackle the various obstacles.

> Florence needs a new stadium, local sports grounds and swimming pools, the province has other vital needs. There are zones in which sport is still at the very beginning. In Valdarno, from Compiobbi to edge of the province of Arezzo there is not a sports field worthy of the name, the Mugello high and low, with the exception of Borgo San Lorenzo, is in the same condition. Here the work of the Fasci and the communes needs to be more fervent.[98]

Of course, constructing stadia throughout the region was far from simple, with cost one of the most prohibitive factors. So, when submitting their request for mayoral support to develop a major stadium in Florence, Ridolfi and Pavolini proposed a number of ways in which the commune might recoup or justify some of the expense. Besides organizing festivals and lotteries and directly approaching various central government bodies for funding, they suggested contacting the prefecture to stress the stadium's contribution to the alleviation of local unemployment.[99] As they explained in their letter to the *podestà*, they did not consider financial difficulties a reason for inaction: 'The problem of sports grounds is a problem of means, but first and foremost it is a problem of faith. The communes of the province have been assigned the task of realising a work that has an inestimable social value that moral and physical sacrifices can no longer delay.'[100]

Undoubtedly committed to developing grass roots sport, Ridolfi's vision turned Fiorentina into a national force that boosted the city's pride. It was the type of dynamic radical progress that Fascist Florence believed it was capable of in all fields of life. Besides warranting a stadium that was both worthy and capable of hosting Serie A football, the new 'superclub' commanded a united fan base that provided loud vocal support and significant income from gate receipts. Echoing similar appeals for money towards the construction costs of the Littoriale, Fiorentina fans were also asked to help ease the club's economic burdens. Partly due to onerous taxation demands in the club's early years, they also derived from a match against Genoa that resulted in Fiorentina losing four championship points and two gate receipts that had left a deficit of over 50,000 lire.[101]

In return for a donation of no less than 50 lire, each supporter was given free entry to the popular seats for the remainder of the championship, in addition to having their names published in *Lo Stadio*.[102] By the following week, perhaps due to a lack of success, the minimum donation guaranteeing entry for the remainder of the season was reduced to 10 lire.[103] In an effort to secure the best response, the appeal was directed at the 'social mass' of supporters, rather than Florentine citizens, which *Lo Stadio* attempted to draw into a definite sense of community by valuing all contributions irrespective of their worth:

> More than anything we insist not on the size of the amount but on the number of subscribers, because all present members need to respond to the appeal . . . it is not obligatory to give L.100, ten Lire are enough to express a tangible sign of attachment to the colours and this truly derisive figure cannot weigh heavily against the family of the red and whites.[104]

Lo Stadio's attempt to construct a sense of community around Fiorentina indicated the importance of the club's continued representation at the national level for the city, although it would be unrealistic to suggest that all supporters stood by the team through good times and bad. The reality was that many were only interested in success and when this was hard to come by in the 1929/30 season, *Lo Stadio* issued a rallying cry:

> [Fiorentina] needs members who, even in hard times, do not lose themselves in trifling matters, but know how to close around the players, to give them that strength of will that sometimes compensates for technical deficiencies. And these fans know that Fiorentina still has more to say in the championship; they know that all is not lost, because if it does fall it needs to fall on its feet.[105]

Despite this plea Fiorentina was relegated from Serie A that season. Nonetheless, the unification of Florentine forces and the experience of competing in the highest division for the first time had undoubtedly strengthened the sense of local identity and stimulated the desire for a quick return to the top flight among the club's supporters and its directors. After all, only in Serie A could supporters enjoy the Apennine derby with the famous Bologna FC. As *Lo Stadio* had previously noted, this was the greatest opportunity for the city, the club and the fans to distinguish their superior qualities from the rest:

> Do we truly want to show that we know how to be Florentines in the nicest sense of the word? To show that this, our sweet city, is truly the master of good taste and manners? . . . Do you remember the first day of the season?

Yes, it is true. We were beaten, well beaten, indeed, but our conduct especially . . . was simply marvellous and I remember having applauded and seen many of you too . . . applauding the talented Ambrosiana that knew how to win with elegance and good taste.[106]

Lo Stadio's contributor showed how the local identity was not being defined and strengthened through victories alone, but also through the achievements, reputation and general comportment of the football club. So important had Fiorentina become to the city's identity that *Il Bargello* reminded the local press of its responsibility to restrain such dangerous sentiments. 'Campanilismo is a wound from past times, of which vestiges still unfortunately exist, which spring to light particularly through minor sporting competitions; it is one of the ills towards which journalism needs to complete its demolition work.'[107] As Mussolini had stipulated, the sports press had to support the regime's work actively to combat this malady. Merely pointing out the mistakes and the bad examples of *campanilismo* was no longer enough, it now needed to provide the remedy: 'Above all sports journalism needs to be far from all profiteering and needs to give sport every help as an impartial apostolate, where occasionally bitterness cannot be overcome by the pride of success . . . Today sports journalism is a living working force in the domain of Fascism and needs to be necessarily at the top of its mission.'[108]

Yet, it was impossible for the city's newspapers and reporters not to be passionate about Fiorentina, especially following the club's achievements from such modest beginnings when compared to the long-established big city Goliaths of the game. The stadium's inaugural fixture, in 1932, also marked Fiorentina's return to the heights of the national league and the beginning of a momentous season in which it incredibly finished in fourth position, level on points with Milan. It was a huge boost to the city's sporting reputation, which was recognized in the commune's monthly publication as 'the brilliant and enviable affirmation of sporting Florence in the Italian football championship'.[109]

While Ridolfi took many of the plaudits for having knocked some of the bigger teams off their pedestals, the success was primarily due to Pedro Petrone's thirty-seven goals in forty-four matches. Ridolfi could not refrain from congratulating himself on the wisdom of his 30,000 lire investment, which had been a calculated gamble to raise the overall ability of the team to a standard that was worthy of the stadium and the national league. Beyond simply basking in the fourth-place finish, the *Rassegna del Comune* showed how *calcio* and Fiorentina had become an extension of the city's identity politics:

In fact, it is always necessary to remember that there are squads boasting glorious and ancient traditions, which have always represented the aristocracy of Italian football, that comprise of players of the highest class and reputation that are still no better [than Fiorentina] – like Roma – and below like Torino, Genoa, Milan, Lazio etc . . . it is opportune to note how the Marchese Luigi Ridolfi . . . dedicates all of his passion and competence, making sacrifices that are not recognized or appreciated enough.[110]

In 1934/5 Fiorentina went one better, finishing third in Serie A after leading the division for much of the season. However, as *viola* fans were to find out, the club's successes always seem to proceed a fall, and in 1938 it returned to Serie B for twenty years. Yet even from such a lowly position Fiorentina continued to impart a modernizing influence on the Italian game through coach Giuseppe Galluzzi's adaptation of a *metodo* style of play that was as much about players' attitudes as it was tactics. The change again showed the city's ease at being the vanguard of change. While it did not bear immediate rewards in the championship, Fiorentina surprised the big names of Milan, Juventus, Lazio and Genoa on the way to claiming the 1940 Coppa Italia, its first national success.

However, such achievements coupled with the new national league strengthened the team's support within the city, intensifying *campanilismo*, which was most evident during the Apennine derby with Bologna, when the embers of the ancient city rivalries were fanned by the game. While celebrating Fiorentina's famous victory over Bologna in 1932, *Lo Stadio* continued to rail against the developing trend of such strong local sentiments. In an editorial headlined 'Finiamola' (Let's end it), the 'football fan' was described as little more than 'an outlet for old provincial grievances that Fascism has never tolerated and has energetically crushed wherever it has manifested itself'.[111]

While directly vilifying *campanilismo*, it was still a veiled attack upon the Bologna supporters who were said to have abused many Fiorentina fans returning along the main road from the Littoriale, after their team's unexpected win. According to *Lo Stadio*: 'Whoever was tempted to react ran the risk of being quickly packed off to the hospital and whoever was instead disposed to have justice . . . was forced to take all the "complements" that the primitive and ignorant could have invented.'[112] *Lo Stadio* naturally highlighted the excellent behaviour of the travelling Florentines whose vocal support from the first minute until the last contributed much to the team's victory. Moreover, the sporting nature of their support merited special praise, 'despite provocation from the Bolognese fans (if one can call them that)'.[113] The impartiality of *Lo Stadio*'s account is open to question, but it does show how serious the problem was considered to have been. Ironically, the newspaper's campaign against such excesses and its defence of the Fiorentina fans, only exacerbated the problem, thereby risking a further escalation the next time the two clubs met.

Besides these particular victories, it was the consistency of Fiorentina's play that boded well for the future, the *Rassegna* assuring fans that: 'the athletes of our squad will be capable and prepared, spiritually, physically and technically, for new affirmations and conquests in the name of sporting Florence.'[114] The emergence of Fiorentina as a squad of national repute completed the city's football holy trinity that consisted of the fans, the stadium and the team, each of which was equally proud of the other. As the *Rassegna* emphasized: 'The Florentine public is among the most enthusiastic and affectionate of all Italy towards the colours of its squad the Viola. The Stadio Comunale "Giovanni Berta" is certainly the most beautiful in Italy, even if not the most complete or the biggest. That is still its value!'[115]

Despite general reservations about extreme *campanilismo*, healthy competition and rivalry was encouraged, the 1934 Tuscan derby between Fiorentina and Livorno being portrayed by *La Nazione* as a triumph for sport in the region: 'The fans of both clubs will come observant, like so many soldiers of sport, and they will bring with them their healthy weapons of enthusiasm and chivalry to fight a fair battle of spirits in the name of sport.'[116] *Lo Stadio* was equally realistic to accept that passionate fans were a vital part of sporting competition, although it must be recognized that these two local publications only referred to the good, competitive ethics of Tuscan supporters. By further highlighting apparent cultural and ethical differences between its readers and those in the rest of Italy, in the classic way of the Fascist regime this also intensified the Tuscan identity by defining the bad characteristics of those outsiders from beyond the region.

Fans from outside of Tuscany were rarely paid complements, as in the earlier case of Fiorentina-Bologna where the levels of acceptability had apparently been transgressed so badly by the Bolognesi, that the incident was declared a sign of sporting and civil decadence.[117] Having identified this evil, *Lo Stadio* questioned whether some of the most drastic measures imaginable might be necessary to quell the excesses: 'On the other hand if a football match needs to mobilize such public force, as much as used to be necessary to check an attempt against the powers of the State, it has to be asked if it is right to allow the public the opportunity to participate in certain sporting events.'[118]

Realistically this was probably impossible given the huge public interest in the game and the inevitable strength of reaction that would have resulted from any prohibition. Aware that any serious suggestion to outlaw football by *Lo Stadio* would also have been tantamount to the paper cutting its own throat, Florentines were urged to take the pacifist route in response to aggression, which only further reinforced their parochialism:

> As interpreters of the feeling of our sporting public we do not want Florentines to forget the offence in the Bolognese city, when 'Fiorentina' hosts 'Bologna' and its supporters. But we also demand for the prestige of Italian sport, for that spirit of fraternity and brotherhood that needs to tie all of the sporting masses of Italy, for the good name of our people . . . the hour has truly arrived to end certain habits that, in the 11th year of the Fascist Revolution, cannot and need not be tolerated.[119]

Another interesting aspect of this report was its reference to the number of female Fiorentina fans that had travelled to Bologna, despite the regime's reservations about female involvement. As Victoria de Grazia noted: 'So-called male games, in particular soccer, were discouraged; with trepidation, Arpinati acquiesced to the formation of a single 'women's soccer group' at Milan, on the condition that it never played in public.'[120]

Although women were undoubtedly in the minority at the Bologna-Fiorentina match, their presence indicated the growing importance of *calcio* among both genders and the way in which teams were increasingly representing larger percentages of the local population. Such was the importance of women that *Lo Stadio* returned to the theme only a few weeks later, encouraging more to attend matches: 'In the feminine field there is also the phenomenon of women and girls who are fans . . . yet they have not been to a match . . . Nevertheless, I know they would like the pure air and the sport . . . Should they find themselves at the Berta stadium they would not regret it.'[121] Perhaps it was hoped that women might curb the less desirable aspects of male behaviour at football matches, for *campanilismo* continued to preoccupy the press and not just in Florence.

After supplying six or seven players to compete for the national team in an unimportant friendly, Juventus wrote to the FIGC questioning whether such a commitment on its part, had really been necessary. In response, one Roman daily that was apparently renowned for its criticisms of anything outside of the capital, lambasted not only Juventus but also the national team manager Vittorio Pozzo. In response, *Lo Stadio* drew attention to the unidentified weekly paper's own outbreaks of partiality:

If 'Roma' loses a match on the field do not worry (it is pointless reading certain Roman papers) that it will be the fault of the referee . . . we should say that the Roman sports weekly does not completely benefit the interests of its squad, or of the team of its heart, with indecent behaviour . . . And this will happen while it does not cease to give the impression, to the rest of Italy (and there is much of it outside of the capital) that Rome wants to win the *scudetto* by hook or by crook.[122]

As ever, this quotation needs to be read in context, *Lo Stadio* having already demonstrated its own extreme parochialism. However, it once again illustrated the strong, local, city-based identities that were being developed and expressed via football teams throughout the country. Moreover, it had also broached a relatively new problem that was emerging from the national and international expansion of the game; that of players' responsibilities towards their club and country. While this debate never reached the heights of the modern game, where money and expanded competitions at both levels have blurred their points of difference, international football was becoming an increasingly important preoccupation of players and fans alike.

At the local level, despite failing to create a side anywhere near as strong as Bologna's, Fascist Florence had put itself on the *calcio* map by using Fiorentina as the hub around which the local, city-based identity could be expressed and its population united. Created from the merger of formerly antagonistic clubs, Fiorentina brought Florentines together where their mass strength was directed towards supporting the team on the national stage. In itself, this was not an unusual feature, Roma having also been created by the local Fascist Italo Foschi in 1926, following the merger of three smaller teams.

However, the strength and identity of Fiorentina was imposed most strongly through the avant-garde construction of the Giovanni Berta stadium. Not only did it dramatically contrast with the aesthetics and style of the Littoriale in Bologna, its revolutionary design and construction symbolized the radical rebirth of Florentine architecture in this period, which reflected the historically dynamic, radical and independent local party. Despite its unquestionable importance for the regime's image and prestige, the stadium was Florentine first and foremost, a point that Francesco Varrasi illustrated by comparing it to Wembley Stadium in London: 'When we think of Wembley we think of its symbolic national value, we see the FA Cup Final, the English national team matches and we do not see a strong connection to the local identity of the city of London. Whereas from the moment of its construction the "G. Berta" became a symbol of Florence and of Fiorentina.'[123]

If the stadium's style stimulated many arguments about the nature of Fascist architecture, art and design, it was in no way so radical that it threatened to exceed the regime's bounds of acceptability. In fact, especially when compared to Bologna, it illustrated the many paths to Fascism that were open to the localities, thereby enabling independent minded cities, such as Florence, to maintain and develop their proud, independent, historical traditions within the confines of the regime's notion of the organic national society.

–7–

Shooting for Italy:
Foreign Bodies on Foreign Fields

The norms that govern the game impose the principle of authority, without which order cannot exist. V. Pozzo, *Campioni del Mondo*

The inaugural World Football Championship in 1930, which later became the World Cup, considerably raised the stakes in international football. In a fit of pique, having been refused the honour of hosting the tournament, the Fascist regime declined to send its team to Uruguay. Yet, even before the host nation had lifted the trophy in victory Mussolini was planning a similar celebration for Rome in four years time. The 1934 World Football Championship was his Berlin Olympics; an opportunity to show the world the achievements of Fascism while further uniting the nation behind the regime's *calcio* creations.

The Giovanni Berta stadium in Florence, the Littoriale in Bologna, plus six others throughout the peninsula,[1] showcased Fascist Italy's heritage and will to embrace technological advance. The regime's creative bent was not restricted merely to bricks, mortar and reinforced concrete either; it also extended to the bodies, minds and souls of the nation that had been tempered in the crucible of the revolution, for Fascism had also built a new man who knew how to play football.

The Italian national team's World Cup victory in 1934 confirmed the emergence of a generation that was to dominate international football for the rest of the decade. Before retaining the trophy in France in 1938, a team of university students affirmed Italian football supremacy by winning the 1936 Olympic football tournament in Berlin, which was the greatest amateur international accolade. Italian clubs were also making a serious impact in Europe. Most notable were Bologna FC's victories in the Coppa d'Europa in 1932 and 1934, before claiming the Paris Exhibition tournament trophy in 1937, which apparently shook the world.[2]

The regime was naturally enthusiastic about such talented teams, viewing their success as the interest on its investment in the physical education of the first Fascist generation. It was also suggested that the victories were achieved using an intrinsically Italian style. While such claims often represent typical racial stereotypes, on this occasion the Italian press employed them positively.

With Fascist foreign policy proving disastrous or embarrassing at best, there was a huge source of pride to be exploited in *calcio*'s European domination, especially as 'the movement and Mussolini's regime constantly proclaimed national greatness, measured in terms of international prestige.'[3] However, so deliberately did Fascism associate itself with the successes of the era that both club and international teams competing abroad were increasingly viewed as direct representatives of the regime, and were thus exposed to the increasing anti-Fascist ire. Tournaments, such as the Coppa d'Europa, began to show the negative and positive aspects of international club competition, while politically motivated incidents showed how *calcio* had become more than just a game. Well aware of the situation, the regime fiercely condemned such attacks on its club sides and the national team, while continuing to exploit the domestic and diplomatic capital that their international victories brought.

Having already established how Fascism restructured *calcio* into a formidable system that reflected, represented and responded to the domestic needs of the new order, it remains to be seen how and with what effect the game was pushed into its diplomatic service.

Sporting Ambassadors

When the *azzurri* claimed the World Cup in 1934, there were already many indications that Italian sport was growing in strength and quality. The huge growth of competitive athletics in schools, universities and youth groups reflected sport's diffusion throughout the mass of young Italians, which corresponded to a noticeable improvement in competitive and technical standards.[4] However, as Luigi Ferrario warned *La Gazzetta*'s readers, patience was required if Italian youth was to mature into a significant, international force: 'Athleticism has made great progress among the young. The Amsterdam Olympics will certainly not confirm it, but the reserves are being created and the future will show that a good wine is coming.'[5]

Nonetheless, the 1928 and 1932 Olympic Games still provided opportunities to assess the improvement of Italian sport under Fascism quantitatively and qualitatively, and the results were better than expected. The athletes departed for Amsterdam from the Littoriale, behind a rally of fifty or more cars from the automobile clubs of Milan and Bologna bound for the capital of the Netherlands. Organized by Bologna's Fascist daily *Il Resto del Carlino*, it was intended to publicize the paper domestically while also giving 'other people a visible demonstration of the national solidarity that reigns in Italy today . . . of how much youth and fervour has brought this country to life'.[6]

With international sport increasingly important, *Il Carlino* reminded the athletes of their duty to assert themselves, as victories were 'clear signs of racial superiority that are destined to reflect in many fields outside of sport'.[7] According to Arpinati's *Il Littoriale*, success commanded foreign respect while encouraging Italians to rediscover 'the glow of *Italianità*'.[8] Following the *azzurri*'s 4–3 victory over Hungary in 1928, Mussolini praised Arpinati 'for the perfect organization that had taken Italian football to victory; and, in a sign of his satisfaction with the young athletes, gave an autographed photo to each member of the squad'.[9] It was an early indication of how Mussolini would personally associate himself with the team's every success.

The national team's first major achievement was a semi-final appearance in the 1928 Olympic Games when it narrowly lost to Uruguay. According to *La Gazzetta*, it was a performance and result that confounded the harshest critics as 'nobody believed . . . the Italian team had the means, passion and enthusiasm to throw a serious obstacle at the feet of the irresistible Uruguayan squad'.[10] It boded well for the future.

Eighteen medals at Amsterdam was no reason for Italian over-confidence, but with France, England and Belgium reportedly in decline, *La Gazzetta* believed the successes showed how Fascist society was incontrovertibly 'marching at the vanguard of modern sport'.[11] Yet Mussolini demanded more, assigning Lando Ferretti the task of making CONI an organ of the party to ensure that the organization and preparations for the 1932 Los Angeles Olympics were even more thorough. In the intervening years athletes became state concerns, competing not just as ambassadors of Italy but also of *Italianità*.[12] Sport assumed a more visible political aspect; Mussolini's black-shirted 'boys', who sang the 'Giovinezza' at the opening ceremony, were a far cry from the allegedly dishevelled team that had arrived in Antwerp for the 1920 Games singing the 'Red Flag'.[13]

Twelve gold, silver and as many bronze medals gave the team overall second place in Los Angeles. After an audience with Mussolini, his 'boys' went to Milan where Arpinati awarded them with the 'medal of steel', 'the highest official recognition' possible according to *La Gazzetta*.[14] While the lesser value of steel, when compared to gold, was probably significant, the medal was a sign of how the regime would continually attempt to devalue the importance of established international prizes with its own tin-pot trophies.

Yet if Olympic success demonstrated the progress of Italian sport in general, the Coppa d'Europa/Mitropa Cup was the litmus test for Italy's premier football teams in Europe. Although no rival to the World Cup, it proved to be a fiercely contested event that often reflected the diplomatic strains of the decade and the degree to which the regime had politicized *calcio*. In 1932, both Juventus (Turin) and Bologna FC reached the Coppa d'Europa semifinals. Whereas Bologna reached the final relatively untroubled, Juventus's tempestuous meeting with Slavia Prague was the clearest demonstration yet of the way that *calcio* had become the regime's representative abroad and a diplomatic barometer.

For Club and Country

With the English Football Association's minimalist participation in European football, Italy was perfectly placed to align itself with the associations of the successor states of central Europe that were intent on making their collective weight felt within FIFA. As Lanfranchi and Taylor have observed, international football was used to symbolize and commemorate international friendships and diplomatic alliances.[15] Regular competition between Italian teams and those of central Europe also provided a convenient opportunity for the regime to involve itself in the region, where the creation of successor states from the former territories of the German and Austro-Hungarian Empires had resulted in a power vacuum in central Europe. Fascist Italy had considerable interests in this volatile area of prime political real estate that continued to be unsettled by revisionist grievances.

The football associations of Italy, Switzerland, Austria, Czechoslovakia and Hungary had a close relationship that was 'cemented in the fierce dispute for the Coppa Internazionale', launched in 1927.[16] However, *calcio* was also stressing Fascism's diplomatic relations as early as 1923, when the Communist party of 'Red Vienna' urged its members to oppose the visit of 2,000 Italian fans for an international between the two countries.[17] Thereafter, animosity between the fans and players of the two nations was a regular feature of the era, which culminated in 1937 when the Austrian fans and team apparently forced the referee to abandon the contest after 29 minutes of the second half. Although the Italian press attributed it to a waterlogged pitch, Pozzo later recalled the shouts, whistles and curses as part of a demonstration that 'was clearly political'.[18]

Such events were not unusual. The treatment of South Tyrolean Germans was a source of great ire, which was further heightened by Mussolini's long-term ambition to stake out the Danube as an Italian sphere of influence in a three-way relationship with Austria and Hungary.

Unlike revisionist Hungary, Austria was content with maintaining the status quo in the hope that it might preserve its democracy.[19] Such issues were reflected during the internationals between the two teams, as the state attempted to defend itself against the ambitions of Mussolini and the extreme right Austrian Heimwehr. By the late 1920s, a programme had emerged whereby the central European extreme right hoped to combine and challenge the French hegemony, established since 1918.

Bilateral agreements between Italy, Austria and Hungary in 1927, preceded a customs union in 1932 and the 1934 Rome Protocols that rubber-stamped the Italian ascendancy and directly threatened the Little Entente states of Czechoslovakia and Yugoslavia. Despite the 1924 treaty of friendship with Czechoslovakia, Fascist Italy's Danubian policy had resulted in its almost complete isolation and encirclement by revisionist states intent on rectifying the 'wrongs' of 1918. This was the background to Juventus's visit to Prague that year.

Having lost the first-leg of the Coppa Europa match with Slavia Prague 4–0, *La Gazzetta*'s correspondent attributed the victory to more than just superior technique:

> We intend to speak of the public that, after the usual pitch invasion during the match, abandoned itself to disgraceful violence against our players. This issue of the disgusting incidents on the football field of Prague is becoming a sad Bohemian tradition and its significance is aggravated when one sees that they always have the corollary of wild demonstrations against Italy.[20]

Following a collision between Cesarini and an opponent, the Slavia coach was said to have thrown a bottle at the Italian before making a number of gestures towards other members of the Juventus team.[21] While the attack was clearly directed at the team, a government source recorded it as having provoked 'public demonstrations towards our players, but above all against Italy'.[22] Following more contentious decisions, *La Gazzetta* described 'the ire of the public that invaded the pitch once again and assaulted our courageous players. Cesarini defended himself well, helped by his companions among whom Orsi, Vecchina and Caligaris were severely and repeatedly hit.'[23] The Ministry of Foreign Affairs' account of the incident was equally biased:

> The public invaded the field and savagely beat the Italian players who defended themselves. Some Italian players were bullied and taken away from the field of play by the arm, where repercussions took place. In the meantime those not taking part in the beatings screamed and shouted abuse at Italy, Fascism and the Duce. Particularly bitter were those under the stand who

turned towards the Italian delegation . . . causing uproar, insulting and threatening them.[24]

Interestingly, the Ministry of Foreign Affairs correspondence refered to
the 'deplorable incidents that took place in the course of the Italy-
Czechoslovakia football match',[25] thereby indicating the extent to which
the identities of Italian city clubs playing abroad were becoming increasingly and officially blurred, as they were perceived to be representing the
regime. The incident became an international concern, the FIGC secretary Zanetti communicating with Juventus, the Italian embassy in Prague
and Ugo Meisl the competition's secretary. Despite apologizing for the
behaviour of the fans, the Czechoslovak representative, Kroft, attacked
the Italian press for escalating the incident. In response, Francesco
Giunta, the under-secretary of state, recommended the suspension 'of
future participation in sporting competitions in Czechoslovakia' until
such time 'as the public will be more civil, and that will take a long
time',[26] although this never seems to have been put into practice.[27]

Unsurprisingly, the return leg on 10 July further exposed the tensions
between the two countries, *La Gazzetta* billing it as an opportunity for
Juventus to show 'Slavia the true measure of its ability, and the
uncivilised crowd of Prague . . . its spirit of hospitality'.[28] The importance of the tournament for the regime was evident in the presence of
Zanetti at the game in Turin and Arpinati at the semi-final in Bologna:
'With this act our Federation wants to show its great interest in these
matches and its desire to show to the outside world that Italy knows how
to overcome, with preventive arrangements and direct intervention, the
stormy incidents.'[29]

If Juventus could not win the tie, the directors were intent on gaining
a moral victory. As *La Gazzetta* pleaded with fans: 'Thus no recriminations; a dignified and admonishing silence towards the hosts and a continu-
ous and warm encouragement to the town's team.'[30] Despite an extra 500
stewards inside and outside of the ground, over 1,000 people were said to
have 'put on a hostile show' for the Slavia team's arrival at the station
that, according to the Ministry of the Interior, the police did well to
contain.[31]

With Juventus winning 2–0 at half-time, a missile thrown from the
crowd apparently struck the Slavia goalkeeper, Frantisek Planicka, after
which his team refused to continue. Claiming the incident was stage-
managed, the Italian press declared the Slavia reaction unjustifiable,[32]
which was later supported by the referee who stated that Slavia had no
right to leave the field.[33] The tie, which was now more of a matter of pride
between the two respective countries than the football clubs, reflected their

strained diplomatic relations that were not improved by the Slavia players' return to Prague. According to Italian Foreign Ministry's records, crowds at the principal stations saluted 'the victims of the fascist violence', who were 'covered in bandages as if returning from a war zone'.[34]

Predictably the Czech and Italian press sprung to their respective team's defence, sparking an ugly war of words. Drawing attention to the political nature of the events of Prague in particular, *Il Tevere*, the staunchly Fascist Roman daily, launched a stinging attack:

> When one has, let us not say the courage – it is stupid to speak of courage from hundreds of kilometres away – but the nerve to print a litany of such vileness, one loses every right to be treated on equal terms. Thus we will not be refuting or answering the nonsense that has been written and said in Prague. It is only important for us to reveal that a sporting boycott and cowardice are being discussed. For the first, there is no need for Czechoslovakia to exert itself . . . On the theme of cowardice, we know with what authority Prague can speak of it.[35]

Although stressing his concern for the harm done 'to the cause of sport and the cordiality of international relations',[36] the FIGC secretary, Zanetti, continued to try and undermine Slavia's position, thereby easing Juventus's passage into the final. It was far from the ideals of brotherhood, cultural exchange and cooperation upon which the competition had been established. The issue was settled on 15 August in Klagenfurth, Austria, where the Austrian and Hungarian dominated tournament committee was expected to order a play-off between the two. However, in a punitive measure intended to restore order to the competition rather than please either club, both were disqualified,[37] which resulted in Bologna's victory by default.

The press of both countries were reportedly asked not to exacerbate the incident further,[38] and following the Czechoslovak government's specific order for its media to employ 'favourable language towards Italy' in the future,[39] *La Gazzetta* responded positively to an international match of good will. Deliberately restricting its reports to avoid any misunderstandings, the paper believed the match would 'seal a complete reconciliation between the players and public, between fans and journalists'.[40] Others, such as Amadeo Fani, the under-secretary for the Ministry of Foreign Affairs, feared its potential for worsening the situation: 'it is evidently in our interest not to provide new occasions to rekindle a polemic that in the political field is indisputably useless and dangerous.'[41]

So tense was the atmosphere four days before the match of 'reconciliation' that the FIGC publicly accepted responsibility for its part in the

incident to the Czechoslovak media. Contrary to its true belief, the declaration was to reaffirm: 'the cordiality of relations and sentiments of
esteem of the Italian sports fans towards the Czechoslovak nation'.[42] The
gesture, which ratified an earlier official confirmation that relations
between the two were now 'cordial',[43] was enough for *La Gazzetta* to
claim that 'every misunderstanding and every preconception' about the
match had been 'officially resolved'.[44] Nonetheless, a metal fence was
still erected around the pitch and observers from Austria, Hungary and
Switzerland were sent to ensure it was played in the correct atmosphere.
On the same day an alternative friendly match was also organized to try
and distract any Czechoslovak fans that may have still held a grudge
against Italy.[45]

Clearly neither government could afford, nor did they want, the match
to degenerate into one where every shot was taken on their behalf.
Recognizing 'the political aspect of the event',[46] *La Gazzetta* implored
the *azzurri* to counter everything thrown at them 'with that enthusiasm,
correctness and prowess that has made them the greatest representatives
of our sport in the entire world: good combatants in all regions and in
front of all adversaries'.[47] Under the circumstances, all were undoubtedly
content to see the match pass without incident, irrespective of Italy's 2–1
defeat. Football and politics were the winners, but in the ideological
decade of the 1930s it was a sign of what was to come for the Duce's
special envoys.

Win, lose or draw, so important was international competition for the
regime that, when such chances did materialize, the *azzurri* needed to be
able to call upon their strongest players, but this was not always possible.
In 1932, Giuseppe Meazza, Italy's most potent striker and goalscorer, was
also committed to his role in the Fifth Alpine Regiment as part of his
national service. His potential omission from the team to face
Switzerland provoked Alberto Santini, 'on behalf of all sports fans in
Milan', to ask an unidentified member of government to:

> put in a good word to the number one Italian sportsman, our beloved Duce,
> who knows his and our passion, so that Meazza might be allowed to resume
> his Sunday football match. Our great champion, who elevated the motherland
> in memorable victories over the Hungarian, German and Spanish crowds, is
> now inactive during the next important international meetings.[48]

The fans also had a role in the developing the regime's prestige abroad:
the 1933 match with England, in Rome, being a perfect opportunity to
show the regime's apparent mass support. Besides the sporting nature of
the crowd, *La Nazione* was keen to report the reaction of the head of the

English party, Mr Kingscott: 'I was profoundly moved by the warm demonstration the crowd gave to the head of government . . . today I had the true impression of the fondness the crowd has for the Duce.'[49] Mussolini attended the match with PNF Secretary Starace, their entrance to the tribune of honour reportedly inspiring mass cheering and the waving of handkerchiefs by over 60,000 people. Meanwhile, the public address system informed everybody that: 'With the Duce one is never lost: neither will we lose today.'[50]

As already seen, football crowds outside of Italy often responded to the politicized nature of *calcio Italiano* and, on the cusp of war, the 1938 World Cup tournament in France did not lack controversy. Italian hopes were buoyed by the various *calcio* successes since 1934, especially the 1937 victory of Bologna's young team in Paris. The European press also concurred with *La Gazzetta's* confidence that the team would again defend the nation with honour: 'The Italian sporting flag, which needs to be lowered from the stadium flagpole today, will be the same that will rise again tomorrow, more joyous, in the warmth of new victories.'[51]

The *azzurri's* hopes were buoyed by a number of Italian fans who had taken advantage of organized travel packages to Marseilles and Paris,[52] and some notable absentees. There were no South American teams, the Anschluss had swallowed the Austrian squad, the Civil War prevented the Spanish from competing, while the absence of the English remained a double-edged sword. More than just a chance for revenge after the 1934 'battle of Highbury', Sisto Favre wanted the English to participate for diplomatic reasons, as sport remained: 'the best instrument of cordiality and understanding between countries both near and far.'[53] His views almost certainly reflected the regime's continuing desire to forge positive diplomatic relations through football, even if the opposite was sometimes the case.

The 1938 tournament was always likely to be a tense affair for the regime's representatives, but Mussolini's anti-French, or pro-Franco, statements on 14 May 1938,[54] perhaps combined with the recent collapse of the French Popular Front, resulted in anti-Fascist protests during the tournament.[55] According to Papa and Panico, the first incident occurred as the team arrived in Marseilles, which contained a considerable number of exiled Italians. Some fifty years later, Ugo Locatelli recalled 3,000 or more French and Italian anti-Fascists being controlled by baton-wielding mounted police.[56] His account contrasted with the Italian press's record of a courteous reception at the station by a number of dignitaries, the only problem being the apparent overenthusiasm of local and Italian supporters.[57] Piero Rava, the only surviving member of that team in 2001, was also unable to remember the alleged protest.[58] However, given that such incidents continued throughout the competition, it seems likely that Locatelli's recollections were closer to the truth. What protests did take place were almost certainly directed more against the team as the representative of the regime than as a football entity. In fact, it was the most recent example of the team reaping what the regime had sown during the 12 years in which it had politicized *calcio*.

Five years earlier in 1933, during Italy's friendly match against Belgium, exiled Italians in Brussels seized Niccolò Carosio's microphone to broadcast to the nation back home.[59] Although the protest went unmentioned in a Ministry of Foreign Affairs telegram,[60] it showed the importance of Carosio's broadcasts for the diffusion, popularization and politicization of the game among the masses.

The *azzurri* entered the tournament carrying the heavy baggage of success that made them everybody's favourites to win, if not everybody's favourites! At the opening match in Marseilles, they met Norway on the field and an estimated 10,000 Italian political exiles in the terraces. Pozzo recalled: 'a background of political-polemic. Unjustly. Because our players did not even dream of making it something political. They represented their country and naturally and worthily wore the colours and insignia',[61] which just happened to be the *fasces*. Above all, it was the Roman salute that most angered the hostile crowd, especially when Pozzo ordered the players to perform it twice: 'At the salute, as predicted, we were greeted by a solemn and deafening barrage of whistles and insults . . . We had just put down our hands when the violent demonstration started again. Straight away: "Team be ready. Salute." And we raised our hands again, to confirm we had no fear . . . Having won the battle of intimidation, we played.'[62]

Not surprisingly, the *azzurri* made a less than impressive start to the tournament, snatching a 2–1 victory in extra time, 'Vittoria ma non basta' (Victory but not enough) summing up the general disappointment among the press.[63] General Vaccaro was also unhappy and asked Pozzo to explain why he had played the ageing Eraldo Monzeglio and not Alfredo Foni, one of the discoveries of Berlin. Pozzo claimed pressure from Villa Torlonia, Mussolini's residence in Rome where Monzeglio was often to be found coaching football to the Duce and his sons.[64] Vaccaro's intervention brought an end to both Monzeglio's international career and the type of political interference in team selection that Pozzo claimed had forced him to pick only players that were party members in 1934.[65]

The aftershocks of the events of Marseilles were felt in Paris when Italy met France in the quarter-final. However, if the anti-Fascist protests undermined the *azzurri's* confidence in Marseilles they inspired them in the capital. With both coutries normally playing in blue, lots were drawn to decide which team would change. Italy lost, but rather than wear the traditional change colour of white, the team was ordered to play in all-black. The decision is often cited as having emanated directly from Mussolini[66] who was still smarting from the earlier poor reception, although there appears to be no archival evidence supporting this. Nonetheless, given the *maglia nera* (black shirt) was never worn again, one can safely assume it was intended to both represent the regime and confront the vocal anti-Fascists.

The Italian team's actions were provocative and the protests were continued in the semifinal by a crowd that was 'manifestly hostile', according to *La Nazione*.[67] Confronting hostility and adversity, *Il Popolo d'Italia* recorded how the entire squad: 'fought the greatest match in this tournament, it is Italy – the blue shirt with the Sabaudo shield and the Fascio Littorio on the chest – that has won the right to contest the final in Paris.'[68] It was a lesson for organic Fascist society that was repeated time and time again, where the team's individual parts combined to form a stronger unit capable of overcoming all obstacles and opposition.

Mussolini's *Mondiale*: The Politicization of the 1934 World Cup

Four years earlier, Fascist Italy had shown its strength when hosting the 1934 World Cup tournament. Although less contentious than France, the competition was Mussolini's opportunity to put his nation on the world stage and gain international prestige 'as much for the technical value of its game as its organizational knowledge'.[69]

Despite the huge burden of expectation from the public and the regime, Pozzo's team preparations were restricted to only three competitive matches that year. In February 1934, Hugo Meisl's Austrian 'Wunder-team' gave the Italians a harsh lesson in technique and psychology, imposing a comfortable 4–2 defeat that forced Pozzo to end his loyalty to ageing players and turn to the new generation of athletes that had been educated and honed in the crucible of Fascism.

While the 1934 tournament was the first step on the road to interna-tional football domination, it was also seen as an opportunity for the regime to demonstrate its ardour, achievements and creative potential to Italians and the rest of the world. As identified in one anonymous govern-ment note to the CONI president, Achille Starace, the 'attention of the world of sport will turn itself on Italy; huge crowds of foreign sports fans are predicted'.[70] More than just a chance to display its athletic elite, this official continued to stress the opportunity to demonstrate the regime's entire range of skills by perfectly organizing a tournament that he deemed 'worthy of an Olympics in every respect, and for the mass attention and passion is perhaps superior to the same competition'.[71]

The statement contrasted with Ferretti's opinion in 1926, when the regime was trying to win the right to host the 1936 Games. Writing to Giacomo Sguardo, the Prime Minister's under-secretary, he stated: 'There is no need to tell you of what global importance an Olympics can have, the significance of which goes beyond the greatest sporting competition, raising it to a political event of the first order.'[72] The exact value of the World Cup in comparison to the Olympic Games is a moot point, but as Augusto Parboni argued in *Lo Sport Fascista* the World Cup said something significant about the regime: 'An event as colossal as this, in which the squads of four continents will be represented, could only have been organized by Benito Mussolini's Italy, that has given to the world . . . the norms of genial and perfect sporting organization, which it envies and tries to copy in vain.'[73]

Although writing for one of the regime's better funded monthly magazines, Parboni was correct to identify the impact of the competition's organization and the diffusion of sport throughout Italy, within foreign circles. One such observer was Mr Fischer, from the influential Hungarian Football Association, who commented on what he saw as the miraculous discipline in society following ten years of Fascist rule. More specifically, he was said to have been particularly impressed by the nation's sporting progress, as 'from Torino and Trieste to Tàranto and Palermo, Italy shakes with healthy sporting enthusiasm, while ten years ago sport, as it is understood today, had not reached Rome.'[74]

While FIFA's organizing committee, headed by Giovanni Mauro, hoped to maximize its earning potential and ensure the tournament's smooth organization, the FIGC also created a number of its own offices, including one for travel and accommodation. Foreign fans from France, Holland, Switzerland and Germany were enticed by journies subsidized by 70 per cent, with internal transport also discounted for those travelling between the host cities.[75]

With any profits from the tournament to be divided among the world governing body and competing countries, the FIFA General Secretary, Mr Schricker, was naturally keen to encourage a successful competition, which may have stimulated some of his public praise on the improvements of life under the regime. During a visit to Rome he was apparently 'amazed by the enormous progress . . . the perfection reached by the new Italy in all fields and, in particular, in the tourist and hotel industries. This will tempt the foreigners to make the journey.'[76] Following the Duce's demand that all foreign visitors experience a show of the utmost efficiency, the propaganda machine went into overdrive, so much so that FIFA President Jules Rimet is said to have felt that during the tournament Mussolini had in fact been the true President.[77]

Such attention to the international market also had considerable domestic value; positive foreign reactions to Fascist Italy's organization featuring regularly in the press. *La Gazzetta* gave Schricker's visit considerable space and having declared the tournament 'a prize that Italy merited', he reportedly thanked the nation for the way it had been organized 'without giving a thought for the benefits or costs involved'.[78] In fact, Fascist Italy cared considerably about costs and profits.

To complement its exemplary athletes, monumental modern stadia and a self-proclaimed ability to put on a good show, the regime's publicity campaign knew no bounds as the tournament was commodified to a new level. Match tickets were printed on good quality paper with an elegant design in the hope they would become popular souvenirs that travelling fans would take back home. A competition to design a promotional poster was won by the Futurist Marinetti, with his image of a goal with a black ball and the *fasces*. One hundred thousand billposters were placed throughout the country and cigarette packets, consumed in huge quantities by the masses, also carried the image of a ball in the net. Commemorative postage stamps featuring the *fasces* plus all of the stadia with an aeroplane flying above were also issued, promoting a similar message to that conveyed during the opening of the Giovanni Berta stadium linking the two forms of Fascist modernity.

As interesting as the stamps themselves was the dispute that erupted between the regime and FIFA over their production. Besides showing the regime's growing confidence to challenge the hegemony of the game's traditional powers, the dispute reflected the government's awareness of the merchandising opportunities available and its desire to maximize profits and propaganda. As one government document records, the stamps' global exposure would make them 'a great work of world propaganda for *Italianità*, connecting in everlasting signs the characteristics of sport with the Fascio Littorio, reconfirming to all the world that Italian Sport had been strengthened by Fascism'.[79]

However, rather than allow the stamps to be printed and distributed through the Italian postal service, FIFA wanted to issue them through the Association's Swiss base. Host countries of the Olympic Games and the previous World Cup had traditionally been awarded this right, and it was not something the regime was prepared to relinquish. As detailed in a letter from the secretary of the organizing committee, Doctor Barassi, to the Prime Minister's under-secretary of state, Edmondo Rossoni: 'it would undoubtedly take prestige away from Italian sport and the nation and would unjustifiably link Italy's onerous and honorary world event to another country.'[80]

The Ministry for Communications also appreciated that such stamps had 'always been most sought after abroad by collectors because of their rarity', and in this case they would be in even greater demand due to Italy's 'avant-garde position in the game of football'.[81] Given their expected future increase in value, plus anticipated sales within the region of one million,[82] it was hoped their issue from Italy would guarantee the regime an income of at least 100,000 lire, which would 'serve to alleviate the huge costs that the Italian Federation has incurred'.[83]

Despite the domestic and diplomatic capital to be gained from the tournament, the regime could not afford to ignore its financial burden that was estimated at around 3.5 million lire.[84] Naturally costs needed to be covered and income from the stamps would have been supplemented by that from tourism and gate receipts. Money itself also had a propaganda angle, as for the first time FIFA's tournament payments were made in lire, the currency of the host nation. The decision not to use sterling or dollars was portrayed in *La Nazione* as an 'official recognition that Italian currency offers a greater confidence and guarantee than that of other foreign currencies'.[85]

To ensure participating teams were sufficiently motivated, FIFA's organizing committee, with heavy Italian representation, requested that CONI supply a prize on behalf of Mussolini. Its response was the Coppa del Duce, which consisted of a group of footballers fixed in an action scene in front of the *fasces*. Carved in bronze by the sculptor Grazes, who was responsible for the winged statue of 'Victory' on the roof of the Littoriale's Marathon Tower, the trophy cost in the region 1,500 lire.[86] According to one official press release: 'Besides the 'World Cup' offered by FIFA, the football world championship is blessed by some of the richest prizes, among which, unique in moral value, is that offered by the Duce, who wanted to recognize the exceptional importance of the event in such a way.'[87]

Rome was also given the honour of hosting FIFA's International Congress during the tournament, only eight years after it had last taken place in the capital. Held in the civic centre of the Campodoglio, it was another feather of respectability in the regime's cap.[88] As General Vaccaro later reported, the Congress had made 'those ties of esteem and reciprocation among nations, the moral value of which is worthy of recognition by each of us'.[89]

With stadia already groaning under the weight of Fascist symbolism, the politicization of the tournament began with the draw for the first-round matches that, according to *Il Resto del Carlino*: 'assumed a special solemn character due to the presence of S.E. Starace, the Secretary of the Party and head of CONI.'[90] In a room of the Ambassadors Hotel flanked by a squad of armed Blackshirts, with the Coppa del Duce as the focal point, two young Balilla members dressed in naval uniforms, one of which was General Vaccaro's son, drew the cards from each urn. The draw did not favour Italy, which Vaccaro said confirmed the tournament's honest organization: 'If we win, the legitimacy of our victory will be brighter and more persuasive.'[91]

The regime demanded victory, but if it failed to arrive the tournament's diplomatic benefits still made its organization worthwhile. One example was the Brazilian Federation's allegedly deliberate appointment of a journalist and writer as head of the squad. Renowned more for his Fascist sympathies than football knowledge, the Brazilians apparently made it known that he had been appointed with the firm intention of strengthening the existing ties between the two governments.[92] As the teams arrived to prepare for the tournament, messages of gratitude and admiration were sent to the Duce from the various national federations.[93] Others paid alternative homage to Mussolini; the Argentine squad visiting his birth village of Predappio and the tomb of the Duce's family, where a wreath of Italian and Argentine national colours was laid.[94] Prior to the quarter-final match in Bologna between Hungary and Austria, both teams met the local organizing committee and Fascist hierarchy during which *podestà* Manaresi referred to the way in which sport and *calcio* was reuniting former enemy nations. Whereas 'in war they fought each other in opposite camps, so in peace they find themselves united by a sincere friendship. And sport . . . intensifies and strengthens such sentiments among diverse nations.'[95] Besides developing good diplomatic relations between Italy and the various competing nations, such demonstrations of friendship were also used to convince Italian citizens of the regime's growing international respect and recognition.

The competition was also a good opportunity to impart a number of lessons throughout society that were intended to contribute to establishing consensus. Mussolini attended most of the Italian matches and while his presence was always as a high-profile supporter, his actions – if deconstructed – often suggest an alternative meaning. At the *azzurri*'s opening match against the USA, which he attended with two of his sons to stress the importance of supporting the team, Mussolini deliberately paid to enter in order to put a definitive end to the 'immoral' system of complementary tickets. As stated in *La Nazione*, those 'Portoghesi'[96] who sought such tickets were an example of 'a bad moral attitude that they believe can be justified by their social position, sporting connections and other means that are condemned in the Fascist regime. The

Duce wanted to set an example: an example of healthy Fascist morality.'[97]

If certain members of Fascist society could enter for free, this undermined the regime's meritocratic promotion of *calcio*, which was intended to reflect its supposed ideals and placate or subtly mobilize the working classes. However small, there was also concern about the impact upon the tournament's income generation, which was intensified by the regime's early fears of poor attendance figures. In fact, Italians turned out in force, *Lo Sport Fascista* declaring gate receipts of 1.2 million lire a sign of 'a disciplined and intelligent public that had learnt to watch sport for itself with interest and passion'.[98]

A passionate and united support for the *azzurri* was yet another metaphor for the nation that was being brought together by Fascism, even in those localities and cities such as Florence that had developed problematic local identities. Following the *azzurri*'s quarter-final in the Giovanni Berta stadium against Spain, one of the strongest teams in world football at the time, *La Nazione* deemed the Florentines' display of undivided support for the national team crucial to its ultimate success: 'The crowd was crazy, it was a screaming monster of thousands and thousands of mouths. And still it was beautiful. In it you find an overwhelming sense of life, a febrile passion capable of knocking over any obstacle, almost capable of opposing the force of nature.'[99]

The huge mass of *calcio* followers was prompted each day by the increasingly nationalist sports press that made the most of the *azzurri*'s achievements. Following Italy's semi-final victory over Austria, Bruno

Figure 6 A postcard capturing Mussolini's 'Soldiers of Sport' against the background of the Partito Nazionale Fascista stadium in Rome. Note General Vaccaro second right and FIFA's Jules Rimet trophy juxtaposed with the *Fasces*. © Fondazione del Museo del Calcio.

Roghi declared in *La Gazzetta*: 'the *Wunderteam* is no more.'[100] Typical of the immodest and occasionally subtle patriotism that made Roghi's name, it also indicated the growing sense of national pride, confidence and superiority that the team's success was engendering among the nation, the ultimate swagger being reserved for the final in Rome.

The match against Czechoslovakia was contested in the PNF stadium in front of 50,000 people, which included many Czechoslovak fans that had taken advantage of the subsidized trains. According to Luigi Freddi in *Il Popolo d'Italia*, on the Duce's arrival, having 'forgot they were here for a sporting contest', the fans offered him 'the staggering sight of their uncontainable passion. The tender acclamation exploded in the immense bowl with a supernatural persistence.'[101] The display continued as the teams entered the stadium, handkerchiefs being waved to cries of 'Duce, Duce', as the Militia band played a selection of Fascist hymns.

More like a Fascist rally than a sporting contest, it was the type of support that had earlier caused Mussolini to ask: 'how can Italy not be the champions?'[102] An extra time goal from Angelo Schiavio secured the title, after which the Italian players paid homage to the Fascist hierarchy in the stand, before respecting both national anthems and the 'Giovinezza' once more. For their efforts, the players were rewarded with the World Cup trophy, the Coppa del Duce, a signed photograph of Mussolini, plus the *medaglia d'oro* (gold medal) in recognition of their conquest of the football world in the name of Mussolini and Fascism. It was an apparent paradigm of national destiny (Figure 6).

It's not just the Competing, It's the Winning that Counts

Following the first of three consecutive international tournament victories, which enabled the regime to claim to be the world's dominant football nation, a number of manufacturers were keen to link their products with the team's achievement and the game's natural association with health. One such product was 'RIM', an intestinal cleansing agent that claimed to keep women young, sluggishness and obesity at bay, make children healthy and strong, in addition to its general benefits for all sportsmen. To ratify the claim, the advert carried a letter from the *azzurri* squad masseurs, Angeli and Bortolotti, who had apparently requested an adequate amount of 'RIM' for the team's tournament preparations.[103] Perfect product placement, thereafter no marketing campaign for any Italian commodity, even beer and chocolate, was complete without a footballer's image or endorsement.

Besides confirming the *azzurri* as arguably the strongest team in world football, the tournament enabled Fascist Italy to project itself as a welcoming country capable of hosting large, expensive events. Positive reports from across Europe were reprinted in the Italian press,[104] not only to sell the regime's achievements to the domestic market but also to stake a claim for another big event in the future, namely the Olympic Games, which Mussolini coveted with a passion. As Bruno Roghi wrote in *La Gazzetta*:

> the spontaneous and most heartfelt statements of our foreign colleagues are more than sufficient to show that Mussolini's Italy – that was once little Italy of all improvizations and apologies – has organized the festival of football with the style, flexibility, precision, even the courtesy and the meticulousness that indicate an absolute maturity and preparedness ... For this the Italian Football Federation is worthy of Fascist sport not only by virtue of the primacy reached on the fields of the eight superb stadia, but because it knew how to guarantee the perfect functioning of the massive organizational task.[105]

The press naturally exploited the victory's full potential, setting it in the imagery and language of national struggle and football patriotism. According to Vaccaro, it was an expression of the national will based upon the merits of collective organization and discipline that derived from Mussolini's inspiration.[106] As Roghi expanded in his article headlined 'Soldati dello Sport' (soldiers of sport):

> They are rare, the rarest of matches in which you see the metamorphosis of the players, no longer little coloured boys who go about their work, with the ball at their feet, but little, gallant soldiers that fight for an idea that is greater than them but who work for the divine unknown, that is the genius of the soldier on the charge. They are the matches, in other words, where not one squad of eleven men but a race shows itself with its feelings and instincts, its anger and its ecstasy, its character and attitude. The game that the Italians won at the stadium was this type of match.[107]

Complying with the Fascist vision, Vaccaro used the team's success as another allegory for organic society; 'Team Italy's' victory indicating what could be achieved if everybody worked together.[108] It was a theory that the Florentine Fascist weekly *Il Bargello* supported with even greater gusto, denoting the national success an example of how to meet and overcome future challenges.

> [It was] the affirmation of an entire people, the indication of its virile and moral strength and not an essentially sporting fact. We Fascists cannot

understand how this indispensable contribution of the national spirit can be separated from the result that needs to be attained. Working in every field of human activity, you struggle in the name of the motherland, it is the motherland that triumphs over everything, it is the entire nation that participates towards the objective, spurs on and encourages the protagonists that become anonymous but aware instruments of this will.[109]

Calcio had become a victim of its own success and Italian teams were now expected to dominate. As Vaccaro stated: the *'azzurri*, wherever they go, will need to defend and confirm the primacy won'.[110] Fortunately, the regime's restructuring of the game had created a generation of players capable of responding to the almost impossible demand.

This was demonstrated by the victory of the Italian Universities team in the 1936 Olympic football tournament in Berlin. Ten years after the formation of the Ballila movement and the restructuring of CONI, the entire Italian Olympic squad was hugely improved.[111] However, the success of the football team was as unexpected as it was sweet, the amateur products of the regime's investment in compulsory physical education defeating a succession of professional opponents.

By deciding to adhere completely to the amateur ethos of the Games – and thus exclude the stars of 1934 – Fascism claimed the moral high ground. Basking in the warm glow of success, Leone Boccali reaffirmed how: 'occupied by the evident moral reasons and . . . protocols not to participate with its best national team, but rather with a formation in order with the Olympic laws, as usual, Italy chose an original solution, sending the national student team.'[112] FIGC President Vaccaro was less bullish prior to the tournament, his hopes going no further than avoiding any unforeseen shocks that might have tarnished Italy's World Champion status. Nonetheless, he knew that amateur *calcio* had strength in depth beyond what any other nation could offer,[113] the Italian Universities XI having won the World Student Games in 1927, 1928, 1930 and 1933.[114]

It was these graduates of Fascist education that many saw sweeping all before them on the football field. According to *La Gazzetta's* Emilio Colombo, it was their 'Latin Blood' that had enabled the *azzurri* to defeat an obdurate Norwegian team earlier in the tournament: 'In the crucial moments of the rough struggle, the Norwegian players did not find the ardour, the flame of passion, the fighting spirit, the overpowering thrusting characteristic of the Italians.'[115] Although his remark echoed much of what was generally being written at the time, his reference to blood made the link between victory, success and racial fitness, which had thus far been underplayed. In an indication of changing times, Boccali attributed similar importance to the victory that had 'been stubbornly wanted and beautifully won, not by the use of exceptional players, of which some are 'repatriates', rather by 14 boys that have been selected exponents of national breeding'.[116]

Boccali went one step further by differentiating between pure Italian athletes and those repatriates or *oriundi* (first-generation Italians from Latin America) that had featured in the 1934 World Cup. It was a bold and unusual distinction. Nobody had previously complained about the presence of five *oriundi* in the victorious 1934 squad.[117] In fact, the masses were more likely to have agreed with *La Nazione*'s correspondent Giuseppe Ambrosini, who saw the athletes as: 'our best, dearest, flourishing youth, that knew how to hold the tricolour high abroad, in the name of Italy and the Duce.'[118] Nonetheless, such comments indicated a directional shift in the regime's attitude to race that became even more apparent after the 1938 success in France.

Whatever contradictions the *oriundi* or *rimpatriati* might have exposed, the regime was still intent on exploiting every potential scrap of propaganda. Combined with Gino Bartali's victory in the Tour de France cycling race that year, the *azzurri*'s triumph further underlined the sporting progress of Fascist Italy. It was, according to *Il Bargello*: 'the synthesis of Italian and Fascist technical and moral superiority, reached with the tenacious will and absolute discipline of the athletes in the style of the time of Mussolini.'[119] The *azzurri*'s victories were linked to the regime and the Duce at every opportunity, Vaccaro also proclaiming that: 'the flag of the revolution has triumphed in your [Mussolini] name'.[120]

The Italian press was naturally keen to publicize foreign appreciation, especially those Parisians that reportedly replaced the angry fists of the supporters in Marseilles with smiles and applause of genuine recognition.[121] The often-quoted French journalist Maurice Pefferkorn, writing in *Auto*, was also said to have drawn attention to the standards that Italian football was setting throughout the world. The *azzurri* 'appeared as a model of play, a dazzling example of style, and an Italian school is already talked of, to which one needs to aspire. This is perhaps the greatest recognition, the most significant eulogy: the azzurri have become the masters.'[122]

In Rome, a mass celebration in the Stadio Olimpico drew a crowd of 50,000 people that, along with the Duce, sang a rousing collection of Fascist anthems.[123] Past athletes who had died serving the motherland were commemorated while the future was represented by a display of young sportsmen and Dopolavoro members. Beyond celebrating the *azzurri*'s achievement, the display was intended to show how the Italian sporting renaissance extended to the masses.

In a more private ceremony in the Palazzo Venezia in Rome, on 29 June 1938, the team and coach were received by the Duce and the

President of CONI, Achille Starace, where they were awarded the medal of athletic valour. It was 'a cold and hasty affair', as Piero Rava recalled, the event little more than a 15-minute photoshoot for Mussolini after which the players were rewarded with their 8,000 lire win bonuses.[124] When asked what the event had meant to him, the team captain Giuseppe Meazza described a more inspiring event:

> It made a magnificent impression! Above all because it gave me the opportunity of being received by the Duce for a second time . . . I hope to be present also in 1942 to be able to contribute to the third azzurri victory that would make us definite owners of the trophy. This is the burning desire for me and my companions and for this reason we will prepare ourselves with Fascist will, driven by today's extensive eulogy from the Duce.[125]

This success was also used to demonstrate that the Italian victory four years earlier had been neither a fluke nor attributable to home advantage. There was also the distinct flavour of foreign military conquest, *Il Popolo d'Italia* referring to 'the victory . . . on foreign ground even hostile territory',[126] a theme that Bruno Roghi exploited in his patriotic acclamation of the success in *La Gazzetta*:

> It takes faith. You don't win an international match, played thousands of kilometres from the motherland, just with the bravura of well-honed bodies and with the fire of well-tempered courage. It takes a high ideal pulsating in the spirit . . .
> A match like this is not just a sporting episode. It is, above all, patriotic fact. To win it is necessary to know in every moment that even the ball can be a means to show to the foreigners that you are worthy of belonging to the earth that has given us life and honour.127

Roghi's references to faith, well-honed bodies and high ideals summed up the characteristics of the *Italiano nuovo*, which Lando Ferretti further developed in *Lo Sport Fascista*. Not just a sporting victory, the triumph was evidence of Fascism's successful breeding programme that was now driving the nation forward in all fields of life:

> But if this renewed triumph of Fascist sport in the most popular and widespread game of times (it could be said that football is a physiognomic expression of mass life at the moment like cinema) represents only a consolidation of positions already reached, the victory . . . has brought us other targets, it has revealed the world to us in the new light of our agricultural and industrial organization. Because creating a race, the production of exceptional animals, raising and managing them to the ultimate victories in the international arena

is not only a sign of the sporting maturity of a people, but rather of the ability to create and win in every sector of productive activity.[128]

With Roghi also arguing that 'beyond the athletic victory shines the victory of the race',[129] a general belief began to emerge that Fascism had created a type of Nietzschean superman.

Oriundo? Rimpatriato? Italiano Nuovo?

Giuseppe Meazza was the most obvious 'superman', although while he personified much of what the regime wished to convey to the masses, he also exposed a number of contradictions that Fascist society was unable to resolve or accommodate. Known by his nickname of Balilla, due to the young age at which he made his Serie A debut, Meazza was the team's irreplaceable goal-scorer, a naturally individualistic role that exposed the ethical dilemma of outstanding individual contributions to the collective good.

By nature of their role, strikers were individuals less easily restricted to the confines of the collective and Meazza, as the leading exponent in Italy, symbolized a fetish for goals that threatened to undermine the organic team ethic. As Mario Rossi noted in *Lo Sport Fascista*: 'Calcio should shun the 'prima donna' because it is essentially a collective sport. However in every city and town, each squad has a player – it is worth saying one eleventh of the group – who, rising above the others through intrinsic quality, [. . .] comes to symbolise those cities.'[130]

No striker could prosper without the service and support of his team-mates and, however successful that individual might be, his achievements had to be placed within the context of the team. It was yet another un-subtle allegory for the relationship between the individual and society that *Il Popolo d'Italia* specifically applied to Meazza: 'The secret of our strength is in the type of game that the Italian half-back knows how to adopt. With two men of the highest class, like Meazza and Ferrari, it needs a half-back of class that passes the ball precisely, who knows how to use cunning.'[131] Moreover, in the light of growing racial awareness, Meazza's representation as the identikit Fascist Italian male set an example that some believed the *oriundi/rimpatriati* could never match.

Although a loose cannon in the *azzurri*'s armoury, as the quintessential *Italiano nuovo* Meazza also provided a direct contrast with the *oriundi* that formed the core of the successful teams of the 1930s. For primarily economic motives, mass emigration from southern Italy began in the period of unification (1861) and, although there are no exact statistics, by 1914 there were an estimated five to six million Italians living abroad.[132]

Consequently, by the mid 1920s, there was no shortage of high-class footballers with Italian roots playing in South America, where the game had an even stronger history. Unfortunately, their recruitment was outlawed by one of the Carta di Viareggio's more short-sighted measures. Quick to exploit this untapped source of talent, rather than repeal the law, the regime overcame it by introducing joint citizenship. As Pozzo recalled: 'I spoke with Arpinati. And he told me: "According to Italian law, the sons of Italians born abroad are considered Italians".'[133] The *rimpatriato* – returnee – was immediately eligible to play not only in Serie A but also for the national team.

After impressing at the 1928 Olympic Games for Argentina, one of the first to make an impact on *calcio* was Raimondo Orsi, signed by Juventus for 100,000 lire, a Fiat 509 and a salary of 8,000 lire per month. So controversial was his transfer the Argentine Federation forced him to remain in a type of *calcio* quarantine for one season, before finally making his debut.[134] In a portentous complaint to the FIGC, the Argentine Federation condemned the regime's unscrupulous and unprincipled strengthening of its team: 'The Italians want to form a national team at the cost of Argentine football . . . The Fascist government, impressed by the value of Argentine players and wanting to make Fascist football appear the best in the world, has set its eyes on well known Creole players and wants to tie them to Italian clubs to make them Italian players.'[135]

Among the forty-seven players that came from South America to play in Italy during the interwar period, Guaita, Cesarini, the Brazilian Filo and Luisito Monti all followed Orsi into the Italian national team, with Monti proving an especially interesting case having already represented Argentina in the 1930 World Cup. While his dual nationality might have appeared to dilute the Italian success, his Italian roots were deemed to have been identifiable in the robust nature of his game. This way, Monti and some of the other *oriundi/rimpatriati* stars, as outsiders, defined some aspects of the 'true' Italian footballer.

Mario Zappa drew attention to the apparent differences between Latin American and Italian players in *Lo Sport Illustrato*, by arguing that it was more than just an issue of talent; there was also a difference in temperament and mental habits. For the Latin American the prize was the game itself and not the result, their preference for dribbling provoking Zappa's exasperation. With the exceptions of Monti, Orsi and Guaita, he implied that this fetish for dribbling meant South American footballers could not be trusted in the team's key positions: 'The Italian player instead tends towards simplicity, the quick game, the result obtained by the direct route . . . the art of the South American is to play the game, our art is to resolve the game.'[136] According to Zappa's rationale, Monti could be entrusted with the team's crucial central role by virtue of his Italian roots.

Despite such questions about their true right to belong to the Italian race, Tornabuoni refused to deny the fundamental role of *oriundi* in the tactical development of the Italian game, arguing that Italian football could learn much from South America. The issue of joint-nationality players was brought into serious question as early as 1934, following the *azzurri*'s first major international success. After a meeting within the FIGC to consider the impact of the *oriundi* following accusations that their presence was weakening the Italian game, it was decided that their commitment to Italy was the most important issue. As *La Gazzetta* made clear, if they came to Italy and made use of dual nationality, they needed to do so as Italians otherwise they would meet tough sanctions.[137]

While there was clearly a general desire to make full use of the excellent *rimpatriati* that were available, there was opposition to the likes of De Maria who returned to Argentina to carry out his national service. His exploitation of joint nationality was contrary to the Fascist spirit as players were either completely Italian or not. As *Il Bargello* argued, it was 'time to resolve this situation that is compromising the good name of Fascist Italy . . . we say that one who has not carried out his military obligations cannot and should not be considered an Italian citizen.'[138]

The issue was further intensified by the impending Ethiopian campaign that prompted World Cup winner Guaita plus two other *rimpatriati*, Scopelli and Stagnaro, to attempt to leave the country before their military call-up.[139] All three were discovered at the Italian-French border complete with their considerable earnings, which further reduced the credibility of returnees. Military service was certainly an obligation that the identikit Italian Giuseppe Meazza carried out,[140] which reflected badly upon those *rimpatriati* that were less enthusiastic about performing their patriotic duties. Despite their contribution to Italy's international football success, questions continued to be asked about their right to a place in the national team.

However, despite appearing as yet another obvious allegory for society as a whole, the issue shed new light on the requirements of an Italian. While it continued to be suggested that the *oriundi/rimpatriati* were not Italian, Zanetti and Tornabuoni argued that the original restrictions had not been introduced to promote ties of race and blood but to defend the concept of Italian citizenship. Blood was less important than a 'clear and general proof of patriotism'.[141] Highlighting Fascism's concern with commitment to the cause more than blood and genes, it demonstrated the flexible nature of the Italian Fascist identity. Replicating the way various cities throughout the peninsula were able to establish their own, often contrasting, identities, there was also space for individuals to express themselves within the broad boundaries of acceptability.

Italy Breaks the Mould: *Metodo* v *Sistema*

If there were question marks over the nationality of some players in the *azzurri*'s incredible success story, the manner and style of the victories were deemed Italian beyond doubt, Mario Zappa commenting upon how the Italian squad showed 'a model of play that is the synthesis of the best elements in all of the most admired systems'.[142] If correct – and there is convincing evidence for this – it questions the justification of numerous references to a specifically Italian style play, as this claim suggests the success was built on a mixture of the best elements of European football. Moreover, when necessary, the team was more than capable of matching the brute force of others that was so maligned in the Italian press.

Calcio's 'Duce', in control of the *azzurri*'s organic collective from 1929 to 1948, was the Italian coach or *commissario unico*, Vittorio Pozzo, whose strategy was also to create a group of players that was stronger than the sum of its constituent parts. As Bruno Roghi explained: 'Football is a collective game. Much will and many brains need to converge and immerse themselves in the unity of the squad. From the multiplicity of strengths needs to emerge the harmony of the collective.'[143]

The squad also represented the idealized Fascist society by blending survivors from the 1934 and 1936 triumphs with a number of debutantes. Reflecting the Futurist-inspired theory of regeneration through conflict, permanent change and the consistent introduction of new blood, the new faces revitalized the team by providing competition within the collective unit. Combined with the regime's physical, moral and spiritual education, the *Italiano nuovo* could be relied upon to struggle to the death, *La Nazione* observing a squad with 'the quality to defend the colours of Italy and also the spirit of Fascism. It will fight serenely without arrogance and a false sense of modesty.'[144]

It was not just the press that increasingly made militaristic references to *calcio*, as Pozzo also used nationalist imagery and combative techniques to stress the players' roles as representatives of the nation and the regime. It was an especially important aspect of preparation that Tornabuoni had already highlighted in his detailed chronicle of *calcio*'s rise:

> The psychological factor is decisive and instrumental for the Latin people and Italians in particular! It is necessary however that our people be motivated . . . by the spring of passion, that naturally has the most beautiful and noble expression of love for the motherland . . .

The Italian soldier needs to have strong feelings for a noble cause: then he overcomes every obstacle and becomes irresistible.[145]

In his biography, published in the 1960s, Pozzo attempted to play down the extent of his nationalist mind games: 'I have read a lot in recent years . . . that before sending the team onto the field, I more or less served the players a strong dose of patriotic and nationalistic ideas . . . They are all stories from people who were neither there nor interested in football.'[146] However, he was unable to completely deny juxtaposing the players' contemporary responsibilities with the wartime sacrifices of their ancestors. The most frequently cited example came before the team's match against Hungary in 1930 when, during the journey to Budapest, the squad was taken to the First World War battlefields of Oslavia and Gorizia before stopping at the monumental cemetery at Redupiglia. As the players paused among the tombs of the war dead, Pozzo drew attention to the sacrifices their forefathers had made for the motherland: 'I told them it was good that the sad and terrible spectacle might have struck them: that whatever would be asked of us on that occasion, was nothing compared with those that had lost their lives on those surrounding hills.'[147] The *azzurri*'s subsequent 5–0 destruction of the Magyar team was warmly received by the regime, the visit thereafter contributing to the media's metaphorical militarization of the squad.

Pozzo never received any payment for his work as *commissario unico*, choosing instead to rely upon one of his many established careers, namely that as a football journalist.[148] He proved to be a prolific and, more often than not, objective writer, even if it did seem rather like putting the wolf in charge of the sheep pen. In his regular, lengthy submissions – to publications such as *La Nazione*, *Il Resto del Carlino*, *La Gazzetta dello Sport*, and *La Stampa*, to name but a few – it was not unusual for him to criticize his team's performances, or to pen more portentous pieces that seem to prepare the readership – and perhaps the regime – for the possibility of defeat.

Pozzo's skills undoubtedly included tactical awareness, but diplomacy, man-management and cunning were equal factors in his success. He used the latter particularly well to cloud the issue of his party membership, which, when combined with the continued restriction of access to his personal archive, explains why the nature of his relationship with the regime hierarchy has remained an area of considerable speculation.[149] As he stated in his biography: 'I was not even a member of the Party. I was a free citizen that had his profession that had nothing in common with politics.'[150] However, this was contradicted by his statement in an earlier article referring to the abuse the players received from the French public in 1938: 'They did not know . . . that we were for sport and not politics, and that a great number of us had Party membership in 1934, in the preceding World Cup.'[151] In fact, the Party membership, or otherwise, of Pozzo and the players tells us little, especially as it has already been established that they were all members of CONI, an organ of the party. However, if Pozzo had never been a PNF member and if, as he said, he was rarely under pressure from the regime, his nationalistic motivational techniques may indicate the extent to which the regime's ideas were penetrating the masses through *calcio*.

The sports press also helped to create a certain mythology around the team's tactical and technical merits, plus its alleged spirit of fair play. Fascist Italy was not only proud of the *azzurri*'s victories, but also of the way the team had apparently torn up the *calcio* rule book and tactically transformed the game, the three victories testimony to their superiority over all but the English. However, when necessary, the allegedly skilful *Italiano nuovo* could easily transform into the *Italiano duro* (hard man).

As a 1932 *Lo Stadio* editorial noted: 'In the 10th year of the Fascist era the youth are toughened for battle, and for the battle, and more for the game itself, courage, determination, gladiatorial pride, chosen sentiments of our race, cannot be excluded.'[152] Not surprisingly, players from such a combative physical education system, who were trained to fight and never concede defeat, began to earn a reputation abroad for aggression, which contrasted with the subtlety, style and fair play that was promoted at home. An early example was brought to the attention of the Ministry of the Interior in 1929, prior to an encounter with Germany. Recalling the *azzurri*'s earlier performances against Czechoslovakia and Austria, which were memorable for their violence and aggression, the German representative, Kurt Schimmer, warned the Italians that his team was 'well prepared for the Italian 'game' and that if [they] repeat the effort of Prague and Vienna, they will have many broken tibia'.[153]

Despite the 2–1 victory for Germany the match passed without incident, but the opposition's fears were a sign that the Italian game plan included more than just superior technique and tactics. Foul play was a practice that some parts of the press, such as *Lo Stadio*, decried as contrary to the tradition and the spirit of *calcio*: 'Such spectacles disgust. And as it is more often the home player committing such disgraceful acts, the public does not shout or protest so as not to harm its player, often because it consents to such acts.'[154]

In his various newspaper columns, even Pozzo railed against the increasing use of rough and violent play that, in his opinion, was disrupting the game's technical development: 'some of the squads in the championship go onto the pitch in a mood that is clearly hostile, which is contrary to the good of the game. It is win at all costs, it is the bitter grudge against the adversary, it is the preoccupation of the result to the ends of the league table.'[155]

Although responsibility for this change was heaped upon the players themselves, the increasing 'win at all costs' approach was clearly related to the formation of the national league and the consequent intensification of *campanilismo* that had stimulated the win bonuses that Pozzo so despised: 'The win bonus guarantees genuine competition ... but it constitutes one of the strongest springs to that "win at all costs" spirit and sense of intolerance that have the consequences we all know.'[156] It was yet another contradiction for which the regime had no answer. While win bonuses guaranteed the type of competition that had been lacking in the old league system, they also intensified local rivalries and increased the need to win so much as to threaten the technical development of the game.

Following the *azzurri*'s defeat by Germany in Turin, in 1929, Pozzo openly criticized the Italian team's obsession with victory. Arguing that this explained its continuing lack of progress, he prescribed a combination of calm, caution, precision and technique within a single game plan.[157] His prioritization of the collective and imposition of discipline and obedience upon the individual clearly appealed to Arpinati, who appointed him as *commissario unico* soon after. The most interesting aspect of the article, however, was the insight into how Pozzo's team might have been expected to play: 'The game is beautiful, technical, interesting and fascinating when it constructs, when it gives life to something, when it thinks and works, not when it simply demolishes, defends, destroys and suffocates. Man has true merit when he does something of his own, that is alone: not when he limits himself to knocking down what others have built.'[158]

His commitment to constructive play was open to sacrifice, nonetheless, when the all-important result looked in danger, his side proving on more than one occasion that brawn rather than brain could also be effective. Facing the Spanish in Bilbao in 1931, Pozzo identified the main threat as Aguirrezabala and planned accordingly: 'I reasoned that, if I succeeded in cutting off the head with which the eleven adversaries thought, the whole system would collapse. I told Cesarini ... to permanently mark and disturb him.'[159] Negative and ruthlessly effective, Italy secured a draw with one of the strongest teams in Europe.

The teams met again in Florence during the 1934 World Cup, Pozzo's mixture of subtlety and steel once again designed to frustrate the Spanish and stop them playing. Contested in front of an impassioned Florentine crowd and an array of local and national Fascist figures, it was more akin to a battle than a football match; exactly the type of contest that the *Italiano nuovo* had been trained/bred for. After a combative draw, Pozzo likened the dressing rooms to an infirmary[160] and was forced to use four new players in the scheduled replay the following day. With the *azzurri's* excesses, led by Monti, forcing the Spanish to make seven changes, only eleven of the original twenty-two appeared in the second match, when, according to Phil Ball's history of Spanish football, they kicked 'the remaining Spaniards into oblivion'.[161]

The essence of Pozzo's tactic was an adaptation of the English 'WM' system to the Italian game, thereby forming the *metodo* style that was more flexible and difficult to defeat. Most importantly, it differed from the English game and the Danubian *'sistema'*. While the Italian playing positions, as part of the *metodo*, were more specific and do not satisfactorily translate into English, the technical innovation saw the 'WM' central defender move into the midfield area of play, to become a third, central *terzino, centro mediano* or half-back. It was this subtle change that adapted the English 'WM' into Italy's 'WW', Pozzo building the team around the key *centro mediano* role that Luisito Monti made his own with aggression more than creativity.

The tactical twist, which had actually been more or less employed by the dominant Juventus team since 1930, laid the foundations of the *azzurri's* incredible success while apparently rejecting the English orthodoxy. In fact, so subtle and complex were the differences that there is no general agreement as to when the concept of *metodo* entered *calcio's* lexicon or even if it ever specifically referred to the Italian game.[162]

Following the World Cup victory in 1938, Mario Zappa cut through the technical jargon to describe in lay terms what he saw as the impact of Pozzo's changes. The 'big secret of the Italian squad is its capacity to attack with the least amount of men possible, without ever distracting the half-backs from their defensive work.'[163] Others, though, were less convinced about the significance of the tactical innovation, the journalist Scipione Picchi[164] suggesting in *Lo Stadio* as early as 1932, that tactical considerations were something of a red herring as an outstanding team like Juventus would succeed irrespective of its strategy.[165] Although developing tactical awareness cannot be underestimated, if Picchi's argument is applied to the national team, the merits of Pozzo's new and apparently Italian system of play must be questioned: he may just have been the fortunate heir to the regime's talented generation. Furthermore, as Christian Bromberger has observed, style needs to be considered not just as a simple reflex from practice but as a stereotyped image that a collective has for itself and hopes to transmit to others: 'In this sense, the style of a squad is part of a "mentality" or of a "public imagination . . . It is a valid compromise between a real and imagined identity"', all of which accords with the *azzurri* in this period.[166]

Either way, the most important thing for the regime was that the *azzurri* were winning, and winning in a style that was perceived to be undermining the notion of English supremacy. Unfortunately for Italy, the English Football Association's decision not to enter the World Cup tournaments and its desire to keep the team's continental appearances to a minimum, meant meetings with the *azzurri* were few and far between. They were also highly charged, as besides aesthetic and tactical comparisons there was also a political edge. For the regime, results between the two held a deeper national significance as achievement on the field was equated with success off of it.

However tactical innovation was dressed up, England was still the ultimate hurdle for Italy. Prior to 1933, some British club teams had played in Italy, one occasion being the visit of Newcastle United in 1929. The robust nature of Newcastle's play provoked a strong reaction from Italian supporters, who had already been incited by the nationalist press prior to the game. The agitated Ambrosiana (Inter) fans gave the English players a hot, rather than warm, welcome and an even livelier post match reception at their hotel, where a government telegram referred to a police presence that was required to protect them from 300 or so protesting fans.[167]

When the national teams met for the first time in 1933, Pozzo declared it: 'A decisive meeting between the best continental footballers and the prodigious maestros of the art.'[168] The contrast between the two teams was always portrayed in terms of their differing styles of play; the English strength rooted in efficiency, preparation and fitness more than technique. Undeterred by the 1–1 draw, Giuseppe Centauro extolled the more virtuous Italian style:

> because it is more in keeping with the spectacular content of a football match, more varied in its stylistic displays, richer in imagination and thus more picturesque and artistic. Our eminently Latin temperament feels more the charm of a match that might have something abstract, that sharp creative spirit of the athletes, rather than a game duty bound to calculations and multiplication tables.[169]

In November 1934, having just won the second World Cup, the *azzurri* went to London to face England in what was portrayed as not only a contest between the two best teams in the world but also one between the respective nations' political ideologies. The regime coveted the opportunity so much that Pozzo, an accomplished speaker of English, was despatched to the English FA to organize the fixture. Contrary to what he believed was in the *azzurri*'s best interests, Pozzo claimed he was forced to accept the fixture in London for the autumn of 1934: 'In London, when I heard, as I feared, that we would have to play immediately in October (sic) and at Arsenal's ground, I objected. I telephoned Rome to express my contrary thoughts. Nothing doing. In Rome, at a high level – and it was a political interference – somebody was in high spirits. It was necessary to accept.'[170]

Pozzo's recollection of the game's importance for the regime was supported by the secretary of the English FA, Stanley Rous, who naturally had his own agenda when recalling the match as the unofficial world title decider: 'The England team [was] the side that every country wanted to play and beat. Mussolini's offer of huge bonuses to his team for the Highbury game in 1934 was only a reflection of the immense prestige that was gained by any country beating England. Italy at least clearly regarded this as just as important as winning the World Cup!'[171] While it is difficult to substantiate Rous's claims about Italian win bonuses, his remarks do indicate the high profile and important nature of the match in the 1934 football calendar, which was also reflected in the Italian press.

In the build up to the 'battle of Highbury', Bruno Roghi stabbed his pen at those across the Channel: 'These people show a very enjoyable ignorance of too many things that happen in the sporting world of the continent. They ask questions that alarm more than surprise . . . Are the English so ignorant of sport on the continent because of ostentation, naivety or lack of interest?'[172] Albeit offensively phrased he had a point, for if England had lost the match there would have been a general sense of amazement, when the difference in quality between the two was negligible. Furthermore, perceptions of the English island mentality were strengthened by a cartoon in *The Daily Mail*, reprinted in *La Gazzetta*, whereby each member of the Italian team was stereotypically portrayed with a ridiculous moustache.[173]

Nonetheless, Roghi's article, in which he referred to Highbury Stadium as 'the theatre of international war', was provocative and clearly designed to stir the home market.[174] As the match approached he became more reticent, publishing a list of reasons why Italy might not win and, most importantly, why it was not possible to consider it as *the* World Cup final. His argument was again logical, but there was also an overriding sense of him preparing the way for a dignified defeat, from which Italy would cling on to its world champion status. It was a prescient move. Following the 3–2 defeat, which was recorded in *calcio* folklore for the English foul play and Italian resilience, the press salvaged whatever positives it could muster from the match.

Emilio Colombo underlined the numerous disadvantages that the Italian team had faced, among which was an extreme sense of outrage at the loss of Monti following a heavy challenge four minutes into the game: 'No, they were not enough the advantages offered to the rivals: the field, fans, date, surroundings, climate. The match also wanted Monti sacrificed.'[175] This sense of injustice contrasted strongly with the cheers that had accompanied Monti's liquidation of the Spanish team in June, before he stamped his mark on the final; after which the Swedish referee Eklind commented that 'some Italians were initially a little excessive, and I refer to Monti.'[176]

Pozzo also took exception to the rough treatment Monti received in London, defending him as the most correct player around, who played the ball and not the man. It was somewhat incongruous with his declaration that the player had 'a big personal problem with the danubians – who he considered all the same, and made him "see red"'.[177] While such a contradictory sense of injustice is probably a consistent feature among many football fans, it drew further attention to the fundamental weakness in the argument that *calcio* had developed a sense of style and fair play that compared so positively with English football.

Nonetheless, the Italian press continued to vindicate its team by suggesting it had exposed the physical English approach; the Fascist magazine *Libro e Moschetto* making the unsubstantiated claim that, unlike the English, Italian players did not know how to charge and obstruct adversaries illegally, nor did they want to.[178] Similarly, in *La Gazzetta*, Colombo argued that the Italian players had morally triumphed with their greater intelligence and technical skills in the face of brute force and ignorance: 'The English overwhelmed our squad with the same impetus and with the same – how to say it? crude violence that we saw unfurl against the Wunderteam in the first twenty-five minutes of the England-Austria match two years or so ago.'[179] It was indicative of how the most patriotic elements of the press hoped the English would accept their weaknesses and recognize the apparent 'ruins of their grotesque system of play, thrown into the air by the Italians'.[180]

Numerically disadvantaged, it was the spirit of struggle that apparently enabled the *azzurri* to strike back when down and out, scoring twice in the second half to run England close. As Colombo saw it, the 'boxer with the better technique imposed his real style upon the violent rival. The heart, intelligence, passionate flame of the azzurri players achieved everything that our Italian and Fascist faith was desperately waiting for.'[181] Even though England had won on points, the *azzurri*'s refusal to submit to the reported English aggression was enough for the press to turn the defeat into a moral victory, Colombo's comments in *La Gazzetta* representing the general mood: 'The Englishman is a colossus or . . . seems a colossus. The Italian is more elegant, subtler. Art against force? . . . The colossus threw itself violently against the stylist that defended itself as it could.'[182]

Giovanni Ferrari picked up the baton in *Lo Sport Fascista*: 'We have morally beaten them abroad, in the heart, and we more than matched them in the technique of the game',[183] while Bruno Roghi went even further in suggesting that England had, in fact, won nothing: 'There is an English phrase that literally translates like so: "Saving face". And they have saved face.'[184] Ignoring the result, he declared the *azzurri*'s efforts vengeance on behalf of Europe and a victory for the game itself. 'The Italian squad, splendid representatives of Fascism and at the same time avengers for sporting Europe, gave the English a terrible lesson. It said clearly that calcio is first of all an art. It said that the destructive game . . . is the mortification of the sport.'[185]

Once again, even in defeat, the 'soldiers of sport' had apparently defended the nation and the Fascist faith on a hostile foreign field. As Roghi explained to the English, but with more significance for the Italian readership: 'the azzurri players came into your house, on your sports ground (the Arsenal ground is the Oxford of English football), and by a whisker failed to give you the biggest shock of your life.'[186] It was an argument that Colombo further developed on *La Gazzetta*'s front page: 'What other squad and what other champions, if not those toughened at the school and raised in the climate of Fascist sport, would have been able to write a page so rich of deeds and so full of lessons that the ten men of the Italian national team added to the history of international football?'[187]

Intoxicated by the achievement of the 'Athletes of Fascism', he even went so far as to refer to the 'victory' of the organic unit representing the regime and the nation. They 'emanated, the class and the style, the technique and the skill . . . the ten athletes played like a platoon of gladiators. Ten combatants, one heart.'[188] Roghi added the final polish to *La Gazzetta*'s veneered presentation of the result: 'the Italian squad returns to the Motherland with a defeat that is worth twice as much as a victory.'[189]

Despite such extreme patriotism, criticisms of the English game had some justification, based as it was upon a mixture of technique and strength. However, by attacking it so virulently, these articles were further developing the idea of an innovative and unique style Italian play. As with many aspects of life under the regime, defining the characteristics of the outsider helped establish what was essentially Italian. Thus, identifying and castigating the English game created the perceived or desired identity of the preferred Italian version: fair play, style, superior technique, tactical improvization and imagination being the prominent features. Certainly *calcio* did possess elements of all of these, but the created myth was different to reality.

With skill and aggression, *calcio Italiano* had kicked the nation into world supremacy on the football field, winning it international respect in the process. Diplomatically, the *azzurri* success plus the successful organization of the 1934 World Cup won Fascist Italy international kudos while domestically, to a certain degree, it united the nation around the national team.

As the victories and the positive benefits of sporting success became more apparent, so the regime increasingly associated itself through words and symbols, with the champions that its policies had contributed to creating. The quality of the *azzurri*'s play in the 1934 World Cup tournament won global respect, providing Fascism with the opportunity to parade its athletic elite, organizational skills, imagination and new sense of nation.

Success also had a positive domestic impact, as in addition to becoming a cause célèbre behind which the regime could attempt to mobilize the masses, the team exemplified an ideal Fascist society where the individual gave his all for the good of the whole. Its victories enabled the regime (and those who wrote on its behalf) to claim that Italy was progressing under Fascism, thanks to its investment in the new generation that was now commanding international respect and recognition.

More negatively, the changes imposed by the Carta di Viareggio politicized *calcio* to such a degree that even club teams, when competing abroad, were hijacked by the regime and robbed of their individual city based identities. Consequently, their matches often reflected and sometimes worsened Italian foreign relations in this period, although the press attempted to redress the balance by reporting all positive foreign reaction.

While *calcio* was the perfect allegory for the merits of the idealized Fascist society, it failed to resolve – and thereby exposed – many of the contradictions that existed within the constructed Italian Fascist identity. If its merit as a team game was consistently promoted, the superstars and talented individuals that emerged could not be ignored, thereby undermining the organic ethic of 'Team Italy'. Moreover, while the *azzurri* victories were triumphs for Fascist Italy, the presence of first generation Italians, some of which had already competed for other national teams, forced a certain amount of national and sometimes racial introspection. Without implying that the *oriundi/rimpatriati* undermined the *azzurri*'s achievements in anyway, their presence did force the leaders and opinion formers in Fascist Italy to consider exactly what their crucial roles in the sporting flagship meant for the nation's identity.

Ultimately, their presence only became a serious issue following the introduction of the racial laws, under pressure from Nazi Germany, in 1938. Thus, in a similar way to the architectural diversity that was permitted during the stadium building era, it seems reasonable to suggest that their presence, in fact, indicated the flexible nature of Italian identity. Although some question marks placed against the players' commitment had racial undertones, their commitment to the regime was of more concern than the nature of their blood. Aware that *calcio* was a most effective tool to not only reach out and touch the masses but also to improve its international respect, the regime allowed considerable space for diversity and individual expression in all aspects of the game. This accounts for the eclectic mix of individuals, ideas and projects that have been considered in this book, which the majority of Fascism's hierarchy believed would serve and strengthen the regime's hegemony.

–8–

Conclusion

In 1926, Fascism intervened in *calcio* because it was the biggest mass cultural leisure-time activity in the country. Whether as players, spectators, newspaper readers or radio listeners, the masses had made the game their own. For Fascism, *calcio* was a ready-made opportunity to mass mobilize society, and through its restructuring of the phenomenon the regime attempted to construct a sense of Italian identity and community that it was hoped might contribute to the establishment of consensus among the masses, thereby further legitimizing the regime's rule.

The first and perhaps most obvious conclusion is that *calcio* was unquestionably politicized towards Fascism's needs in a variety of ways. Although it might be somewhat deterministic to expect the sociocultural features of northern Europe's Labour movement to apply to Italy's more agrarian working class, Italian cities were industrializing and the urban masses expanding in this period. Exploiting this opportunity, and that presented by the failure of Socialism and the Church to recognize sport's potential to mobilize mass interest and support, the Fascist regime developed and directed the masses' passion as part of its programme to regenerate the nation physically, morally and spiritually.

Creating or inventing a sense of collective identity and tradition was a significant aspect of the regime's regeneration programme, with buildings and bodies focal points in the process. However, while they undoubtedly contributed to the formation a new, national, Fascist identity, somewhat contradictorily they also exposed and intensified many already existing identities throughout the peninsula. New Fascist rituals deliberately communed with past identities by blending tradition and innovation. However, as Cavazza's study of the restoration of provincial festivals and folklore under the regime suggests, this only resulted in a resumption or manipulation of former historical traditions and legends that were applied to the needs of the era.[1]

The same can be said about football, *calcio fiorentino* being the obvious example of a long-established football-type game that was successfully resurrected in the 1930s. Unlike the tennis-style game of *volata*, which was invented as a specifically Fascist game but failed to capture the public's imagination, the ancient Florentine form of *calcio* provided a long-standing tradition to complement the modern format. Even if *calcio fiorentino* is rejected as the ancient predecessor of the modern game, Italian association football still had approximately thirty years of history behind it. Rather than invent a new tradition, the regime seized that of *calcio* and adapted it to display and promulgate its vision of society. To what extent this vision was idealized and falsified naturally warrants consideration, but neither does this detract from the value of assessing exactly what this idealized society consisted of, as seen through the prism of *calcio*.

It should be noted how *calcio* was an obvious opportunity for the regime to express its view of organic society, whereby individuals were depersonalized and their needs subsumed into those of the collective mass which was ruled by a leader figure. Although subservient to the organic whole every individual was nonetheless crucial to its function, which demanded all were physically and psychologically able to meet their commitments and responsibilities. The regime's national regeneration programme was embodied by the *Italiano nuovo*, whose mythical characteristics were theoretically evident within Fascist footballers showing heroism, sacrifice and commitment to the team's cause. In this way, footballers set examples to the masses on two levels: first, by displaying the importance of individual physical and mental fitness and secondly, by showing how this should be directed towards benefiting the organic whole.

If society was to be regenerated to the levels of mental and physical fitness demanded, Fascism needed more than just schools and training programmes. For this reason society was honed and bound into a collective experience through metaphorical and occasionally very real struggles, battles and wars. Politicized *calcio* provided regular imaginary and real combat opportunities, especially once international competitions for clubs and countries assumed significance that went beyond mere sporting contests. For the regime, while confirming the Italian presence abroad, international football acted as focus around which national unity could be encouraged, directed and disciplined, as *La Gazzetta* observed on the eve of the 1938 World Cup in France.

> The Fascist revolution . . . has stirred the vigour of the race in sport, it has created the sporting spirit among the masses, of which a warlike spirit is known to be a direct descendant.
>
> Thus the gymnasia and stadia have been increased tenfold, the legions of militant youngsters have multiplied by hundreds, and within a decade the most functional and perfect facilities have brought us the strongest and best prepared athletes.

The Olympics, European championships, World Cup and International Student Games have been the sieve and the evidence of our rise. The blue shirt has become, in all fields, a symbol of ability . . . of ardour, of assertion.

The number of individual successes blend into the bright dazzling size of the collective success, and abroad our superiority is recognized, admired and envied.[2]

Undoubtedly, international sporting success enabled the regime to make claims about the merits and achievements of Fascist rule to both international and domestic audiences, and there was significant national progress in this field. Nonetheless, such achievements did not always unite society around the national Fascist identity as promoted by the regime through sport, for as Berezin correctly notes: 'rituals are as capable of creating disorder as order.'[3] In reality, Fascism's idealized national identity contained and exposed many contradictions and inconsistencies that had the potential to undermine its message.

Despite the portrayal of the *Italiano nuovo* as a heroic combatant, fighting in the name of the regime, *calcio* drew much of its inspiration and many of its best international players from outside Italy, thereby slightly undermining any nationalist pride in these 'pure' Italian players. Yet this also indicates the key, non-biological nature of belonging to the nation. As Falasca-Zamponi notes: 'total obedience and faith in the regime were fundamental requirements for membership in the community. Passive acceptance of Mussolini's rule did not suffice for one to be considered a loyal fascist. Participation was a duty and dictated the inclusion and exclusion of the true believers.'[4]

While some questions were raised about the presence of *oriundi* in the national team, their commitment to the cause was more important than any question marks over their nationality and Italian bloodline. In return for its investment in the physical education and preparation of the masses, plus its huge development of the national sporting infrastructure, the regime demanded the utmost loyalty from participants in sport at every level. It reflected the nature of Italian Fascist society up until the Ethiopia campaign in 1935 and the introduction of racial laws in 1938, whereby total commitment to the regime was the fundamental factor in an individual's 'membership' of the national community.

If commitment was the keyword in the Italian Fascist identity, it left room for manoeuvre among the finer small print, which was particularly visible in the general field of culture where considerable individuality was permitted within the broad parameters of Fascism. The national stadium-building programme demonstrated this, the stark difference between the Littoriale in Bologna and the Giovanni Berta in Florence revealing the scope for individual expression within the field of art and architecture. Unable to formulate any definitive guidelines as to what exactly constituted Fascist art, these stadia were huge examples of the regime's attempt to include rather than exclude its cultural exponents and practitioners. Ensuring broader mass public appeal as much as it avoided alienation, this cultural flexibility and openness also questioned the extent to which such loosely defined cultural forms could realistically be called Fascist, thereby undermining the regime's attempt to invent a sense of tradition and shared experience.

As seen, the products of this cultural flexibility, particularly in the field of architecture, varied between modernist and more traditional neo-Roman styles. Besides enabling such apparently contradictory forms to coexist peaceably, this flexibility facilitated the construction of buildings that helped form and establish a unifying Fascist identity and invented tradition. In this way, the Giovanni Berta stadium and the Santa Maria Novella station in Florence symbolized the modernization of Italian cities throughout the peninsula, while the Littoriale strengthened Fascism's imperial roots and the myth of Rome.

Although Benedetto Croce's assertion that Fascism and culture were diametrically opposed[5] was supported by a number of historians in the 1970s who failed to see the connection,[6] recent research has revealed how the regime actually embraced it; the dramatically contrasting stadia in Bologna and Florence perfectly illustrating this. In fact, *calcio* and stadia further support Cavazza's argument that the regime used regional culture as a moderately conservative form of national education. This clearly applies to the presented case studies of Bologna and Florence, where the respective city teams and their stadia were employed to present, sustain and develop myths around the physical and spiritual rebirth of the nation.

Irrespective of the system of government, football thrives upon strong associations and affinities to town, city and national representative teams. It is, of course, possible to support both with equal degrees of passion, but under Fascism an intense support for the local side, even if combined with equally strong sentiments for the national team, increasingly undermined the regime's organic view of the nation. For Fascism, the unfortunate and often uncontrollable result of *calcio*'s national development and politicization, which it hoped would act as a societal bonding agent, was the creation of strong, local, city-based identities that required teams, and occasionally encouraged fans, to do battle across the peninsula. Ironically, once again, the nationalization of *calcio* resulted in the atomization of identity.

In Bologna, it appears that Arpinati's motives for building the stadium and supporting the club as much as possible were stimulated by his desire to restore the city's former glory. However, while the team required a stadium worthy of its status, the Littoriale's excessive size was indicative of national and international ambitions. These were also reflected in Arpinati's encouragement of the commune's financial support for the club that it was hoped would ensure it remained competitive in the emerging transfer market and national and international competition. The net result of this strategy was the intensification of *campanilismo*, which was exactly what the regime had been trying to avoid. However, if local fans were identifying strongly with the club, its Coppa d'Europa campaigns revealed another side to Bologna FC's identity, as foreign supporters and political campaigners chose to attack what they saw as a symbol of Fascism.

The comparison of Bologna with Fiorentina shows how *campanilismo* was not just stimulated by success in *calcio*. In the case of Fiorentina, the radical local party chose to put the city on the national *calcio* map by merging two smaller clubs into one, around which the city could unite. However, given the new club's relative lack of success, the Giovanni Berta stadium best illustrated the city's independent spirit and rebirth under its avant-garde Fascist leadership.

Such radical buildings were an acceptable form of identity politics for the regime, as they were able to represent the strength of local pride adequately without crossing the boundaries of architectural acceptability and undermining its national organic vision. Once again, this concurs neatly with Cavazza's investigation into the revival of folk-traditions and festivals in which he argues that the recourse to a local ideology seems to have been greatest where men from the old Fascist elite were strongest; like Tuscany or Friuli.[7]

Despite the peaceable coexistence of such examples of architectural diversity, *calcio* also provoked a number of dilemmas and contradictions that the regime was unable to resolve. It is tempting to view the many irreconcilable differences mentioned throughout this book as a failure of the regime's attempt to create a shared sense of identity through *calcio*, but even if true, this cannot undermine its undoubted efforts in this field. Of course, assessing the extent to which people believed in Fascism and consented to the regime through football is an almost impossible task, as participation in whatever form of the game, be it as a spectator or player, cannot necessarily be read as a sign of consensus or support.

Nonetheless, while this study has concentrated on the regime's attempt to mobilize mass support and project its identity upon the nation through football, some conclusions as to its effectiveness can also be drawn. Irrespective of Fascism's success in this field, the mere fact that it delib-erately chose this cultural format indicates its awareness of sport as arguably the most widespread cultural activity in society, and certainly one in which its involvement was unlikely to experience too much resistance.

Yet, this is not to say that football supporters formed a simplistic, easily manipulated amorphous mass. As Falasca-Zamponi has argued:

> One needs to contextualise the popular reception of fascism by looking specifically at the way the regime conceived its audience and the implications of the perception on the audience's response. We cannot think of a 'public' as an already established entity, an objectified unchanging reality, nor a spontaneous outgrowth. Audiences are a social construction, the product of social processes that situate them within a discursive space characterized by distinctive power relations.[8]

Thus, if the regime's exploitation of *calcio* is to be considered a failure in any way, it would have to be on the basis that people cannot merely be considered passive objects, as they are subjects capable of autonomous thought and judgement. Yet even this reality did not deter the regime, as Le Bon's theory of crowds suggested that the mass collective mind was open to manipulation and suggestion. In fact, this suited Fascism's desire to create the impression, as much as the reality, of mass participation in society.

Domestically, there is little recorded sense of opposition having been expressed through *calcio*, and while external anti-Fascist forces did organize collective action against travelling teams, it is impossible to suggest this might have undermined support for the regime. In fact, it may even have indirectly achieved the opposite as fans took offence at attacks upon their local representatives.

Violent examples of *campanilismo* that threatened the concept of the nation did require close surveillance, threats and acts of repression, if order was to be maintained. However, as in the cases of Bologna and Florence, one could argue that such sentiments were stimulated by an appreciation of the work of the respective local party in financing and constructing clubs and stadia that citizens could be proud of. Expressions of local identity through *calcio* varied considerably from area to area, and although they were occasionally strong enough to undermine the idealized image of the Fascist nation, one cannot suggest that they represented politically motivated opposition to the regime.

Again, it would be unwise to portray this as Fascism's failure to impose its identity upon the masses, for permitting the existence of individual expressions of local identity may have acted as a necessary safety valve that averted the need for stronger acts of repression. Whether or not the regime succeeded in mobilizing mass support, its takeover and manipulation of *calcio* was a deliberate attempt to establish subservience and consensus among society.

An investigation beyond the period of this study and the rule of the Fascist regime would further develop this assessment of the long-term extent to which the regime's politicization of *calcio* impacted upon the game's identity. A superficial assessment of this period shows how many of the game's structures and leading figures remained in place, while the stadia were divested of their Fascist names, imagery and iconography. Many of the old issues that the regime attempted to tackle, such as regionalism, the role of foreign players, the organizational structure and the importance of the national team, quickly resurfaced. This contributed to a general sense of bankruptcy within the game and the FIGC, which demanded further, radical restructuring by the late 1940s. Although it is impossible to state categorically from the research undertaken here, many of the structures established by the regime still endured even beyond these post-war changes, which could either suggest the depth or the superficiality of the regime's impact.

In many respects, assessing the degree to which Fascist policy towards sport and *calcio* succeeded in mobilizing the masses and contributed to the long-term survival of the regime, is almost impossible. However, the game's efficacy as a political tool may be evident in the dictatorships that applied and adapted the Italian blueprint to their own needs. Fascist states as diverse as Bulgaria, Norway, Holland, Finland and Slovakia all embraced sport and planned European Sports Federation in 1942 'to co-ordinate fascist sport and counteract the Anglo-American domination in many international sports federations'.[9] The collapse of the German campaign on the Eastern front focused minds on more pressing issues, but the concept alone demonstrated the impact of Italy's example throughout Europe.

The Italian formula was replicated most obviously in Nazi Germany where the old sports federations were 'co-ordinated', Nazified and brought under the control of the Party. A significant difference however, was the emphasis on purifying and strengthening the race, which naturally excluded Jews and Marxists. Unfortunately for Nazism, German football could not match the Italian success story, even after the talented Austrian team was consumed by the Anschluss in 1938. Besides emphasizing the risk and boldness of the Italian project, it also highlights the Fascist regime's effective skill in constructing national victories even from defeats.

In Francoist Spain, football was used as both a diversion from reality and a medium to unite the nation behind the regime. While Italian

Fascism and German Nazism invested in elite and mass sport, Franco's refusal to follow suit left only self-financing, money-generating sports capable of adequately representing the regime. With its mass popular support, football was an ideal representative that acted on the regime's behalf in two ways: 'it demonstrated Spanish unity, so important for the nationalists after the Civil War and it created the culture of evasion, the chance to talk about something other than the war, economic problems, lack of freedom, police brutality.'[10] As in Italy, the Francoist promotion of football to construct national unity was flawed, as it was through this specific medium that Basque and Catalan nationalism found the best opportunity for public expression.[11] Further mirroring the Italian example, Spanish football was employed to reintegrate the regime into the international community, with South American players of Spanish origin, such as Alfredo Di Stefano, encouraged to return to represent the motherland and dramatically improve its standard of play. National team performances were impressive, although nowhere near as much as Franco's favourite team Real Madrid, which won the European Cup from 1955 to 1960.

In Argentina, President Péron's military dictatorship also exploited football to mobilize the masses' support and divert their attention from the regime's less pleasant aspects. With Péron portrayed as the number one national sportsman, victories dedicated to the leader and his wife, and football and health promoted through the Social Aid Foundation's 'Evita championship', the parallels with Italy were striking. Decimated by defections to European countries, the Argentine national team went neither to the 1949 South American Championships nor the 1950 World Cup, both held in Brazil. According to Tony Mason: 'One possible explanation is that anxiety about defeat led the government to take the decision not to play ... Critics have suggested that by not risking defeat the supporters of Argentinian football could still think their team was the best.'[12]

Success is a powerful drug and the Italian blueprint was and continues to be a source of great inspiration, Silvio Berlusconi's political career arguably representing its latest incarnation. Of course, no sporting achievement could keep the social, economic and political realities of life under the Fascist regime permanently at bay, yet, as argued throughout this book, *calcio*'s inability to mobilize society on a mass, long-term basis was offset by the image that it projected, of life under Fascism, which was often as powerful as the reality.

On the eve of the 1934 World Cup, Mussolini commented on the educational and recreational organizations and facilities that Fascism had created, which had not only sharpened the muscles and minds of the

Italian population but had also won it the right to host the tournament. Leaving the final word to *Lo Sport Fascista* and Mussolini should not be interpreted as an apology for the regime's exploitation of *calcio* and the leisure time of the masses, as this book is primarily concerned with the image and identity that Fascism attempted to create through the game, be this real or imaginary. Hence, the individual best placed effectively to summarize all that the regime hoped to achieve through its politicization of sport and *calcio*, was Mussolini; even if his statement belies reality and truth:

> Fascism did what the old liberalism and the same democracy had always overlooked: it took itself to the people, it went among the peasants, the workers, the farmers, the middle classes, it approached students, the young, it interpreted the needs of the people, it educated them politically and morally, it organized them not only from the professional and economic point of view but also from the military, cultural, educational and recreational perspective.[13]

Notes

Chapter 1 Introduction

1. E. Bianchi, 'Sport (Dall'Italia)', *Giustizia e Libertà*, 10/2/34, p. 50. Reprinted in G. De Donato (ed.) *Carlo Levi 'Coraggio dei Miti. Scritti contemporanei 1922–1974'*, De Donato Editore, 1975, pp. 41–6.
2. 'Saluto alla palla e al tifoso', *Calcio Illustrato*, I, 1, 2/12/31, p. 2.
3. J. Schnapp, *Staging Fascism. 18 BL and the Theater of Masses for Masses*, Stanford University Press, 1996, p. 9.
4. M. Berezin, 'Cultural Form and Political Meaning: State-subsidized Theater, Ideology, and the Language of Style in Fascist Italy', *American Journal of Sociology*, 99, 5, 1994, pp. 1237–86; M. Berezin, 'The Organization of Political Ideology: Culture, State, and the Theater in Fascist Italy', *American Sociological Review*, 56, 5, 1991, pp. 639–51.
5. R. Ben-Ghiat, *Fascist Modernities. Italy, 1922–1945*, University of California Press, 2001, p. 3.
6. See M. Burleigh & W. Wipperman, *The Racial State. Germany 1933–1945*, Cambridge University Press, 1991; C. Ipsen, *Dictating Demography. The Problem of Population in Fascist Italy*, Cambridge University Press, 1996; D. Pick, *Faces of Degeneration. A European Disorder, c.1848–c.1918*, Cambridge University Press, 1989; M.S. Quine, *Population Politics in Twentieth-Century Europe. Fascist Dictatorships and Liberal Democracies*, Routledge, 1996.
7. T.H. Koon, *Believe, Obey, Fight: Political Socialization of Youth in Fascist Italy 1922–1943*, North Carolina University Press, 1985, pp. xx–xxi.
8. V. de Grazia, *The Culture of Consent. Mass Organisation of Leisure in Fascist Italy*, Cambridge University Press, 1981, p. vii.
9. Koon, *Believe, obey, fight*, p. xxi.
10. S. Cavazza, *Piccole Patrie. Feste popolari tra regione e nazione durante il fascismo*, Mulino, 1997.
11. Ibid., p. 7.

12. E. Gentile, 'Fascism as a Political Religion', *Journal of Contemporary History*, 25, 1990, pp. 229–51; E. Gentile, *The Sacralization of Politics in Fascist Italy*, Harvard University Press, 1996.

13. G. Le Bon, *The Crowd. A Study of the Popular Mind*, Ernest Benn, 1947.

14. Schnapp, *Staging Fascism*, p. 8.

15. Berezin, 'Cultural Form and Political Meaning', *American Journal of Sociology*, p. 1259.

16. M.S. Stone, *The Patron State. Culture & Politics in Fascist Italy*, Princeton University Press, 1998, p. 4.

17. M. Berezin, *Making the Fascist Self: The Political Culture of Interwar Italy*, Cornell University Press, 1997, p. 27.

18. Koon, *Believe, obey, fight*, p. 4.

19. For example of Bologna see Chapter 4, pp. 4–5.

20. A. Lyttelton, *The Seizure of Power. Fascism in Italy 1919–1929*, Princeton University Press, 1987, pp. 396–7.

21. G. Berghaus, *Futurism and Politics. Between Anarchist Rebellion and Fascist Reaction, 1909–1944*, Berghahn Books, 1996, p. 229.

22. Lyttelton, *Seizure of Power*, p. 399.

23. For details of government control over the press under Fascism see V. Castronovo & N. Tranfaglia (eds) *La Stampa Italiana nell'età fascista*, Laterza, 1980, pp. 33–91.

24. V. Castronovo & N. Tranfaglia (eds) *La Stampa Italiana del Neocapitalismo*, Laterza, 1976, p. 315.

25. For short biographies of the principal sports journalists of the era see Ibid., pp. 335–7.

Chapter 2 *'Mens sana in corpore sano'*

1. 'Ogni comune deve avere il proprio campo sportivo', *La Nazione*, 18/12/29, p. 5.

2. See S. Pivato, 'Associazionismo Sportivo e Associazionismo Politico nella Romagna d'Inizio Novecento', *Bolletino del Museo del Risorgimento*, 1987–1988, pp. 167–93.

3. I. Bonomi, 'Lo 'sport' e I giovani', *Avanti!*, 29/9/10, pp. 1–2.

4. Ibid., p. 1.

5. S. Wagg, *Giving the Game Away. Football, Politics and Culture on Five Continents*, Leicester University Press, 1995, p. 2.

6. The example of England is used as the world's first industrialized nation.

7. De Sanctis was minister for public instruction in 1878 and from 1879–81.

8. F.M. Varrasi, *Economia, Politica e Sport in Italia (1925–1935)*, Fondazione Artemio Franchi, 1997, p. 116; R. Bassetti, *Storia e storie dello sport in Italia. Dall'unitá a oggi*, Marsilio, 1999, p. 66.

9. Semeria was one of the best-known Italian Catholics in this period. A talented orator, he participated in the First World War as a military chaplain of the Supreme Command in the Udine area. See, Istituto della Enciclopedia Italiana, *Enciclopedia Italiana di Scienze, Lettere ed Arti*, Roma, Istituto Poligrafico di Stato, 1950.

10. P. McCarthy, 'The Beginnings of Italian Sport', *Journal of Modern Italian Studies*, 5, 3, 2000, p. 324.

11. Varrasi, *Economia, Politica e Sport in Italia*, p. 118.

12. A. Ghirelli, *Storia del Calcio in Italia*, Einaudi, 1990, p. 93.

13. Ibid., p. 110.

14. See V.L. Lidtke, *The Alternative Culture: The Socialist Labor Movement in Imperial Germany*, Oxford University Press, 1985.

15. See R. Bellamy (ed.) *Antonio Gramsci. Pre-Prison Writings*, Cambridge University Press, 1994; D. Forgacs (ed.) *The Antonio Gramsci Reader*, New York University Press, 2000; Q. Hoare, & G. Nowell Smith (eds) *Selections From The Prison Notebooks of Antonio Gramsci*, Lawrence and Wishart, 1971; G. Jarvie, & J. Maguire, *Sport and Leisure in Social Thought*, Routledge, 1994.

16. Jarvie & Maguire, Ibid., p. 114.

17. Bassetti, *Storia e storie dello sport*, p. 64.

18. Quoted in Varrasi, *Economia, Politica e Sport in Italia*, p. 112.

19. I. Bonomi, 'Lo 'sport' e I giovani', *Avanti!*, p. 2.

20. Ibid., p. 2.

21. G. Zibordi, 'Lo sport e I giovani. Una lettera di Zibordi', *Avanti!*, 4/10/10, p. 2.

22. A. Balabanoff, 'Lo sport, I giovani e la coscienza rivoluzionaria', *Avanti!*, 11/10/10, pp. 1–2.

23. Ibid., p. 1.

24. See A. Lorenzini, *I ciclisti rossi. I loro scopi e la loro organizzazione*, Tipografia Caravaggese, 1913; S. Pivato, 'Le pigrizie dello storico. Lo sport fra ideolgia, storia e rimozioni', *Italia Contemporanea*, 174, March 1989, pp. 17–27.

25. Varrasi, *Economia, Politica e Sport in Italia*, p. 112. Also see L. Rossi, 'Per la Montagna Contro l'Alcool. Sei anni di alpinismo proletariato in Italia (1921–1926)', *Lancillotto e Nausica*, 2, 1988, pp. 30–5.

26. G. Zanetti & G. Tornabuoni, *Il Giuoco del Calcio. Commento alla legislazione della F.I.G.C*, Ceschina, 1933, p. 64. See also Varrasi, *Economia, Politica e Sport in Italia*, p. 113.

27. 'Un Movimento Tipicamente Italiano. L'U.L.I.C. e i suoi 50.000 giuocatori', *Il Calcio Illustrato*, I, 3, 16/12/31, p. 6.

28. A. Grospierre, 'Gli sports e la folla', *Sport e Proletariato*, 14/7/23, p. 3.

29. Serrati became director of *Avanti* in 1913 after Mussolini's expulsion. A leading maximalist socialist he played an important role in the formation of the PSI that alligned itself to the III International before merging with the Partito Comunista in 1924. See, Istituto della Enciclopedia Italiana, *Lessico Universale Italiano di Lingua Lettere Arti Scienze e Tecnica Vol XX*, Istituto Poligrafico dello Stato, Roma, 1978, p. 597.

30. G.M. Serrati, 'Lo Sport e la classe lavoratrice', *Sport e Proletariato*, 14/7/23, p. 3.

31. 'L'esperienza di' Sport e Proletariato' ', *Lancillotto e Nausica*, 3, 1986, pp. 66–73.

32. 'Lo Sport e la classe lavoratrice', *Sport e Proletariato*, p. 3.

33. Bianchi, 'Sport (Dall'Italia)', *Giustizia e Libertà*, p. 47.

34. Ibid., p. 49.

35. 'Lo Sport e la classe lavoratrice', *Sport e Proletariato*, p. 3.

36. 'Consensi', *Sport e Proletariato*, 8/9/23, p. 1.

37. 'Come e Perché', *Sport e Proletariato*, 14/7/23, p. 1.

38. 'Lo Sport e la classe lavoratrice', *Sport e Proletariato*, p. 3.

39. J. Riordan, 'The worker sports movement', in J. Riordan & A. Kruger (eds) *The International Politics of Sport in the Twentieth Century*, E & FN Spon, 1999, p. 110.

40. Ibid., p. 26.

41. See P. Brantliger, *Bread and Circuses. Theories of Mass Culture as Social Decay*, Cornell University Press, 1983; H. Eichberg, 'Forward race and the laughter of pygmies: on Olympic Sport', in R. Porter & M. Teich (eds) *Fin de Siecle and its Legacy*, Cambridge University Press, 1990; Anon, 'Sport and Decadence', *The Quarterly Review*, 211, 1909, pp. 486–502; T.H. Hodgkin, 'The Fall of the Roman Empire and Its Lessons For Us', *The Contemporary Review*, 73, January 1898, pp. 51–70.

42. 'La cultura e lo sport in un discorso di Lando Ferretti', *Il Littoriale*, 22/1/29, pp. 1–2.

43. Ibid., pp. 1–2.

44. Vittorio Varale quoted in M. Gallian, *Arpinati Politico e Uomo di Sport*, Pinciana, 1928, p. 125.

45. Costante Girardengo was a famous 1920s cyclist.

46. G. Ambrosini, 'Il ciclismo è in decadenza?', *Lo Sport Fascista*, 7, 1928, p. 64.

47. Bianchi, 'Sport (Dall'Italia)', *Giustizia e Libertà*, p. 48.
48. A. Parboni, 'Nel 'Dopolavoro' Riorganizzato', *Lo Sport Fascista*, 3, 1929, p. 7.
49. For example: the Boer War 1899–1902, Franco-Prussian War 1870–1 and Italo-Ethiopian Wars 1887–95.
50. 'Art.I – On the degeneracy of the human race', *The Journal of Psychological Medicine and Mental Pathology'*, X, 1 April 1857, p. 195.
51. D. Pick, *Faces of Degeneration. A European Disorder, c.1848–c.1918*, Cambridge University Press, 1989, p. 114.
52. L. Ferretti, *Esempi e idee per l'Italiano nuovo*, Libreria del Littorio, 1930, p. 201.
53. P. V. Cannistraro (ed.) *Historical Dictionary Of Fascist Italy*, Greenwood Press, 1982, pp. 148–9.
54. Ben-Ghiat, *Fascist Modernities*, p. 7.
55. de Grazia, *The Culture of Consent*, p. 187.
56. Berghaus, *Futurism and Politics*, p. 232.
57. Gentile, 'Fascism as a Political Religion', *Journal of Contemporary History*, p. 245.
58. T. Benton, 'Speaking Without Adjectives: Architecture in the Service of Totalitarianism', D. Ades, T. Benton, D. Elliot & I.B. Whyte, (compiled and selected by) *Art and Power. Europe under the dictators 1930–45*, Thames & Hudson, 1995, p. 36.
59. L. Ferretti, *Il Libro dello Sport*, Libreria del Littorio, 1928, p. 69.
60. 'La cultura e lo sport in un discorso di Lando Ferretti', *Il Littoriale*, pp. 1–2.
61. G.L. Mosse, *The Image of Man. The Creation of Modern Masculinity*, Oxford University Press, 1996, p. 156.
62. Ibid., p. 158.
63. L. Ferretti ,'Guerra e Sport', *Lo Sport Fascista*, 8, 1935, pp. 7–8.
64. 'Nel decennio della Vittoria ricordiamo il contributo dato dallo sport alla guerra ed esaltiamo il sacrificio degli Sportivi caduti sul campo di battaglia', *Lo Sport Fascista*, 5, 1928, p. 42.
65. L. Ferretti, 'Programma', *Lo Sport Fascista,* 6, 1928, p. 4.
66. G. Gorrieri, 'Programma immutato', *Lo Sport Fascista*, 9, 1928, p. 1.
67. 'Al nostro posto', *Lo Sport Fascista*, 7, 1929, p. 1.
68. Ibid., p. 2.
69. Berezin, *Making the Fascist Self*, p. 205.
70. 'Nel decennio della Vittoria', *Lo Sport Fascista*, pp. 43–8.
71. Ibid., pp. 44–5.
72. Ibid., p. 49.

73. 'Nel nome dei morti, per la gloria dei vivi', *Lo Sport Fascista*, 8, 1936, p. 12.

74. Archivio Storico del Comune di Bologna (ASCB), X, 3, 5, 1937, Protocollo Generale 5531, Lettera, Il Presidente F.I.G.C. Direttorio VII° Zona al Podestà di Bologna, 15/2/37.

75. Ibid.

76. ASCB, CA X, 3, 5, 1937, PG.10080, Lettera, Il Presidente F.I.G.C. Direttorio VII° Zona al Podestà di Bologna, 17/3/37.

77. Gallian, *Arpinati*, pp. 42–3. From a bourgeois family, Gallian participated in the occupation of Fiume led by Gabrielle D'Annunzio and went on to become an original *squadrista*, taking part in the March on Rome. Having socialized among Rome's avant-garde where intellectual Fascist ideas were mixed with those of anarchism and the radical left, he developed a prolific literary career studying the merits of Fascist art and culture before writing a history of Fascism. See Istituto della Enciclopedia Italiana, *Dizionario Biografico Degli Italiani Vol 51*, Arti Grafiche Abramo, pp. 637–9.

78. 'Sportivi, date UN DOLLARO alla Patria', *La Striglia Sportiva*, 25/11/25, p. 1.

79. Ibid., p. 1.

80. 'Presentazione', *La Voce Sportiva*, 10/7/24, p. 1.

81. Ibid., p. 1.

82. 'Il Plebiscito. Il dovere degli sportivi', *Il Littoriale*, 25/3/29, p. 1.

83. Gallian, *Arpinati*, p. 190.

84. O. Fantini, 'Sport e Turismo Potenza Nazionale', C.O.N.I., *L'Italia Turistica Annuario Generale. Sport - Turismo - Industrie Applicate*, Edizioni A.E.S.T.I., 1930, p. 13.

85. M. Bontempelli, *L'avventura novecentista*, Vallecchi, 1938, p. 159.

86. V. Varale, 'Per la sanitá della razza', *Lo Sport Fascista*, 3, 1930, p. 1.

87. 'Sport e Italianità', *Il Littoriale*, 3/2/28, pp. 1–2.

88. 'Per la sanità della razza', *Lo Sport Fascista*, p. 2.

89. 'L'on. Arpinati per la razionalizzazione dello sport,' *Il Resto del Carlino*, 26/6/28, p. 3.

90. Ferretti, 'Il Fascismo e l'educazione sportiva della nazione', in G.L. Pomba (ed.) *La Civiltà, fascista illustrata nella dottrina e nelle opere*, Edit. Torinese, 1928, p. 610.

91. 'Sport e Fascismo', *La Gazzetta*, 8/12/26, p. 3.

92. Parboni, 'Il Partito e Lo Sport', C.O.N.I., *L'Italia Turistica*, p. 695.

93. A. Parboni, 'Lo sport nella concezione fascista', *Lo Sport Fascista*, 6, 1928, pp. 4–5.

94. For further details on Italian education policy see Koon, *Believe,*

Obey, Fight.
95. Mosse, *The Image of Man*, p. 39.
96. E.M. Gray, 'Lo Sport e la Patria', *La Gazzetta*, 24/8/26, p. 1.
97. V. Costa, 'Un'opera veramente Fascista: l'istruzione preatletica nelle scuole di Bologna', *Lo Sport Fascista*, 4, 1929, pp. 11–12.
98. Ferretti, *Il Libro dello Sport*, p. 69.
99. For a brief history of his career see Cannistraro, *Historical Dictionary Of Fascist Italy*, p. 224.
100. 1906–1914 CONI was known as the International Committee for the Olympic Games.
101. P. Dogliani, 'Sport and Fascism', *Journal of Modern Italian Studies*, 5, 3, 2000, p. 329.
102. 'I giovani e la politica', *Lo Sport Fascista*, III, 10, 1930, p. 1.
103. Ferretti, *Il libro dello sport*, pp. 63–4.
104. Ferretti, *Esempi e idee*, p. 191.
105. J. Schnapp (ed.) *A Primer of Italian Fascism*, University of Nebraska Press, 2000, p. 140.
106. Ferretti, *Esempi e idee*, pp. 193–4.
107. 'La cultura e lo sport in un discorso di Lando Ferretti', *Il Littoriale*, 22/1/29, pp. 1–2.
108. de Grazia, *The culture of consent*, p. 188.
109. Lyttelton, *Seizure of Power*, pp. 404–5.
110. Koon, *Believe, Obey, Fight*, p. 33.
111. Lyttelton, *Seizure of Power*, p. 407.
112. Ibid., p. 407.
113. See 'Sport and Fascism', *Journal of Modern Italian Studies*, p. 328; Ferrara, *Italia in Palestra*, pp. 218–22.
114. P. Ferrara, *L'Italia in palestra. Storia documenti e immagini della ginnastica dal 1833 al 1973*, La Meridiana, 1992, p. 219.
115. 'Un'opera veramente Fascista', *Lo Sport Fascista*, p. 14.
116. V. de Grazia, *How Fascism Ruled Women. Italy 1922–1945*, University of California Press, 1992, pp. 218–19.
117. Ibid., p. 12.
118. For more details see Società Sportiva di Bologna (ed.) *Il Littoriale*, Bologna, Tipografia Paolo Neri, 1931, pp. 23–32.
119. 'L'Arte medica nella educazione fisica e nello sport', *Lo Sport Fascista*, 8, 1929, pp. 17–18; 'Sport and Fascism', *Journal of Modern Italian Studies*, p. 332.
120. 'Bologna All'Avanguardia. Il controllo medico degli atleti', *Il Littoriale*, 5/10/28, p. 1.
121. 'L'on. Arpinati per la razionalizzazione dello sport', *Il Resto del Carlino*, p. 3.

122. 'Il Convegno dei medici sportivi inaugurato da S.E. Arpinati', *Il Resto del Carlino*, 29/10/29, p. 4.

123. Ibid., p. 1.

124. Ibid., p. 1.

125. D. Horn, *Social Bodies. Science, Reproduction, and Italian Modernity*, Princeton University Press, 1994, p. 24.

126. 'Lo stadio di Roma aperto al popolo', *Lo Sport Fascista*, 4, 1931, pp. 36–9.

127. See Horn, *Social Bodies*.

128. For the history of this medical symbolism prior to the twentieth century see R. Nye, 'Degeneration and the medical model of cultural crisis in the *French Belle Epoque*', in S. Drescher, D. Sabean & A. Sharlin (eds) *Political symbolism in Modern Europe*, Transaction Books, 1982.

129. Horn, *Social Bodies*, p. 23. Notes to Chapter II, no.10, 'Mussolini, for example, likened Italian society to a cancer-ridden body and himself to an uncompromising surgeon. Mussolini's use of medical metaphor dates from his involvement with socialism before the war.' See also A. Simonini, *Il linguaggio di Mussolini*, Bompiani, 1978; H. Ellwanger, *Sulla lingua di Mussolini*, Mondadori, 1941.

130. Ibid., p. 26.

131. See Lyttelton, *Seizure of Power*, pp. 121–48.

132. Quoted in Horn, *Social Bodies*, p. 44.

133. See E. Susmel & D. Susmel (eds) *Opera Omnia di Benito Mussolini XXII*, La Fenice, 1957, p. 367; Horn, *Social Bodies*, p. 49.

134. Susmel & Susmel, *Opera Omnia*, p. 361 & 68. For a discussion of the address and Italian demographic programs, see D.V. Glass, *Population Policies and Movements in Europe*, Clarendon Press, 1940; P. Meldini, *Sposa e madre esemplare: Ideologia e politica della donna e della famiglia durante il fascismo*, Guaraldi, 1975; M.S. Quine *Italy's Social Revolution. Charity and Welfare from Liberalism to Fascism*, Palgrave, 2002; M.S. Quine, *Population Politics in Twentieth-Century Europe. Fascist Dictatorships and Liberal Democracies*, Routledge, 1996; E. Santarelli, *Storia del movimento e del regime fascista*, Editori Riuniti, 1967.

135. Horn, *Social Bodies*, p. 49.

136. Ibid., p. 57.

137. de Grazia, *How Fascism Ruled Women*, pp. 53–4.

138. For further discussions on the politics of Ricci and the ONB see: P. Bartoli, C. Pasquini Romizi, R. Romizi (eds) *L'organizzazione del consenso nel regime fascista: l'Opera Nazionale Balilla come istituzione di controllo sociale*, Istituto di etnologia e antropologia

culturale della Universita degli studi, 1983; C. Betti, *L'opera Nazionale Balilla e l'educazione Fascista*, La Nuova Italia, 1984; Koon, *Believe, Obey, Fight*; R. Scarpa, *Eravamo tutti balilla*, Ciarrapico, 1984; S. Setta, *Renato Ricci. Dallo squadrismo alla repubblica Sociale Italiana*, Il Mulino, 1986.

139. A. Teja, 'Italian sport and international relations under fascism', in P. Arnaud & J. Riordan, *Sport and International Politics*, E & FN Spon, 1998, p. 150.
140. 'I giovani e la politica', *Lo Sport Fascista*, p. 2.
141. For the principal points of the *Carta dello Sport*, see F. Fabrizio, *Sport e Fascismo*, pp. 39–42.
142. 'Il testo della Carta dello Sport', *Lo Sport Fascista*, 1, 1929, p. 5.
143. 'Sport and Fascism', *Journal of Modern Italian Studies*, pp. 329–30.
144. 'La costituzione dell'Istituto Fascista di Cultura', *La Nazione*, 16/1/29, p. 4.
145. de Grazia, *The Culture of Consent*, p. 188.
146. Commissione Reale per lo studio di un progetto relativo all'ordinamento dell'educazione fisica, see Ferrara, *Italia in palestra*, p. 223.
147. 'L'ordinamento del C.O.N.I., secondo le direttive dell'on Turati', *La Nazione*, 12/10/28, p. 6.
148. Archivio Centrale dello Stato (ACS), PCM 1928–30, f.3.2.5. n.4301, 'Pro-Memoria', 15/9/28, pp. 3–4.
149. A. Parboni, 'Gli Enti Sportivi Provinciali Fascisti', C.O.N.I., *Italia Turistica*, p. 695.
150. Ibid., p. 695.
151. A. Parboni, 'La Soppressione Degli Enti S.P.F.', C.O.N.I., *Italia Turistica*, p. 696.
152. Ibid., p. 697.
153. Bianchi, 'Sport (Dall'Italia)', *Giustizia e Libertà*, p. 48.
154. L. Ferretti, 'Il Fascismo e l'educazione sportiva della nazione', *La Civiltà*, p. 611.
155. 'Sport e Turismo Potenza Nazionale', C.O.N.I., *Italia Turistica*, p. 12.
156. ACS, PCM 1928–30, f.3.2.5. n.4301, 'Pro-memoria', 15/9/28, p. 1.
157. 'Nel 'Dopolavoro' riorganizzato', *Lo Sport Fascista*, 3, 1929, p. 7.
158. 'Sport e Turismo Potenza Nazionale', C.O.N.I., *Italia Turistica*, p. 13.
159. 'L'ordinamento del C.O.N.I,' *La Nazione*, p. 6.
160. de Grazia, *The Culture of Consent*, p. 195.
161. Bianchi, 'Sport (Dall'Italia)', *Giustizia e Libertà*, p. 49.
162. 'Lo sport del Dopolavoro', *Lo Stadio*, 4/12/32, p. 2.
163. *Il Bargello*, 26/4/31, p. 2.

164. Teja, 'Italian sport and international relations under fascism', *Sport and International Politics* p. 165.
165. A. Parboni, 'Lo sport nella vita della nazioni', C.O.N.I., *Italia Turistica*, p. 692.
166. Ibid., pp. 693–4.
167. Ferretti, 'Guerra e Sport', *Lo Sport Fascista*, p. 7.
168. Ibid., p. 1.
169. Ibid., p. 1.
170. A. Cotronei, 'La battaglia delle razze', *La Gazzetta*, 7/7/24, p. 1
171. 'Il CONI e la sua opera', *Lo Sport Fascista*, 9, 1928, p. 4.
172. 'L'Associazione Fiorentina del Calcio', *Firenze: Rassegna del Comune*, June 1934, p. 188.
173. A. Cotronei, 'Fascismo e lo sport', *La Gazzetta*, 25/12/26, p. 1.
174. 'Lo Sport dell'Italia Fascista osservato, studiato ed esaltato dalla stampa straniera', *La Gazzetta*, 4/1/34, p. 1.
175. Bianchi, 'Sport (Dall'Italia)', *Giustizia e Libertà*, pp. 47–8.
176. Gallian, *Arpinati*, p. 61.
177. PNF, *Campo Sportivo del Littorio*, Libreria del Littorio, 1928, p. 4, in ACS, CA 1928–30, f.3.2.5, n.2294, 'Campi Sportivi del Littorio'.
178. 'Educazione fisica e Fascismo', *Lo Sport Fascista*, 4, 1931, p. 57.
179. A. Kruger, "Buying victories is positively degrading.' European origins of government pursuit of national prestige through sport', J.A. Mangan (ed.) *Tribal Identities. Nationalism, Europe, Sport*, Frank Cass, 1996, p. 183.
180. 'Sport e Turismo Potenza Nazionale', C.O.N.I., *Italia Turistica*, p. 14
181. ACS, PCM 1928–30, f.3.2.5. n.2294, 'Campi Sportivi del Littorio', 6/9/27. For the numerous responses from communes throughout the peninsula see folder 'Istituzione dei Campi Sportivi del Littorio'.
182. ACS, PCM 1928–30, f.3.2.5. n.3344, circolare n.19, 18/8/27.
183. P.N.F., *Campo sportivo del Littorio*, Libreria del Littorio, 1928, p. 6. See also 'Ogni comune deve avere il proprio campo sportivo', *La Nazione*, 18/12/29, p. 5.

Chapter 3 Fascist Football Foundations

1. F. Muzzi, 'Cinquecentomila', *Lo Sport Fascista*, 1, 1930, pp. 2–3.
2. Schnapp, *Staging Fascism*, p. 45.
3. A. Papa, & G. Panico, *Storia sociale del calcio in Italia. Dai club pionieri alla nazione sportiva (1887–1945)*, Il Mulino, 1993, p. 116.
4. 'Quel che dice il cassiere federale sulla situazione finanziaria della FIGC', *La Gazzetta*, 23/4/26, p. 3.
5. Ibid., p. 3.

6. 'La preoccupante situazione delle finanze federali', *La Gazzetta*, 4/5/26, p. 3.
7. 'Quel che dice il cassiere', *La Gazzetta*, p. 3.
8. 'Che sará del football italiano', *La Gazzetta*, 18/6/26, p. 1.
9. 'Football', *La Voce Sportiva*, 9/4/25, p. 1.
10. 'Treno speciale per il match Juventus-Bologna', *Il Resto*, 22/7/26, p. 2.
11. 'Treno Ross-Blu', *La Vita Sportiva*, 30/7/26, p. 3.
12. See 'Il problema arbitrale', *La Voce Sportiva*, 4/7/25, p. 2.
13. N.S. Onofri & V. Ottani, *Dal Littoriale allo Stadio. Storia per immagini dell'impianto sportivo bolognese*, Consorzio Cooperative Costruzioni, 1990, p. 19; 'I 'Genoa-Bologna' del '25 e la sparatoria di Torino', *La Gazzetta*, 12/11/73, p. 4.
14. 'Verso il Girone Unico', *La Grande Storia del Calcio Italiano*, 4, 20/2/65, p. 89.
15. 'Intendiamoci', *La Voce Sportiva*, 12/6/25, p. 1.
16. Ibid., p. 1.
17. Ibid., p. 1.
18. Ibid., p. 1.
19. 'Verso il Girone Unico', *La Grande Storia del Calcio*, p. 89.
20. 'Seguendo la nostra strada', *La Vita Sportiva*, 17/6/26, p. 1.
21. 'Casale – Torino: 2–1 (0–1)', *La Gazzetta*, 8/2/26, p. 5.
22. 'I provvedimenti', *La Gazzetta*, 28/4/26, p. 2.
23. 'Il campionato italiano. Verso l'epilogo', *La Gazzetta*, 15/5/26, p. 5.
24. 'I provvedimenti', *La Gazzetta*, p. 2.
25. Ibid., p. 2.
26. 'Casale – Torino', *La Gazzetta*, 29/5/26, p. 4.
27. 'Le vicende del mancato incontro Casale – Torino', *La Gazzetta*, 31/5/26, p. 2.
28. Ghirelli, *Storia del Calcio*, p. 88.
29. 'L'A.I.A. invita I propri soci a restituire la tessera', *La Gazzetta*, 31/5/26, p. 5.
30. Ibid., p. 5.
31. 'Seguendo la nostra strada', *La Vita Sportiva*, p. 1.
32. 'Crisi di Campionato', *La Gazzetta*, 1/6/26, p. 3.
33. 'Che sará del football italiano', *La Gazzetta*, 18/6/26, p. 1.
34. Ibid., p. 1.
35. 'La vertenza degli arbitri verso la soluzione per l'intervento del C.O.N.I.', *La Gazzetta*, 2/6/26, p. 1.
36. 'I pensiero del Presidente del C.O.N.I., per una ripresa normale della vita calcistica e sull'attivitá sportiva nazionale', *La Gazzetta*, 27/7/26, p. 3.

37. 'La vertenza degli arbitri', *La Gazzetta*, p. 1.
38. 'La situazione del football italiano', *La Gazzetta*, 1/7/26, p. 1.
39. Ibid., p. 1.
40. 'I pensiero del Presidente', *La Gazzetta*, p. 3.
41. Ibid., p. 3.
42. 'Il C.O.N.I. ha nominato gli esperti', *La Gazzetta*, 8/7/26, p. 3.
43. Zanetti & Tornabuoni, *Il Giuoco del Calcio*, p. 24.
44. Ghirelli, *Storia del Calcio*, p. 90.
45. Zanetti & Tornabuoni, *Il Giuoco del Calcio*, p. 28.
46. 'L'on Ferretti illustra la riforma calcistica', *La Gazzetta*, 5/8/26, p. 5.
47. Zanetti & Tornabuoni, *Il Giuoco del Calcio*, p. 63.
48. For a detailed discussion of these changes see 'Campi Sportivi', *Il Bargello*, 2 & 30/8/31 and 6/9/31.
49. 'Gli Arbitri del Duce', *Il Bargello*, 16/2/30, p. 2.
50. See 'Sistemiamo I Campionati', *La Voce Sportiva*, 26/6/25, p. 1.
51. 'L'on Ferretti illustra la riforma', *La Gazzetta*, 5/8/26, p. 3.
52. FIGC, *Annuario Italiano Giuoco del Calcio*, Tipo. Modenese, 1928, p. 145.
53. 'Il riasetto della F.I.G.C', *La Gazzetta*, 3/8/26, p. 1.
54. 'Nelle conversazioni di Bruxelles presenti 14 nazioni il problema del dilettantismo é discusso ma non risolto', *La Gazzetta*, 15/3/26, p. 4.
55. 'L'on Ferretti illustra la riforma', *La Gazzetta.*, p. 3.
56. ACS, PCM 1928–30, f.3.2.5. n.4301, 'Pro-Memoria', 15/9/28, p. 1.
57. 'Un problema morale e sportivo', *Lo Sport Fascista*, 8, 1929, p. 50.
58. 'Le 'mediocritá' e le liste di trasferimento', *La Nazione*, 5/8/30, p. 5.
59. 'Un problema morale', *Lo Sport Fascista*, p. 50.
60. 'Le' mediocritá e le liste', *La Nazione*, p. 5.
61. 'Un problema morale', *Lo Sport Fascista, pp.* 50–1.
62. Ibid., p. 51.
63. FIGC, *Annuario Italiano Giuoco del Calcio*, 1928, p. 144.
64. 'Dopo il discorso Turati', *Lo Sport Fascista*, 9, 1928, p. 6.
65. 'Un problema morale', *Lo Sport Fascista*, pp. 51–2.
66. 'Le' mediocritá' e le liste di trasferimento', *La Nazione,* p. 5.
67. 'I problemi del Calcio nazionale nelle chiare parole dell'on Arpinati', *Il Littoriale*, 23/1/29, p. 3.
68. FIGC, *Annuario Italiano Giuoco del Calcio*, 1928, p. 145.
69. 'L'on Ferretti illustra la riforma', *La Gazzetta*, p. 3.
70. Zanetti & Tornabuoni, *Il Giuoco del Calcio*, p. 175.
71. ACS, PCM 1928–30, f.3.2.5. n.3941, Fonogramma n.20930,

124. 'Problemi e questioni sportive in terra redenta', *La Gazzetta*, 5/5/26, p. 5.
125. ASCB, CA X, 3, 5, 1925, PG.17159, Lettera, Club Sportivo 'Olimpia' Fiume to Il Sindaco di Bologna, 1/5/25.
126. 'Epurare lo Sport', *Il Bargello*, 15/12/29, p. 2.
127. ACS, PS 1929, b.180, D.14 Sports e Gare, 'Regia Prefettura di Forlì al Ministero dell'Intero', 16/4/29, p. 1.
128. ACS, PS 1929, b.180, D.14 Sports e Gare, 'Questura di Roma, Pro-Memoria', 14/6/29, p. 1.
129. ACS, PS 1929, b.180, D.14 Sports e Gare, 'L' 'ultima' del Campionato di calcio: Napoli contro Lazio', *Il Piccolo*, 12/6/29.
130. ACS, PS 1929, b.180, D.14 Sports e Gare, 'Lotta senza quartiere', *Il Popolo di Roma*, 14/6/29.
131. ACS, PS 1929, b.180, D.14 Sports e Gare, 'Incontro calcistico 'Lazio Napoli'', 18/6/29.
132. ACS, PS 1929, b.180, D.14 Sports e Gare, 'Fonogramma in arrivo', 16/6/29.
133. ACS, PS 1932, Sez.II, b.59, f.D 242 Gare sportive, Prefettura di Cosenza al Ministero del Interno, 8/3/32, pp. 1–2.
134. ACS, PS 1929, b.180, D.14 Sports e Gare 'Questura di Roma, Pro-Memoria', 14/6/29, pp. 2–3.
135. See M. Bontempelli, 'Tifo e tifi diversi', in F. Ciampitti & G. Titta Rosa, *Prima antologia degli scrittori sportivi*, R. Carabba, 1934.
136. Bianchi, 'Sport (Dall'Italia)', pp. 46–7.

Chapter 4 Building the Future

1. G. De Finetti, 'Gli otto stadi del Campionato del mondo', *Lo Sport Fascista*, 7, 1934, p. 31.
2. Berezin, *Making the Fascist Self*, p. 7.
3. Bontempelli, *L'avventura novecentista*, p. 381.
4. Gentile, *The Sacralization of Politics*, 1996.
5. Bontempelli, *L'avventura novecentista*, p. 163.
6. Benton, 'Speaking without adjectives', D. Ades, T. Benton, D. Elliot & I.B. Whyte (compiled and selected by), *Art and Power. Europe under the dictators*, Thames & Hudson, p. 36.
7. For further details of conditions see Ferrara, *Italia in Palestra*, pp. 188–94.
8. F. Muzzi, 'I campi sportivi comunali', *Lo Sport Fascista*, 8, 1929, p. 4.
9. Terzino, 'Per gli Stadî Municipali', *Sport e Proletariato*, 11/8/23, p. 1.

10. Ibid., p. 1.
11. 'Alcuni dati per le costruzioni sportive', *Casabella*, December 1933, p. 14.
12. Legge 21 giugno 1928, n.1580 (Pubbl. G.U. 18–7–1928, n.166), 'Provvedimenti per la costruzione dei campi sportivi'.
13. PNF, *Campo Sportivo del Littorio*.
14. 'Si costruisce', *Lo Sport Fascista*, 11, 1929, p. 2.
15. 'Ogni comune deve avere il proprio campo sportivo', *La Nazione*, p. 5.
16. ACS, PCM 1928–30, f.3.2.5. n.3344, circolare n.19, 18/8/27.
17. 'Problemi atletici regionali. I campi sportivi', *Il Bargello*, 12/1/30, p. 2.
18. 'I campi sportivi in Italia e la necessità di vigilarne la costruzione', *La Gazzetta*, 18/4/30, p. 3.
19. 'I campi sportivi comunali', *Lo Sport Fascista*, p. 5.
20. 'Problemi atletici regionali', *Il Bargello*, p. 2.
21. Ibid., p. 5.
22. 'I campi sportivi comunali', *Lo Sport Fascista*, p. 6.
23. 'Problemi atletici regionali', *Il Bargello*, p. 2.
24. 'Alcuni Dati', *Casabella*, p. 14.
25. 'I campi sportivi in Italia', *Lo Sport Fascista*, p. 3.
26. Ibid., p. 3.
27. Ibid., p. 3.
28. 'Cinquecentomila', *Lo Sport Fascista*, pp. 1–2.
29. 'Il Campionato del mondo 1933 assegnato all'unanimità all'Italia dal congresso di Zurigo', *La Gazzetta*, 9/10/32, p. 3.
30. G. De Finetti, *Stadi. Esempi – Tendenze – Progetti*, Hoepli, 1934, Prefazione.
31. Ibid., Prefazione.
32. F. Fabrizio, *Sport e Fascismo. La Politica Sportiva del Regime 1924–1936*, Guaraldi, 1976, p. 23.
33. Archivio Storico del Comune di Firenze (ASCF), Belle Arti (BA) 115, Registro Generale (RG) 5711, CONI, Commissione Impianti Sportivi, 'Regolamento', 1934, p. 8.
34. Ibid., p. 5.
35. Ibid., p. 6.
36. Zanetti & Tornabuoni, *Il Giuoco del Calcio*, p. 133.
37. CONI, Commissione Impianti Sportivi, 'Regolamento', pp. 5–6.
38. Ibid., pp. 10–11.
39. Ibid., p. 15.
40. Ibid., p. 10.
41. ACSF, 'Regolamento', p. 12.

42. Ades et al., *Art and Power*, p. 38.
43. ACSF, 'Regolamento', p. 6.
44. Quoted in Ades et al., *Art and Power*, p. 39.
45. 'Un Programma d'Architettura', *Quadrante*, May 1933, p. 5.
46. Ibid., pp. 5–6.
47. Ibid., p. 6.
48. P.L. Nervi, 'Problemi dell'Architetto', *Casabella*, May 1933, p. 34.
49. Ibid., p. 34.
50. ACSF, BA, 115, G. Barbero, 'Architettura Sportiva', *La Città Nuova*, 5, 5/3/34, p. 4.
51. 'La Nuova Architettura', *La Città Nuova*, 6/2/32, p. 4.
52. Ibid., p. 4.
53. See 'Casa per la gioventù', *Parametro. Rivista internazionale di architettura e urbanistica*, 172, May–June 1989. Issue dedicated to design of Fascist youth clubs and Balilla clubs.
54. Gentile, 'Fascism as a Political Religion', *Journal of Contemporary History*, p. 246.
55. ACS, PCM 1928–30, f.3.2.5. n.33125, Memorandum, 15/11/28, p. 2.
56. Ibid., p. 3.
57. E. Bianchini, R. Fagnoni, D. Ortensi, 'Lo stadio Mussolini a Torino', *Casabella*, December 1933, p. 26.
58. Ibid., p. 26.
59. De Finetti, *Stadi. Esempi*, p. 73, refers to praise from respected German architects regarding more than one aspect of the stadium's design.
60. 'Lo Stadio Littorio a Torino', *La Gazzetta*, 5/10/32, p. 5.
61. ACS, PCM 1934–36, f.20.1. n.7113, 'Proposta per intitolare il Campo Sportivo di Napoli', 20/4/34, p. 1.
62. ACS, PCM 1934–36, f.20.1. n.152559, 'Appunto', 3/5/34.
63. Ibid., p. 5.
64. 'Uno studio per le manifestazioni sportive a Tripoli', *La Nazione*, 14/8/30, p. 6.
65. ACS, PCM 1928–30, f.3.2.5. n.33125, Memorandum, 15/11/28, p. 6.
66. Ibid., p. 6.
67. For a discussion of the development of stadium design see F. Agostinelli, 'Stadi / Dalle Prime Olimpiadi Moderne Ai Campionati Del Mondo di Calcio del 1934', *Parametro*, 172, May-June 1989; De Finetti, *Stadi. Esempi*; E. Del Debbio, *Progetti di costruzione Case Balillà, Palestre, Campi Sportivi, Piscine*, Palazzo Viminale, 1930; S. San Pietro (ed.) *1990: Stadi in Italia*, L'archivolta, 1990.

68. San Pietro, *1990: Stadi in Italia*, p. 10.
69. G. De Finetti, 'Stadi antichi e moderni', *Casabella*, December 1933, p. 2.
70. De Finetti, *Stadi. Esempi*, pp. 15–16.
71. San Pietro, *1990: Stadi in Italia*, p. 31.
72. Ibid., pp. 22–3.
73. 'Stadi antichi', *Casabella*, p. 3.
74. Ben-Ghiat, *Fascist Modernities*, p. 4.
75. V. Orazi, 'La Città Eterna', *La Città Nuova*, 5/1/34, p. 5.
76. Ibid., p. 309.
77. San Pietro, *1990: Stadi in Italia*, p. 309.
78. 'Foro Mussolini sorto a Roma per realizzare l'educazione fisica totalitaria', *La Gazzetta*, 3/11/32, p. 3.
79. Ibid., p. 6.
80. 'Fascism as a Political Religion', *Journal of Contemporary History*, p. 247. Also, see AA.VV. *E42: Utopia e scenario del regime*, Marsilio, 1987.
81. Ibid., p. 246.
82. ACSF, BA 115, Fillia, 'Intransigenza', *La Citta Nuova*, 5, 5/3/34, p. 1.
83. Ibid., p. 1.
84. ACSF, BA 117, 'Architettura', *La Città Nuova*, 6, 20/3/34, p. 1.
85. Ibid., p. 1.
86. De Finetti, *Stadi. Esempi*, p. 81.
87. 'Intransigenza', *La Citta Nuova*, p. 1.
88. See F. Legnani, 'Via Roma, 1936–1937', in G. Gresleri and P.G. Massaretti (eds). *Norma e arbitro. Architetti e ingegneri a Bologna 1850–1950*, Bologna, Marsilio, 2000, pp. 287–97.
89. 'Architettura', *La Citta Nuova*, p. 1.
90. 'Intransigenza', *La Citta Nuova*, p. 1.
91. Ibid., p. 1.
92. 'Arte Fascista. I concorsi del C.O.N.I. per opere di pittura e di scultura', *La Gazzetta*, 20–21/1/34, p. 1.
93. G. Pagano, 'Politica e architettura', *Casabella*, April 1935, p. 2.
94. Ibid., p. 3.
95. Berghaus, *Futurism and Politics*, p. 233.
96. 'Dalla Seduta del 20–V-XII', *Casabella*, June 1934, p. 3.
97. 'Comunicato Stefani Del 10–VI-XII', Ibid., p. 3.
98. G. Pagano, 'Mussolini Salva L'Architettura', *Casabella*, June 1934, p. 2.
99. Ben-Ghiat, *Fascist Modernities*, p. 9.
100. 'Alcuni Dati', *Casabella*, p. 14.

101. Ibid., p. 14.
102. Lyttelton, *The Seizure of Power*, p. 364.
103. A. Asor Rosa, *Storia d'Italia, Dall'Unità a oggi, 2, La Cultura*, Einaudi, 1975, p. 1383.
104. Quoted in A. James Gregor, *Interpretations of Fascism*, General Learning Press, 1974, p. 88.
105. Le Bon, *The Crowd*, p. 23.
106. Ibid., p. 27.
107. Ibid., p. 30.
108. R. Nye, *The Origins of Crowd Psychology. Gustave Le Bon and the Crisis of Mass Democracy in the Third Republic*, Sage, 1975, p. 79.
109. J. Van Ginneken, *Crowds, Psychology, and Politics 1871–1899*, Cambridge University Press, 1992, p. 176.
110. Le Bon, *The Crowd*, p. 118.
111. Ibid., p. 19. On revolutionary crowds see G. Rudé, *The Crowd in the French Revolution*, Oxford University Press, 1959.
112. S. Barrows, *Distorting Mirrors. Visions of the Crowd in Late Nineteenth-Century France*, Yale University Press, 1981, p. 173.
113. Schnapp, *Staging Fascism*, p. 32.
114. Ibid., p. 18.
115. Ibid., p. 18.
116. Ibid., p. 25.
117. B. Mussolini, 'Certezza Nelle Forze Dello Spirito e Dell' Intelligenza Italiana', *Quadrante*, June 1933, p. 1.
118. On previous attempts at creating/theorizing utopian theatre see Schnapp, *Staging Fascism*, pp. 8–12; Berghaus, *Fascism and Theatre*.
119. Schnapp, *Staging Fascism*, p. 43.
120. G. Ciocca, '(Servizi a Mussolini) Il Teatro di Masse', *Quadrante*, July 1933, p. 7.
121. Ibid., p. 10.
122. Schnapp, *Staging Fascism*, p. 38.
123. 'Gli otto stadi del Campionato del mondo', *Lo Sport Fascista*, p. 33.
124. 'L'equivoco dello spettacolo di masse', *La Nazione*, 12/5/34, p. 5.
125. Schnapp, *Staging Fascism*, p. 79.
126. Ibid., p. 83, note 2.
127. 'Il Duce e lo sport', *Il Bargello*, 14/12/30, p. 2.
128. 'QUOTE', *Il Bargello*, 26/4/31, p. 2.
129. Stone, *The Patron State*, p. 6.

Chapter 5 Arpinati, Bologna, *Calcio*: The ABC to Success

1. L. Arpinati, 'Il Littoriale', *Lo Sport Fascista*, 1, 1928, p. 13.
2. Gallian, *Arpinati*, p. 13. For biographical detail of Gallian see Chapter 2, Note 77.
3. For more on this argument see Gentile, *The Sacralization of Politics in Fascist Italy*.
4. Ibid., p. 14.
5. 'Le feconda attività del Fascismo Bolognese', *Il Resto del Carlino*, 24/10/24, p. 5.
6. 'Il Littoriale: ideato, voluto', *L'Assalto*, p. 3.
7. P. Lanfranchi and M. Taylor, *Moving with the Ball. The Migration of Professional Footballers*, Berg, 2001, p. 195.
8. Another suggestion is that he avoided the war as the eldest son of a widow. D. Susmel, 'Il Ras del Pallone', *Domenica del Corriere*, 69, 36, 29/8/67, p. 16.
9. For detailed accounts of the Fascist rise to power see Lyttelton, *Seizure of Power*, 1987; R. De Felice, *La Conquista del Potere (1919–1925)*, Einaudi, 1995; E. Ragionieri, *Dalla dittatura fascista alla liberazione 1926–1945*, Einaudi, 1978.
10. Lyttelton, *Seizure of Power*, p. 60.
11. Ibid., p. 38.
12. Onofri & Ottani, *Dal Littoriale allo Stadio*, p. 13; M. Grimaldi, *Leandro Arpinati. Un anarchico alla corte di Mussolini*, Società Stampa Sportiva, 1999, p. 23, quotes the dead at 9.
13. M.M. 'Arpinati', *Lo Sport Fascista*, 10, 1929, p. 9.
14. Grimaldi, *Leandro Arpinati*, p. 13.
15. G. Cantamessa Arpinati, *Arpinati Mio Padre*, Il Sagittario, 1968, pp. 23–4.
16. 'Arpinati', *Lo Sport Fascista*, p. 9.
17. V. Pozzo, 'Il fallimento del calcio italiano', *Successo*, 2, 1959, pp. 107–8.
18. For a detailed discussion of the entire affair see N.S. Onofri, *I Giornali Bolognesi Nel Ventennio Fascista*, Moderna, 1972, pp. 83–122; U. Bellocchi, *Il Resto del Carlino. Giornale di Bologna*, Società Editoriale' Resto del Carlino', pp. 133–46.
19. Onofri, *I Giornali Bolognesi*, p. 104.
20. Cantamessa Arpinati, *Arpinati Mio Padre*, p. 52.
21. Bellocchi, *Il Resto del Carlino*, p. 134.
22. Cantamessa Arpinati, *Arpinati Mio Padre*, p. 55.
23. Arpinati apparently gained the entire package of shares on 16 June

1933, although there is a suggestion they may have been owned by his loyal friend Germano Mastellari. See Onofri, *I Giornali Bolognesi*, p. 116.

24. Onofri, *I Giornali Bolognesi*, p. 53.
25. Lyttelton, *Seizure of Power*, pp. 394–7.
26. Zanetti & Tornabuoni, *Il Giuoco del Calcio*, p. 57.
27. Onofri, *I Giornali Bolognesi*, p. 106.
28. ASCB, Ex-Casa del Fascio, I, 2, 1, 'Comunicato ai Giornali', 26/12/26, p. 2.
29. Ibid., p. 2.
30. Ibid., p. 3.
31. Gallian, *Arpinati*, p. 8.
32. Ibid., p. 34.
33. Grimaldi, *Leandro Arpinati*, p. 82.
34. See Chapter 7, p. 188, n. 97.
35. Cited in Cantamessa Arpinati, *Arpinati Mio Padre*, p. 102.
36. Ibid., pp. 97–8.
37. Gallian, *Arpinati*, p. 42.
38. Ibid., p. 48.
39. De Finetti, *Stadi. Esempi*, p. 63.
40. Gallian, *Arpinati*, pp. 24–5.
41. '"Il Littoriale"', *L'Assalto*, 31/7/26, p. 3.
42. Onofri & Ottani, *Dal Littoriale allo Stadio*, p. 13.
43. Varrasi, *Economia,Politica e Sport in Italia*, p. 251.
44. F. Cristofori, *Bologna gente e vita dal 1914 al 1945*, Edizioni ALFA, 1980, p. 136.
45. ASCB, CA X, 3, 5, 1925, Letter: 9815, Leandro Arpinati, Il Segretario politico, P.N.F., Fascio di Bologna, to Il Sindaco del Comune di Bologna, 25/3/25.
46. Ibid.
47. Ibid.
48. ASCB, CA X, 3, 5, 1925, 'Tornata II della sessione consigliare straordinaria', 20/7/25, p. 2.
49. Ibid., p. 3.
50. Ibid., pp. 3–4.
51. Ibid., p. 4.
52. 'I Campi Sportivi di Bologna Fascista', *L'Assalto*, 28/10/32, p. 7.
53. Ibid., p. 7.
54. 'Arpinati', *Calcio Illustrato*, I, 1, 2/12/31, p. 3.
55. 'Saluto', *La Sberla Sportiva*, I, 9/3/33, p. 1.
56. Interview with Professor G. Gresleri, University of Bologna, 20/8/2001.

57. ASCB, CA X, 3, 5, 1925, Letter: 9815, Leandro Arpinati, Il Segretario politico, P.N.F. Fascio di Bologna, to Il Sindaco del Comune di Bologna, 25/3/25.

58. Comité Organisateur des Championnats de Natation, Plongeons et Water Polo (ed.) *Bologne et le Littoriale*, Stabilimenti Poligrafici Riuniti, 1927, p. 6.

59. 'Il Campo polisportivo', *Il Comune di Bologna*, p. 443.

60. 'Un Primato', *Il Resto del Carlino*, p. 4.

61. Ibid., p. 4.

62. 'L'inaugurazione del Littoriale segna un superbo trionfo del calcio italiano', *L'Assalto*, 4/6/27, p. 6.

63. ASCB, CA X, 3, 5, PG 1116.

64. De Finetti, *Stadi. Esempi*, p. 63.

65. ASCB, Ex-Casa del Fascio II, 'Operazione Cambiaria a Debito Soc. Anon Civile. Pro Casa del Fascio', 9/1/36, p. 1.

66. Ibid., p. 1.

67. ASCB, Ex-Casa del Fascio II, PG 6396, 'Il Podestà di Bologna', 28/3/27, p. 2. See also ACS, PCM 1926, f.3.15. n.4154, 8/11/26.

68. Ibid., p. 2.

69. ASCB, Ex-Casa del Fascio II, PG 17767, letter from Cassa di Risparmio in Bologna to the Comune del Bologna, 30/4/35 XIII, pp. 1–2.

70. See Varrasi, *Economia, Politica e Sport in Italia*, pp. 255–7.

71. For the conditions under which the Littoriale was transferred see ASCB, Ex-Casa del Fascio, PG 7799.

72. ASCB, Ex-Casa del Fascio II, Foglio aggiunto al PG 25524, 6/8/34 XII.

73. Ibid.

74. ASCB, Ex-Casa del Fascio II, PG 7080, 21/2/38 XVI.

75. See ASCB, Ex-Casa del Fascio II, PG 17767, letter from Cassa di Risparmio in Bologna to the Commune del Bologna, 30/4/35 XIII, pp. 1–2.

76. Varrasi, *Economia, Politica e Sport in Italia*, p. 251.

77. Onofri & Ottani, *Dal Littoriale allo Stadio*, p. 18.

78. 'DATE AL LITTORIALE', *Il Resto del Carlino*, 14/10/26, p. 4.

79. 'DATE AL LITTORIALE', *Il Resto del Carlino*, 15/10/26, p. 4.

80. 'DATE AL LITTORIALE', *Il Resto del Carlino*, 16/10/26, p. 4.

81. Ibid., p. 4.

82. G. Bonuzzi, *Le Grandi Realizzazioni Fasciste. Il Littoriale di Bologna*, Edizioni di' Arte Fascista' , 1927, p. 3.

83. 'DATE AL LITTORIALE', *Il Resto del Carlino*, 16/10/26, p. 4.

84. A. Galluzzo, C. Battiloro, F. Varrasi, *La Grande Vicenda dello Stadio di Firenze*, Edifir, 2000, p. 66.

85. 'Il Littoriale', *Lo Sport Fascista*, p. 13.

86. For more details see Onofri & Ottani, *Dal Littoriale allo Stadio*, pp. 17–18.
87. See Varrasi, *Economia, Politica e Sport in Italia*, p. 252.
88. 'Untitled', *L'Assalto*, 22/8/25, p. 3.
89. 'La struttura del campo', *L'Assalto*, 28/5/27, p. 3.
90. Gresleri & Massaretti (eds) *Norma e arbitrio*, p. 231.
91. S. Sani, 'Il Campo Polisportivo del Fascio di Bologna', *Il Comune di Bologna*, 7, 1925, p. 440.
92. Bologna Sportiva, *Il Littoriale*, p. 19; I. Luminasi, *Il Littoriale*, Società Tipografica Mareggiani, 1927, pp. 19–20. For further details on the excavations see C.M. Govi & D. Vitali, 'Il sepolcro etrusco dello Stadio Communale', Onofri & Ottani, *Dal Littoriale allo Stadio*, pp. 25–6.
93. 'La 1 Assemblea quinquennale del Regime. Il bilancio della rinascita', *Il Littoriale*, 11/3/29, p. 1.
94. Koon, *Believe, Obey, Fight*, p. 20.
95. 'Il Littoriale', *Lo Sport Fascista*, p. 13.
96. San Pietro, *Stadi in Italia*, pp. 100–1.
97. Bologna Sportiva (ed.) *Il Littoriale*, p. 17.
98. S. Inglis, *The Football Grounds of Europe*, Willow, 1990, p. 33. San Pietro measures the portico at 2 km with 666 arches.
99. 'Speaking without Adjectives: Architecture in the Service of Totalitarianism', Ades et al., *Art and Power*, p. 41.
100. R. Mazzucconi, *La Città Fascista. Il governo fisico degli abitati secondo alcuni nuovi principi di politica edilizia*, Maremma, 1928, p. 84.
101. 'Dopo il trionfo', *L'Assalto*, 4/6/27, p. 3.
102. 'Considerazioni sul' "Littoriale"', *L'Assalto*, 23/4/27, p. 3.
103. Ibid., p. 3.
104. '"Il Littoriale"', *L'Assalto*, 3/7/26, p. 3
105. Bonuzzi, *Le Grandi Realizzazioni*, p. 4.
106. '"Eugenéo" o "Littoriale"', *L'Assalto*, 20/2/26, p. 1.
107. Ibid., p. 1.
108. 'La struttura del campo', *L'Assalto*, p. 3.
109. ASCB, Ex-Casa del Fascio I, PG 12736, 9/4/28.
110. 'Il Duce a Bologna', *Il Resto del Carlino*, p. 4.
111. 'Vendicare l'offesa', *L'Assalto*, 6/11/26, p. 1.
112. 'Un'opera grandiosa', *Il Littoriale*, 29/5/27, p. 3.
113. Berezin, *Making the Fascist Self*, p. 73.
114. J. Ridley, *Mussolini*, Constable, 1997, p. 183.
115. 'Vendicare l'offesa', *L'Assalto*, p. 1.
116. Ridley, *Mussolini*, p. 183.

117. 'Vendicare l'offesa', *L'Assalto*, p. 1.
118. 'Il messaggio del Duce al Fascismo bolognese', *L'Assalto*, 6/11/26, p. 3.
119. Luminasi, *Il Littoriale*, p. 23
120. 'La Federazione Italiana Giuoco Calcio, pubblica, per la fausta ricorrenza, il seguente manifesto', *L'Assalto*, 28/5/27, p. 3.
121. ASCB, CA X, 3, 5, 1927, Official invitation to opening of Littoriale.
122. 'Un primato', *Il Resto del Carlino*, 31/5/27, p. 4.
123. Luminasi, *Il Littoriale*, p. 30.
124. 'Dopo il trionfo', *L'Assalto*, p. 3.
125. Luminasi, *Il Littoriale*, p. 28.
126. Ibid., p. 24.
127. Ibid., p. 30.
128. ASCB, CA X, 3, 5, PG 6949, 31/1/30.
129. ASCB, CA X, 3, 5, PG 1095, 'R. Consolato D'Italia', 6/1/34.
130. ASCB, CA X, 3, 5, PG 15547, 'R. Agenzia Consolare D'Italia in Vigo', 21/4/34.
131. ASCB, CA X, 3, 5, PG 9771, 11/3/35.
132. Comité Organisateur des Championnats de Natation, Plongeons et Water Polo, *Bologne et le Littoriale*, pp. 25–7.
133. 'I Campionati Europei di nuoto al Littoriale', *Vita Nuova*, 9, III, 1927, pp. 600–1.
134. Ibid., p. 601.
135. ASCB, CA X, 3, 5, PG.5850, 11/3/26, p. 1.
136. Ibid., p. 2.
137. ASCB, CA X, 3, 5, PG.16307, 14/6/26.
138. ASCB, CA X, 3, 5, PG 2504, 22/2/27.
139. ASCB, CA X, 3, 5, PG 2504, 7/10/27.
140. ASCB, CA X, 3, 5, PG 33307, 11/10/27.
141. ASCB, CA X, 3, 5, PG 30737, 29/8/28.
142. ASCB, CA X, 3, 5, PG 20885, 7/6/30.
143. ASCB, CA X, 3, 5, PG 22003, 14/6/30.
144. ASCB, CA X, 3, 5, PG 33374, 26/10/31.
145. Ex-Casa del Fascio II, 'Comune di Bologna', 30/11/33, p. 1.
146. Ibid., pp. 1–2.
147. Ibid., Allegato N.1, 'Riassunto Bilanci dal 1927/8 al 1932–33'.
148. Ibid., p. 2.
149. Ibid., p. 3.
150. Ibid., p. 4.
151. 'La più grande vittoria alla presenza del Duce', *La Gazzetta*, 8/7/29, p. 1.
152. 'Il Bologna e il campionato', *Lo Sport Fascista*, 7, 1929, p. 16.

153. Ibid., p. 17.
154. 'Importanti dichiarazioni dell'on Arpinati nel banchetto rosso-bleu di Bologna', *Il Littoriale*, 10/5/28, p. 1.
155. 'Arpinati', *Calcio Illustrato*, p. 3.

Chapter 6 Radical Florence: The Cradle of *Calcio*

1. P. Lanfranchi & S. Wagg, 'Cathedrals in Concrete: Football in Southern European Society' in S. Wagg (ed.) *Giving the Game Away. Football, Politics and Culture on Five Continents*, Leicester University Press, 1995, p. 125. The traditional theory that football was imported into Italy by the English has also been challenged by: S. Pivato, 'Il football: un fenomeno di frontiera. Il caso del Friuli Venezia Giulia, *Italia Contemporanea*, 183, 1991; 'Il' Calcio Fiorentino!', *Il Calcio Illustrato*, II, 19, 11/5/32, p. 7.
2. Ben-Ghiat, *Fascist Modernities*, p. 10.
3. A. Galluzzo, 'Il Marchese Luigi Ridolfi e lo Stadio "Berta"', in Galluzzo et al., *La Grande Vicenda*, pp. 22–3.
4. 'Vita della Fiorentina', *Il Bargello*, 27/10/29, p. 4.
5. The intransigents wanted the radical elimination of all non-Fascists from political life while the revisionists urged reconciliation with at least other parties.
6. Lyttelton, *Seizure of Power*, p. 152.
7. For more detailed accounts see M. Palla, *Firenze nel regime fascista (1929–1934)*, Olschki, 1978, Chapter II; Lyttelton, *Seizure of Power*, pp. 277–82.
8. Lyttelton, *Seizure of Power*, p 281.
9. Ibid., p. 281.
10. Ibid., pp. 282–3.
11. Formed in 1924 as the 'independent' voice of Florentine Fascism, the weekly was essentially an organ of Tamburini.
12. 'Il Duce ordina la ricostituzione del Fascio di Firenze', *Battaglie Fasciste*, 11/6/26, p. 1.
13. 'Monito categorico dell'on. Augusto Turati', *Il Nuovo Giornale*, 22/12/26, p. 4.
14. 'L'insediamento del nuovo Segretario Federale', *Il Nuovo Giornale*, 22/12/26, p. 1.
15. Galluzzo, 'Il Marchese Luigi Ridolfi e lo Stadio "Berta"', p. 20.
16. 'La costituzione dell'Associaz. Fiorentina del Calcio è in pericolo!', *Il Nuovo Giornale*, 1/9/26, p. 5.
17. A. Galluzzo, *Il Fiorentino. Vita e Opere del Marchese Luigi Ridolfi*, Società Stampa Sportiva, 1999, p. 167.

18. 'L'inizio del campionato del calcio', *La Nazione*, 30/9–1/10/28, p. 5.
19. Ibid., p. 165.
20. 'Vin Buono', *Il Bargello*, I, 1, 9/6/29, p. 1.
21. de Grazia, *How Fascism Ruled women*, p. 162.
22. A. Petacco, *Il superfascista. Vita e morte di Alessandro Pavolini*, Mondadori, 1998, p. 46.
23. Palla, *Firenze nel regime fascista*, p. 171.
24. Galluzzo, *Il Fiorentino*, p. 76.
25. Galluzzo, 'Il Marchese Luigi Ridolfi e lo Stadio "Berta"', p. 20.
26. A. Turati, *Un anno di vita del partito*, Libreria d'Italia, 1929, p. 43.
27. Lyttelton, *Seizure of Power*, p. 303.
28. Ibid., p. 183.
29. D. Mack Smith, *Mazzini*, Yale University Press, p. 169
30. H. Hearder, *Italy in the Age of Risorgimento*, Longman, 1990, p. 242.
31. FIGC, *Azzurri 1990. Storia bibliografica emerografica iconografica della Nazionale Italiana di Calcio e del Calcio a Firenze*, La Meridiana Editori, 1990, p. 109.
32. San Pietro, *Stadi in Italia*, p. 156.
33. FIGC, *Azzurri 1990 . . . Firenze*, p. 110.
34. Susmel & Susmel, *Opera Omnia*, p. 367.
35. 'Cifre e deduzioni: sfollare le città', *Il Popolo d'Italia*, 22/11/28, p. 1.
36. Mazzucconi, *Città Fascista*, pp. 22–3.
37. 'Piani regolatore', *Il Bargello*, III, 24, 14/6/31, p. 1.
38. P.M. Bardi, *Rapporto sull'Architettura (per Mussolini)*, Civiltà Fascista, 1931, p. 138.
39. For details of the various plans and polemics see Palla, *Firenze nel regime fascista*, pp. 354–62.
40. Ades et al., *Art and Power*, p. 42.
41. 'Perché siamo per il progetto Michelucci', *L'Universale*, III, 5, 10/3/33, p. 1.
42. 'Architettura', *L'Universale*, III, 6, 25/3/33, p. 1.
43. Ibid., p. 1.
44. G. Pagano Pogatchnig, 'La Nuova Stazione di Firenze', *L'Universale*, 10/4/33, p. 1.
45. Palla, *Firenze nel regime fascista*, pp. 361–2.
46. Ades et al., *Art and Power*, p. 37. (Note 11. Apart from Florence railway station, won in competition among much public controversy by a group of young Florentine architects led by Giovanni Michelucci (1932–4), Ufficio V (a design department in the

Ministry of Communications) and one of its architects Angiolo Mazzoni, built post offices and railway stations all over Italy which were always original and often very striking.)

47. 'Mussolini riceve gli architetti della nuova stazione di Firenze', *Il Bargello*, 17/6/34, p. 3.
48. Ibid., p. 3.
49. Ibid., p. 3.
50. 'La Nuova Stazione S.M.N.', *Firenze: Rassegna del Comune*, October 1935, pp. 268–72.
51. E. Detti, *Firenze Scomparsa*, Firenze, Vallechi, 1970, p. 101.
52. 'Il problema dello stadio', *Lo Stadio*, 8/12/28, p. 1.
53. 'I Martiri di Fascisti Fiorentini. Giovanni Berta', *Firenze: Rassegna del Comune*, November 1933, p. 344.
54. Ibid., p. 344.
55. 'ANNO X', *Lo Stadio*, 30/10/32, p. 1.
56. ASCF, BA 116, 'Lettera dal P.N.F. Gruppo Rionale Fascista' Giovanni Berta' al Podestà', 30/5/30.
57. Galluzzo etc, *La Grande Vicenda*, pp. 36 & 66; Petacco, *Il superfascista*, p. 38.
58. C. Battiloro, 'Lo Stadio "Giovanni Berta" in Firenze di Pier Luigi Nervi', Unpublished Laurea thesis 1995–1996, Università di Firenze, Facoltà di Architettura, p. 107.
59. ASCF, BA 116, 'NORME e condizioni alle quali dovrà ottemperarsi nello studio del progetto e nella costruzione delle Tribune in cemento armato per il Campo sportivo 'Giovanni Berta' ', undated.
60. G. Michelucci, 'Lo Stadio 'Giovanni Berta' in Firenze dell'ing., Pier Luigi Nervi', *Architettura*, III, March 1932, p. 105.
61. ASCF, BA 13623, 'Deliberazione del Podestà', 17/7/30.
62. ASCF, BA 13623, 'Contratto (Brutta copia) fra Il Comune di Firenze e la Società in Nome Collettivo Ing. Nervi e Nebbiosi Sedente in Firenze', 1/12/30.
63. Galluzzo et al., *La Grande Vicenda*, p. 66.
64. ASCF, BA 13623, 'Deliberazione del Podestà', 17/7/30.
65. Galluzzo et al., *La Grande Vicenda*, p. 38. Varrasi also estimates the total cost as 6,800.000 lire, p. 65.
66. ASCF, BA 13623, 'Deliberazione del Podestà', 17/7/30.
67. Galluzzo et al., *La Grande Vicenda*, pp. 66–7.
68. Ibid., p. 26.
69. ASCF, BA 116, 'NORME e condizioni'.
70. ASCF, BA 13623, Dall'Ufficio Tecnica al Podestà del Comune di Firenze: 'Campo Sportivo "G. Berta" – Costruzione di Tribune', 6/5/30.

71. ACSF, BA 13263, 'Lettera dalla Società per Costruzioni Ing. Nervi & Nebbiosi al Podestà del Comune di Firenze', 16/9/30.
72. Inglis, *Football Grounds of Europe*, p. 38.
73. G.K. Koenig, 'Pier Luigo Nervi e lo Stadio Comunale fiorentino', reprinted in M. Piccardi & M. Settimelli (eds) *Lo Stadio di Firenze di Ieri di Oggi*, Arnaud, 1990, p. 46.
74. Quoted in Galluzzo etc, *La Grande Vicenda*, p. 42.
75. San Pietro, *1990 Stadi in Italia*, p. 156.
76. ASCF, BA 102, 'Deliberazione del Podestà N. 1687', 9/7/31.
77. ASCF, BA 116, 'NORME e condizioni'.
78. De Finetti, *Stadi. Esempi*, p. 67.
79. Quoted in San Pietro, *Stadi in Italia*, p. 154.
80. ASCF, BA 13668, 'Missiva dell'Ufficio Tecnico al Podestà del 9/6/32'.
81. 'Architettura Sportiva', *Città Nuova*, p. 3.
82. Koenig, 'Pier Luigi Nervi e lo Stadio Comunale fiorentino', p. 46.
83. Inglis, *The Football Grounds of Europe*, p. 36.
84. Battiloro, 'Lo stadio "Giovanni Berta"', p. 159; Galluzzo, *Il Fiorentino*, p. 162.
85. 'Il debutto casalingo dei viola', *Il Bargello*, 11/9/32, p. 2.
86. P.M. Bardi, 'Lo Stadio di Firenze', *Casabella*, April 1933, reprinted in Piccardi & Settimelli, *Lo Stadio di Firenze*, p. 44.
87. Palla, *Firenze nel regime fascista*, p. 332.
88. ASCF, BA 117, Lettera dal Federazione Atletica Ungherese al Podestà, 27/12/33.
89. See various letters in ASCF, BA 119.
90. F. Agostinelli, 'Stadi / Dalle Prime Olipiadi Moderne ai Campionati del Mondo', *Parametro*, 1989, p. 63.
91. For a comprehensive list of articles on the stadiums see Ibid., pp. 63–4, note 13.
92. 'Azzurri in campo viola', *Il Calcio Illustrato*, III, 18, 3/5/33, p. 1.
93. 'Gli otto stadi del Campionato del mondo', *Lo Sport Fascista*, p. 32.
94. ASCF, BA 115, Lettera dalla R. Agenzia Consolare D'Italia in Vigo al Podestà di Firenze, 7/5/34.
95. 'Disciplina Fascista – Il nuovo inquadramento sportivo delle società e gruppi rionali di Firenze', *Lo Stadio*, 12/1/29, p. 1.
96. ASCF, BA 13623, Lettera dal Vice Podestà del Comune di Firenze al Podestà del Comune di Firenze, 4/3/30.
97. ASCF, f. 5481, 'Missiva del Ente Sportivo del Partito Nazionale Fascista Federazione Provinciale Fiorentina al Podestà di Firenze, 14/12/29, p. 2.
98. 'Lo sport e il Regime', *Il Bargello*, 27/10/29, p. 4.

99. ASCF, f. 5481, 'Missiva del Ente Sportivo del Partito Nazionale Fascista Federazione Provinciale Fiorentina', p. 2.
100. Ibid., p. 2.
101. 'Un appello della 'Fiorentina' ai soci' *Lo Stadio*, 12/1/29, p. 2.
102. Ibid., p. 2.
103. 'La Sottoscrizione Bianco-rossa', *Lo Stadio*, 19/1/29, p. 2
104. 'Appello ai soci della Fiorentina', *Lo Stadio*, 26/1/29, p. 2.
105. 'Nervi a Posto Signori', *Lo Stadio*, 2/2/29, p. 2.
106. Lèlle, 'O Tifosi, via c'è il Bologna!', *Lo Stadio*, 24/11/28, p. 7.
107. 'Giornalismo sportivo', *Il Bargello*, 4/8/29, p. 6.
108. Ibid., p. 6.
109. 'Note di Sport. Calcio', *Firenze: Rassegna del Comune*, June 1933, p. 188.
110. Ibid., p. 188.
111. 'Finiamola!', *Lo Stadio*, 20/11/32, p. 1.
112. Ibid., p. 1.
113. 'dalla torre di Maratona', *Lo Stadio*, 20/11/32, p. 6.
114. 'Note di Sport. Calcio', *Rassegna del Comune*, p. 188.
115. 'L'Associazione Fiorentina del Calcio', *Firenze: Rassegna del Comune*, June 1934, p. 188.
116. 'Il derby', *La Nazione*, 18/2/34, p. 6.
117. 'Finiamola!', *Lo Stadio*, p. 1.
118. Ibid., p. 1.
119. Ibid., p. 1.
120. de Grazia, *How Fascism Ruled Women*, pp. 219–20.
121. 'dalla torre di Maratona', *Lo Stadio*, 11/12/32, p. 6.
122. 'Siamo serî', *Lo Stadio*, 26/2/33, p. 1.
123. Varrasi, *Economia, Politica e Sport in Italia*, p. 242.

Chapter 7 Shooting for Italy: Foreign Bodies on Foreign Fields

1. Other cities included Genoa, Turin, Milan, Trieste, Florence, Bologna, Rome and Naples.
2. Lanfranchi, "Bologna:' The Team that Shook the World', pp. 336–46; see also E. Monzeglio, 'Il Bologna che tremare il mondo fa!', *La Grande Storia del Calcio Italiano*, 4, 20/2/65, pp. 100–1.
3. Lyttelton, *Seizure of Power*, pp. 421–2.
4. 'Cinquecentomila', *Lo Sport Fascista*, 1, 1930, pp. 2–5.
5. 'I frutti della buona propaganda rivelati dai progressi realizzati dagli atleti italiani', *La Gazzetta*, 28/6/28, pp. 1–2.

6. 'Dal Littoriale partono stanotte i messaggeri dell'augurio di tutta l'Italia sportiva per gli Azzurri', *Il Littoriale*, 25/5/28, p. 5.
7. Ibid., p. 5.
8. 'ITALIA', *Il Littoriale*, 24/4/28, p. 1.
9. ACS, SPD, CO 1922–43, B.345, Nos.119850/2 & 10698, 26/3/28.
10. 'La sconfitta vale più di una vittoria', *La Gazzetta*, 8/6/28, p. 1.
11. Ibid., p. 1.
12. 'L'idea olimpionica e le vittorie degli ambasciatori straordinarî a Los Angeles', *La Gazzetta*, 5/10/32, p. 1.
13. Ibid., p. 2.
14. 'Le medaglie d'acciaio', *La Gazzetta*, 2/10/32, p. 1.
15. Lanfranchi and Taylor, *Moving with the Ball*, p. 192.
16. Zanetti & Tornabuoni, *Il Giuoco del calcio*, p. 44.
17. D. Cante, 'Propaganda e sport negli anni trenta. Gli incontri di calcio tra Italia e Austria', *Italia Contemporanea*, 204, September 1996, p. 527.
18. Pozzo, *Campioni del Mondo*, p. 253.
19. On Mussolini's Danubian ambitions and the diplomacy of the era see H.J. Burgwyn, *Italian Foreign Policy in the Interwar Period, 1918–1940*, Praeger, 1997; F.L. Carsten, *The First Austrian republic 1918–1938*, Cambridge University Press, 1986; C.J. Lowe & F. Marzari, *Italian Foreign Policy, 1870–1940*, Routledge & Kegan Paul, 1975; C.A. Macartney, *Independent Eastern Europe*, Macmillan, 1962; J. Rothschild, *East Central Europe between the Two World Wars*, University of Washington Press, 1974.
20. 'La semifinali della Coppa d'Europa', *La Gazzetta*, 8/7/32, p. 3.
21. Archivio del Ministero degli Affari Esteri (AdMAdE), AP 1931–45 Cecoslovacchia, Busta 4, 'Affari Politici, Incontro di Calcio a Praga fra 'Juventus' e 'Slavia'', Telespresso N.221125 'Incidenti alla partita a Praga', 9/7/32. p. 1.
22. ACS, PCM 1931–33, f.14.3, n.6102, 'Incidenti alla Partita di calcio a Praga', 9/7/32, p. 1.
23. 'La semifinali della Coppa d'Europa', *La Gazzetta*, 8/7/32, p. 3.
24. ACS, PCM 1931–33, f.14.3, n.6102, 'Incidenti alla Partita di calcio a Praga', 9/7/32, pp. 1–2.
25. Ibid., p. 1.
26. Ibid., pp. 2–3.
27. ACS, PCM 1931–33, f.14.3. n.6103, 'Appunto per S.E. Il Capo del Governo', 16/7/32.
28. 'La Juventus darà allo Slavia la misura del suo valore stilistico e alla folla incivile di Praga la misura del spirito d'ospitalità', *La Gazzetta*, 9–10/7/32, p. 1.

29. 'Le semifinali della Coppa d'Europa', *La Gazzetta della Domenica*, 10/7/32, p. 3.
30. Ibid., p. 3.
31. ACS, PS 1932, Sezione II, b.59, f.D.80, Telegramma No.32827(6), 8/7/32.
32. Ibid., p. 5.
33. 'Gli strascichi della Coppa d'Europa', *La Gazzetta*, 14/7/32, p. 4.
34. AdMAdE, AP 1931–45 Cecoslovacchia, Busta 4, 'Affari Politici, Incontro calcistico a Torino fra 'Juventus' e 'Slavia'', 1656, 'Dimostrazioni antitaliano in Cecoslovacchia al ritorno'.
35. Ibid., p. 4.
36. 'La Juventus è finalista della Coppa d'Europa', *La Gazzetta*, 12/7/32, p. 5.
37. 'Le decisioni di Klagenfurth per la Coppa d'Europa', *La Gazzetta*, 16/8/32, p. 5.
38. Ibid., p. 5.
39. AdMAdE, AP 1931–45 Cecoslovacchia, Busta 3, Rapporti Politici, Telespresso N.4511–AI/2633, 'Italia e Cecoslovacchia', 1/12/32.
40. 'Dichiarazioni del delegato Italiano e favorevoli commenti della stampa', *La Gazzetta*, 26/10/32, p. 1.
41. ACS, PCM 1931–33, f.14.3. n.6102, 'Incidenti Italo-Cecoslovacchi per il gioco del calcio', 2/9/32, p. 1.
42. Ibid., p. 1.
43. AdMAdE, AP 1931–45 Cecoslovacchia, Busta 4, Miscellanea-Affari Politici, 'Incontro di calcio a Praga fra Italia e Cecoslovacchia', 6102/14–3, Telegram to Minister of Foreign Affairs, 26/9/32.
44. 'La politica battuto dallo sport', *La Gazzetta*, 26/10/32, pp. 1–2.
45. 'La partita Cecoslovacchia-Italia per la Coppa Internazionale', *La Gazzetta*, 26/10/32, pp. 5–6.
46. 'La partita della nebbia', *La Gazzetta*, 30/12/32, p. 1.
47. 'La politica battuto dallo sport', *La Gazzetta*, pp. 1–2.
48. ACS, SPD, CO 1922–43, B.345, n.119850/2, Letter, 13/1/32.
49. 'Interviste brevi', *La Nazione*, 14–15/5/33, p. 6.
50. 'Anche Mafalda e Maria di Savoia assistono all'incontro', *La Nazione*, 14–15/5/33, p. 1.
51. 'Fiorente primavera dello sport fascista', *La Gazzetta*, 3/5/38, p. 1.
52. 'Viaggi per la Coppa del Mondo di calcio', *La Gazzetta*, 26/5/38, p. 2.
53. S. Favre, 'In attesa che i 'ventidue' siano convocati', *Lo Sport Fascista*, 4, 1938, p. 18.
54. 'Fondamentale discorso del Duce sulle direttive della politica

italiana', *Il Popolo d'Italia*, 15/5/38, p. 1. In this speech, in Genoa, Mussolini publicly stated his desire for Franco to win the Civil War in Spain rather than 'Barcelona', which was supported by the French. His announcement of a political accord with England also threatened the potential encirclement of France when he declared it 'an accord of two Empires that extended from the Mediterranean to the Red Sea to the Indian Ocean'.

55. For other examples of anti-Fascist/Italian protests in France and the deteriorating relations between the respective countries, as recorded by the Italian Foreign Ministry, see AdMAdE, AP, 1931–45 Francia, Busta 33/4, 'Rapporti Politici'.

56. Papa & Panico, *Storia Sociale del Calcio*, p. 197.

57. See 'Gli 'azzurri' in Francia', *La Gazzetta*, 4/6/38, p. 5; 'Marsiglia avvampa d'entusiasmo per l'odierno duello italo-norvegese', *La Gazzetta*, 5–6/6/38, p. 5.

58. Interview conducted 30/11/2001, Turin.

59. For more details on this incident and Carosio's career in general see 'La radiocronaca all'italiana: Nicolò Carosio', *Ludus*, I, 3–4 October 1992–April 1993, pp. 40–9.

60. AdMAdE, AP 1931–45 Belgio, Busta 4, 'Miscellanea', Telespresso N.265747, 23/2/33.

61. Pozzo, *Campioni del Mondo*, p. 265.

62. Ibid., p. 266.

63. 'Vittoria ma non basta', *La Gazzetta*, 6/6/38, p. 3.

64. M. Grimaldi, *Vittorio Pozzo. Storia di un Italiano*, Società Stampa Sportiva, 2001, p. 128. On Monzeglio's relationship with Mussolini see E. Parodi (ed.) *Nove colonne in Prima. Gino Palumbo: L'ultima intervista*, Editrice Portoria, 1989, pp. 35–6.

65. Pozzo, 'Il fallimento del calcio', *Successo*, p. 108.

66. M. Pennacchia, *Il Calcio in Italia*, UTET, 1999, p. 213.

67. 'Come l'Italia è giunta alla conquista del titolo mondiale', *La Nazione*, 2/6/38, p. 5.

68. 'L'Italia elimina il Brasile' *La Gazzetta*, p. 4.

69. Zanetti & Tornabuoni, *Il Giuoco del calcio*, p. 43.

70. ACS, PCM 1934, f.14. 4. n.465, 'Appunto per S.E. Il Presidente del C.O.N.I.', 12/1/34.

71. Ibid.

72. ACS, PCM 1928–30, f.3.2.5. n.269, 'Letter from L. Ferretti President of CONI to G. Sguardo Undersecretary to the President of the Council of Ministers', 10/11/26.

73. A. Parboni, '32 Stati (ma saranno anche di più...) in lotta pei Campionati Mondiali di calcio', *Lo Sport Fascista*, 12, 1933, p. 23.

74. A. Parboni, 'Si prepara la Coppa del Mondo di calcio', *Lo Sport Fascista*, 1, 1934, p. 28.
75. 'L'organizzazione del grande avvenimento in un'intervista con il generale Vaccaro', *Il Popolo d'Italia*, 26/5/34, p. 8.
76. '"È un premio che l'Italia si merita"', *La Gazzetta*, 1/4/34, p. 3.
77. Papa & Panico, *Storia Sociale del Calcio*, p. 190.
78. '"È un premio che l'Italia si merita"', *La Gazzetta*, p. 3.
79. ACS, PCM 1934, f.14.4. n.465.1, 'Emissione serie speciale francobolli', 22/2/34.
80. Ibid.
81. ACS, PCM 1934, f.14.4. n.465.1, 'Ministero delle Communicazioni, copia di lettera del Campionato del Mondo di Calcio', 29/1/34, pp. 1–2.
82. 'L'impressioni del gen. Vaccaro presidente della FIGC', *Il Popolo d'Italia*, 26/5/34, p. 8.
83. ACS, PCM 1934, f.14.4. n.465.1, 'Emissione serie speciale francobolli', 22/2/34.
84. For a complete breakdown of the tournament costs and expenditure see P.L. Marzola, 'Storia economica dei campionati del mondo di calcio dall'Uruguay a "Italia 90"', *Ludus. Sport e loisir*, I, n.1, April 1992, pp. 34–9.
85. 'I campionati mondiale e i pagamenti in moneta italiana', *La Nazione*, 11/1/34, p. 6.
86. ACS, PCM 1934, f.14. 4. n.465, 'Appunto per S.E. Il Sottosegretario di Stato'.
87. ACS, PCM 1934, f.14. 4. n.465, n.1379, 31/8/34.
88. 'S.E. Starace inaugura a Roma il XXII congresso della FIFA', *Il Resto*, 25/5/34, p. 6.
89. 'L'impressioni del gen. Vaccaro', *Il Popolo d'Italia*, p. 8.
90. 'S.E. Starace presiede all'estrazione dei gironi eliminatori fra le seidici nazionali', *Il Resto del Carlino*, 4/5/34, p. 6.
91. 'L'impressioni del gen. Vacarro', *Il Popolo d'Italia*, p. 8.
92. Grimaldi, *Vittorio Pozzo*, pp. 88–9.
93. 'Telegrammi di saluto al Duce', *La Nazione*, 22/5/34, p. 8.
94. 'Gli argentini depongono una corona sulla tomba dei Genitori del Duce', *Il Resto del Carlino*, 25/5/34, p. 6.
95. 'I protagonisti dell'incontro di domani al Littoriale: Austria-Ungheria ricevuti dal Segretario federale e dal Podestà', *Il Resto del Carlino*, 30/5/34, p. 6.
96. The expression 'Portoghese' referred to anybody who gained access to the theatre or any other public spectacle without paying the necessary entry fee. It originated from the eighteenth century when the

Portuguese Embassy in Rome announced a performance at the Teatro Argentina for which tickets had not been issued. It was enough for individuals to present themselves as 'Portoghesi' to gain entry. See *Lessico Universale Italiano di Lingua Lettere Arti Scienze e Tecnica*, Istituto della Enciclopedia Italiana, 1978, pp. 443–4.

97. 'L'esempio del Duce', *La Nazione*, 30/5/34, p. 7.

98. 'I calciatori di 16 Nazioni ospiti dell'Italia fascista per i campionati del Mondo', *Lo Sport Fascista*, 6, VII, 1934, pp. 2–3.

99. 'Una furibonda contesa', *La Nazione*, 1/6/34, p. 6.

100. 'Italia – Austria: 1–0 (1–0)', *La Gazzetta*, 4/6/34, p. 1.

101. 'L'appassionante incontro Italia-Cecoslovacchia', *Il Popolo d'Italia*, 12/6/34, p. 8.

102. 'I calciatori di 16 Nazioni', *Lo Sport Fascista*, p. 8.

103. Advertisment, 'Campionato del Mondo', *Il Popolo d'Italia*, 12/6/34, p. 9.

104. For various foreign press comments see 'La stampa estera concorde nel riconoscere il valore degli azzurri', *La Nazione*, 12/6/34, p. 1.

105. 'Dopo la trionfale giornata di Roma', *La Gazzetta*, 13/6/34, pp. 1–2.

106. G. Vaccaro, 'Le impressioni del gen. Vaccaro e degli 'azzurri' dopo la grande vittoria', *Lo Sport Fascista*, 7, 1934, pp. 25–8.

107. 'Soldati dello Sport', *La Gazzetta*, 11/6/34, p. 1.

108. 'Il trionfo italiano nel Campionato mondiale di calcio', *Il Resto del Carlino*, 12/6/34, p. 4.

109. 'Gli azzurri nel nome del DUCE', *Il Bargello*, 17/6/34, p. 7.

110. 'Il valore della vittoria 'Azzurra' ', *La Nazione*, 14/6/34, p. 6.

111. See 'Maglie Azzurre a Berlino', *La Gazzetta*, 24/7/36, p. 1.

112. See L. Boccali, 'Il Trionfo del 'Goliardi Azzurri' nell'Olimpiade Calcistica', *Lo Sport Fascista*, 9, 1936, p. 20.

113. G. Vaccaro, 'Calcio', *Lo Sport Fascista*, 7, 1936, p. 12.

114. 'Gli azzurri di Pozzo: come hanno vinto e contro chi hanno vinto', *La Gazzetta*, 18/9/36, p. 1.

115. 'Sangue Latino', *La Gazzetta*, 11/8/36, p. 1.

116. 'Il Trionfo del 'Goliardi Azzurri' ', *Lo Sport Fascista*, p. 20.

117. The *oriundi* consisted of four Argentines and one Brazilian, namely De Maria, Orsi, Guaita, Monti and Filo. See O. Duarte, *The Encyclopedia of World Cup Soccer*, McGraw-Hill, 1994, p. 26.

118. 'Clamorosa vittoria dei calciatori azzurri', *La Nazione*, p. 5.

119. 'Nuovo trionfo dello sport fascista nella 'coppa' del mondo', *Il Bargello*, 26/6/38, p. 2.

120. ACS, SPD, CO 1922–43, B.345, n.119.850, 'Telegramma'.

121. Sivre, 'Come gli 'Azzurri' si sono dimostrati maestri', *Lo Sport Fascista*, 7, 1938, p. 18.

122. 'Bisogna imparare dagli italiani', *La Nazione*, 21/6/38, p. 5.
123. 'Il Duce consegna le medaglie al valore atletico', *Il Popolo d'Italia*, 30/6/38, p. 1.
124. Interview conducted 30/11/2001, Turin.
125. 'Il Duce riceve ed elogia gli azzurri del calcio due volte campioni del mondo', *La Gazzetta*, 30/6/38, p. 1.
126. 'Italia conquista la III Coppa del Mondo', *Il Popolo d'Italia*, 20/6/38, p. 5.
127. B. Roghi, 'Per la Bandiera', *La Gazzetta*, 20/6/38, p. 1.
128. Ferretti, 'Uno, due. . .(e tre?)', *Lo Sport Fascista*, p. 14.
129. 'Per la Bandiera', *La Gazzetta*, p. 1.
130. 'La classifica dei 'canonieri' è incentivo al gioco individuale?', *Lo Sport Fascista*, 10, 1933, p. 46.
131. 'In bocca al lupo, calciatori azzurri!', *Il Popolo d'Italia*, 12/6/38, p. 6.
132. Mack Smith, *Modern Italy*, p. 214.
133. Pozzo, *Quarant'anni*, p. 124.
134. Ghirelli, *Storia del Calcio in Italia*, p. 99.
135. Quoted in Ibid., p. 100.
136. 'Calciatori di scuola sudamericana', *Lo Sport Illustrato*, 21/4/1937, p. 13.
137. 'L'importantissima seduta del Direttorio federale', *La Gazzetta*, 22/6/34, p. 1.
138. 'Italiano o argentino?', *Il Bargello*, 13/5/34, p. 2.
139. Fabrizio, *Sport e Fascismo*, pp. 55–6; see also G. Brera, *Storia critica del calcio italiano*, Bompiani, 1975, p. 143.
140. 'Meazza e l'aria di Roma', *Il Calcio Illustrato*, II, 25, 22/6/32, p. 7.
141. Zanetti & Tornabuoni, *Il Giuoco del Calcio*, p. 176.
142. 'Il fresco stile nuovo degli azzurri', *La Gazzetta*, p. 4.
143. 'Per la bandiera', *La Gazzetta*, p. 1.
144. 'La situazione degli italiani', *La Nazione*, 4/6/38, p. 5.
145. G. Tornabuoni, *L'Ascesa del Foot-ball in Italia (Saggio Critico)*, La Gazzetta dello Sport, 1932, p. 137.
146. Pozzo, *Campioni del Mondo*, pp. 143–4.
147. Pozzo, 'Il fallimento del calcio', *Successo*, p. 108.
148. He also worked in Milan as an office manager for Pirelli.
149. See 'La vita di Pozzo diventa storia', *La Repubblica*, 20/5/93, p. 27; 'Pozzo? Macchè Fascista . . .', *La Repubblica*, 21/5/93, p. 27.
150. Pozzo, *Campioni del Mondo*, p. 118.
151. Pozzo, 'Il fallimento del calcio', p. 108.
152. 'Virilità e vigliaccheria', *Lo Stadio*, 9/10/32 p. 1.
153. ACS, PS 1929, b.180, D.14 Sports e Gare, n.34384, 'Prefettura di

Bolzano al Ministero Interno', 18/4/29.

154. 'Virilità e vigliaccheria', *Lo Stadio*, p. 1.

155. 'Fioriture pericolose', *Il Littoriale*, 24/1/29, p. 1.

156. Ibid., p. 1.

157. 'L'opinione italiana e la sconfitta di Torino', *Il Littoriale*, 30/4/29, p. 1.

158. Ibid., p. 1.

159. Pozzo, *Campioni del Mondo*, p. 161.

160. Ibid., p. 191.

161. P. Ball, *Morbo. The Story of Spanish Football*, WSC Books, 2001, p. 219.

162. For a detailed discussion of the various terms and styles of *sistema* and *metodo* see F. Marri, '*Metodo, sistema* e derivati nel linguaggio calcistico', *Ludus. Sport e Loisir*, 3, 1992, pp. 86–101.

163. 'Il fresco stile nuovo degli azzurri', *La Gazzetta*, 22/6/38, p. 4.

164. Picchi was also a Fiorentina vice-president.

165. 'Un fattore essenziale e trascurato dai tanti teoriche filosofano sui sistemi', *Lo Stadio*, 4/12/32, p. 2.

166. C. Bromberger, *La Partita di calcio. Etnologia di una passione*, Riuniti, 1999, p. 89.

167. ACS, PS 1929, b.180, D.14 Sports e Gare, Ministero dell'Interno, Telegramma n.23342, 19/5/29.

168. 'Un confronto decisivo fra I migliori calciatori continentali e I prodigiosi maestri dell'arte', *La Nazione*, 13/5/33, p. 6.

169. 'Arte e geometria', *La Nazione*, 14–15/5/33, p. 6.

170. Pozzo, *Campioni del Mondo*, pp. 213–14.

171. S. Rous, *Football Worlds. A Lifetime in Sport*, Readers Union, 1979, p. 62.

172. 'Al di là della muraglia cinese dell'isolamento sportivo britannico', *La Gazzetta*, 11/11/34, p. 3.

173. 'Spirito Inglese', *La Gazzetta*, 11/11/34, p. 3.

174. 'Al di là della muraglia cinese', *La Gazzetta*, p. 3.

175. E. Colombo, 'Atleti del Fascismo', *La Gazzetta*, 15/11/34, p. 1.

176. 'Dopo la partita Italia-Cecoslovacchia', *La Gazzetta*, 12/6/34, pp. 1–2.

177. Pozzo, *Campioni del Mondo*, p. 215.

178. 'Inghilterra 3 Italia 2', *Libro e Moschetto*, 24/11/34, p. 6.

179. 'Atleti del Fascismo', *La Gazzetta*, p. 1.

180. 'Successo dello spirito della squadra', *La Gazzetta*, p. 1.

181. 'Atleti del Fascismo', *La Gazzetta*, p. 1.

182. Ibid., p. 1.

183. G. Ferrari, 'Esperienze inglesi', *Lo Sport Fascista*, 12, 1934, p. 7.

184. 'Successo dello spirito della squadra', *La Gazzetta*, 15/11/34, p. 1.
185. Ibid., p. 1.
186. 'Successo dello spirito', *La Gazzetta*, p. 3.
187. 'Atleti del Fascismo', *La Gazzetta*, p. 1.
188. Ibid., p. 1.
189. 'Successo dello spirito della squadra', *La Gazzetta*, p. 1.

Chapter 8 Conclusion

1. Cavazza, *Piccole Patrie*, pp. 247–8.
2. 'Fiorente primavera dello sport fascista', *La Gazzetta*, 31/5/38, p. 1.
3. Berezin, *Making the Fascist Self*, p. 247.
4. Falasca-Zamponi, *Fascist Spectacles*, p. 190.
5. Schnapp, *Staging Fascism*, p. 10.
6. W. Laqueur (ed.) *Fascism: A Readers Guide*, Scolar, 1991, p. 143.
7. Cavazza, *Piccole Patrie*, p. 246.
8. Falasca-Zamponi, *Fascist Spectacles*, p. 189.
9. J. Riordan & A. Krüger (eds) *The International Politics of Sport in the 20th Century*, p. 85.
10. Ibid., p. 83.
11. See D. Shaw, 'The Political Instrumentalisation of Football in Francoist Spain', PhD thesis, Queen Mary College, University of London, 1988.
12. T. Mason, *Passion of the People? Football in South America*, Verson, 1995, p. 68.
13. Parboni, '32 Stati (ma saranno anche di più)', *Lo Sport Fascista*, p. 20.

Bibliography

Primary Literature

Archival Sources
Archivio Centrale dello Stato *(ACS)*
Ministero dell'interno, direzione generale pubblica sicurezza, divisione affari generali e riservati (PS), 1925, 1929.
Presidenza del Consiglio dei ministri (PCM)1928–30, 1931–33, 1934.
Segreteria Particolare del Duce (SPD), Carteggio Amministrativo (CA).
Segreteria Particolare del Duce (SPD), Carteggio Ordinario (CO) 1922–43.
Archivio Storico del Comune di Bologna (ACSB)
Carteggio Amministrativo (CA), 1924–36.
Ex-Casa del Fascio.
Archivio del Ministero degli Affari Esteri (AdMdAE)
Affari Politici (AP),1931–45, Austria, Belgio, Cecoslovacchia.
Archivio Storico del Comune di Firenze (ASCF)
Archivio Generale (AG), 1929.
Archivio Legale (AL) 13668.
Belle Arti, 102, 115, 116, 117, 119.

Interviews
Professor G. Gresleri, University of Bologna, 20 August 2001.
Piero Rava, Turin, 5 December 2001.

Unpublished Theses
Alassio, A. *Lo Sport nello stato fascista*, tesi al regio istituto superiore di scienze economiche e commerciali, Genova, 1934.

Contemporary Newspapers and Journals
L'Architettura
L'Assalto
Avanti!

Il Bargello
Battaglie Fasciste
Il Calcio Illustrato
Casabella
Il Cittadino
La Città Nuova
Il Comune di Bologna
La Critica Fascista
Firenze: Rassegna del Comune
La Gazzetta dello Sport
Gerarchia
La Giovane Calabria
Il Littoriale
La Nazione
Il Nuovo Giornale
La Pedata
Il Popolo d'Italia
Il Popolo di Roma
Quadrante
Il Resto del Carlino
La Sberla Sportiva
La Scuola Fascista
Il Secolo
Lo Sport Fascista: rassegna mensile illustrata di tutti gli sport
Sport e Proletariato
Lo Stadio
La Stampa
La Striglia Sportiva
Il Tevere
L'Universale
Vita Nuova
La Vita Sportiva
La Voce Sportiva

Books

AA.VV. *Lo sport in Regime Fascista, 28 Ottobre 1922–I – 28 Ottobre 1935–XIII*, Roma, Lo Sport Fascista, 1935.

Aruga, U. *Organizzazione fascista dello sport'*, Torino, Federazione dei Fasci di Combattimento, 1932.

Barbarito, C. *Lo sport fascista e la razza*, Torino, G.B. Paravia, 1937.

Bardi, P. M. *Rapporto sull'architettura*, Roma, Civiltà Fascista, 1931.

Bianchini, E., Fagnoni, R. & Ortensi, D. *Lo stadio di Torino*, Roma, A.

Armani, 1933.

Bontempelli, M. *L'avventura novecentista*, Firenze, A. Valecchi, 1938.

Bonuzzi, G. *Le Grande Realizzazioni Fasciste. Il Littoriale di Bologna*, Bologna, Arte Fascista, 1927.

Bresci, A. *La questione dell'italianità nel giuoco del calcio*, Prato, Martini, 1926.

Carli, F. *Mussolini e lo Sport*, Mantua, Paladino, 1928.

Ciampitti, F. & Titta Rosa, G. *Prima antologia degli scrittori sportivi*, Milano, R. Carabba, 1934.

Comitato Olimpico Nazionale Italia, *L'Italia Turistica Annuario Generale. Sport – Turismo – Industrie Applicate*, Firenze, Edizioni A.E.S.T.I., 1930.

—— *Commissione Impianti Sportivi. Regolamento*, Roma, C.O.N.I., 1934.

Comité organizateur des Championnats de Natation, Plongeons et Water Polo (ed.) *Bologne et le Littoriale*, Bologna, Stabilimenti Poligrafici Riuniti, 1927.

De Finetti, G. *Stadi. Esempi – Tendenze – Progetti*, Milano, Hoepli, 1934.

De Martino, E. *Tre volte campioni del mondo. Da Berlino a Parigi. Diario di un giornalista*, Milano, Calcio illustrato, 1938.

—— *Campioni del Mondo. Da Roveta a Londra*, Milano, Calcio illustrato, 1936.

Del Debbio, E. *Progetti di costruzione Case Balillà, Palestre, Campi Sportivi, Piscine*, Roma, Palazzo Viminale, 1930.

Del Guerra, G. *Lo sport in regime fascista*, Pisa, Giardino, 1935.

Del Marco, B. & Ottenziali, B. *Le costruzioni di campi sportivi*, Milano, Hoepli, 1938.

Di Crollanza, A. *Le opere pubbliche nel primo decennio fascista*, Milano-Verona, Mondadori, 1933.

Ellwanger, H. *Sulla lingua di Mussolini*, Milan, Mondadori, 1941.

Federazione Italiana Giuoco Calcio, *Annuario Italiano Giuoco del Calcio, Volume I*, Modena, Antica Tipographia Modenese, 1928.

——, *Annuario Italiano Gioco del Calcio (1928–32)*, Modena, Tipographia Modenese Soliani, 1932.

——, *Coppa del Mondo. Cronistoria del II campionato mondiale di calcio 1934*, Roma, F.I.G.C., 1936.

Ferrauto, E. *L'educazione fisica nell'educazione giovanile fascista*, Torino, G.B. Paravia, 1939.

Ferretti, L. *Il libro dello sport*, Roma, Libreria del Littorio, 1928.

—— *Esempi ed idee per l'italiano nuovo*, Roma, Libreria del Littorio, 1930.

Fillia, L.G. (ed.) *La nuova architettura*, Torino, UTET, 1931.

Gallian, M. *Arpinati politico e uomo di sport*, Roma, Casa Editrice Pinciana, 1928.

Glass, D.V. *Population Policies and Movements in Europe*, Oxford, Clarendon Press, 1940.

Le Bon, G. *The Crowd. A Study of the Popular Mind*, London, Ernest Benn, 1896.

Lorenzini, A. *I ciclisti rossi. I loro scopi e la loro organizzazione*, Caravaggio, Tipografia Caravaggese, 1913.

Luminasi, I. *Il Littoriale*, Bologna, Società Tipografica Mareggiani, 1927.

Mazzucconi, R. *La Città Fascista. Il governo fisico degli abitanti secondo alcuni nuovi principii di politica edilizia*, Grosseto, Maremma, 1928.

P.N.F., *Campo sportivo del Littorio*, Roma, Libreria del Littorio, 1928.

Pomba, G.L. (ed.) *La Civiltà, fascista illustrata nella dottrina e nelle opere*, Torino, Edit. Torinese, 1928.

Pozzo, V. *Campioni del mondo: quarant'anni di storia del calcio Italiano*, Roma, CEN, 1960.

Società Sportiva di Bologna (ed.) *Il Littoriale*, Bologna, Tipographia Paolo Neri, 1931.

Susmel, E, & Susmel, D. (eds) *Opera Omnia di Benito Mussolini XXII*, Firenze, La Fenice, 1957.

Tornabuoni, G. *L'Ascesa del Foot-ball in Italia (Saggio Critico)*, Milano, La Gazzetta dello Sport, 1932.

Turati, A. *Un Anno di Vita del Partito*, Milano, Libreria d'Italia, 1929.

Zanetti, G. & Tornabuoni, G. *Il Giuoco del Calcio. Commento alla legislazione della F.I.G.C*, Milano, Ceschina, 1933.

Articles

AA.VV., 'On the degeneracy of the human race', *The Journal of Psychological Medicine and Mental Pathology'*, X, April 1, 1857, pp. 159–208.

Ambrosini, G. 'Il ciclismo è in decadenza?', *Lo Sport Fascista*, 7, 1928, pp. 59–65.

Anon., 'Sport and Decadence', *The Quarterly Review*, 211, 1909, pp. 486–502.

Bardi, p. M. 'Lo stadio di Firenze', *Casabella,* April 1933, pp. 4–11.

Bianchi, E. 'Sport (Dall'Italia)', *Giustizia e Libertà*, 10/2/34, pp. 46–50.

Bianchini, E., Fagnoni, D. & Ortensi, R. 'Lo stadio Mussolini a Torino', 12/33, *Casabella*, pp. 26–7.

Boccali, L. 'Una problema morale e sportivo', *Lo Sport Fascista*, 8, 1929, pp. 49–53.

—— 'Il Trionfo del 'Goliardi Azzurri' nell'Olimpiade Calcistica', *Lo Sport Fascista*, 9, 1936, pp. 20–3.

Ciocca, G. '(Servizi a Mussolini) Il Teatro di Masse', *Quadrante*, July 1933, pp. 7–10.

Costa, V. 'Un'opera veramente Fascista: l'istruzione preatletica nelle scuole di Bologna', *Lo Sport Fascista*, 4, 1929, pp. 11–15.

De Finetti, G. 'Stadi antichi e moderni', *Casabella*, December 1933, pp. 2–9.

—— 'Gli otto stadi del Campionato del mondo', *Lo Sport Fascista*, 7, 1934, pp. 30–4.

Ferrari, G. 'Esperienze inglesi', *Lo Sport Fascista*, 12, 1934, pp. 6–10.

Ferretti, L. 'Programma', *Lo Sport Fascista*, 6, 1928, pp. 3–4.

—— 'Il CONI e la sua opera', *Lo Sport Fascista*, 9, 1928, pp. 2–4.

—— 'Cultura e lo Sport', *Lo Sport Fascista*, 2, 1929, pp. 1–7.

—— 'Guerra e Sport', *Lo Sport Fascista*, 8, 1935, pp. 7–8.

—— 'Nel nome dei morti, per la gloria dei vivi', *Lo Sport Fascista*, 8, 1936, pp. 11–12.

—— 'Il Foro Mussolini, città sportiva splendente di marmi, nasce sulle rive del Tevere', *Lo Sport Fascista*, 2, 1937, pp. 7–10.

—— 'Uno, due . . . (e tre?)', *Lo Sport Fascista*, 7, 1938, pp. 13–14.

Gorrieri, G. 'Programma immutato,' *Lo Sport Fascista*, 4, 1928, p. 1.

Hodgkin, T.H. 'The Fall of the Roman Empire and Its Lessons For Us', *The Contemporary Review*, 73, January 1898, pp. 51–70.

M.M. 'Arpinati', *Lo Sport Fascista*, 10, 1929, pp. 8–10.

Michelucci, G. 'Lo stadio 'Berta' in Firenze', *Architettura*, March 1932, pp. 105–116.

Mussolini, B. 'Certezza Nelle Forze Dello Spirito e Dell'Intelligenza Italiana', *Quadrante*, June 1933, pp. 1–2.

Muzzi, F. 'I campi sportivi comunali', *Lo Sport Fascista*, 8, 1929, pp. 4–7.

—— 'Cinquecentomila', *Lo Sport Fascista*, 1, 1930, pp. 1–5.

Nervi, P. L. 'Problemi dell'Architetto', *Casabella*, May 1933, pp. 34–5.

—— 'Idee Sulla Costruzione di Uno Stadio Per 120,000', *Quadrante*, August 1933, p. 36.

Pagano, G. 'Mussolini Salva L'Architettura', *Casabella*, June 1934, pp. 2–3.

—— 'Politica e architettura', *Casabella*, April, 1935, pp. 2–3.

Paolini, A. 'L'educazione fisica nell'esercito italiano', *Esercito e Nazione. Rivista per l'ufficiale Italiane*, 6–7, 1926, pp. 458–61.

Parboni, A. 'Nel 'Dopolavoro' Riorganizzato', *Lo Sport Fascista*, 3, 1929, pp. 4–8.

—— '32 Stati (ma saranno anche di più . . .) in lotta pei Campionati Mondiali di calcio', *Lo Sport Fascista*, 12, 1933, pp. 18–23.

—— 'Si prepara la Coppa del Mondo di calcio', *Lo Sport Fascista*, 1, 1934, pp. 25–8.

Pavolini, A., 'Vin Buono', *Il Bargello*, 1, 9/6/29, pp. 1–2.

Petroselli, P. 'Stadi Pieni e Stadi Vuoti', *Il Calcio Illustrato*, 2, 13/1/37, pp. 4–5.

Piacentini, M. 'Il Foro Mussolini in Roma', *Architettura*, February 1933, pp. 65–75.

Pini, G. 'L'Arte Medica Nella Educazione Fisica e Nello Sport', *Lo Sport Fascista*, 10, 1929, pp. 16–18.

Pozzo, V. 'Il fallimento del calcio italiano', *Successo*, 2, 1959, pp. 107–8.

Saitta, G. 'Leandro Arpinati e il Fascismo Bolognese', *Vita Nuova. Pubblicazione mensile illustrata dell'Università di Fascista di Bologna*, 1, III, 1927, pp. 3–4.

Sani, S. 'Il campo polisportivo del fascio di Bologna', *Il Comune di Bologna, rassegna mensile di cronaca amministrativa e di statistica*, 7, 1925, pp. 439–43.

Sivre, 'Come gli 'Azzurri' si sono dimostrati maestri', *Lo Sport Fascista*, 7, 1938, pp. 15–18.

Vaccaro, G. 'Le impressioni del gen. Vaccaro e degli 'azzurri' dopo la grande vittoria', *Lo Sport Fascista*, 7, 1934, pp. 25–8.

—— 'Calcio', *Lo Sport Fascista*, 7, 1936, p. 12.

Varale, V. 'Verso la Nazione Sportiva', *Lo Sport Fascista*, 2, 1930, pp. 1–2.

—— 'Per la sanità della razza', *Lo Sport Fascista*, 3, 1930, pp. 1–2.

—— 'Mentalità fascisti degli sportivi', *Lo Sport Fascista*, 5, 1933, pp. 1–4.

Vietti Violi, P. 'Alcuni dati per le costruzioni sportive', *Casabella*, December 1933, pp. 14–15.

Secondary Literature

Unpublished Theses

Battiloro, C. 'Lo Stadio 'Giovanni Berta' In Firenze di Pier Luigi Nervi', Tesi di Laurea, Università di Firenze, Facoltà di Architettura, 1995–6.

Coveney, F. '"Soldati dello sport" la stampa fascista ed il "Mondiale" di calcio del 1934', Tesi di laurea, Università degli studi di Milano, 1989.

Shaw, D. 'The Political Instrumentalization of Football in Francoist Spain', PhD thesis, Queen Mary College, University of London, 1988.

Books

AA.VV. *E42: Utopia e scenario del regime*, Venice, Marsilio, 1987.

Ades, D., Benton, T., Elliot, D. & Whyte, I.B. (compiled and selected by), *Art and Power. Europe under the dictators 1930–45*, London, Thames and Hudson, 1995.

Affron, M. & Antliff, M. (eds) *Fascist Visions. Art and Ideology in Fascist Italy*, Princeton, Princeton University Press, 1997.

Anderson, B. *Imagined Communities: Reflections on the Origin and Spread of Nationalism*, London, Verso, 1991.

Arnaud, P. & Riordan, J. (eds) *Sport and International Politics. The Impact of Fascism and Communism on Sport*, London, E & F.N. Spon, 1998.

Artusi, L. Gheri, R. Nistri, L. *Firenze e il suo gioco del calcio*, Firenze, Lucio Pugliese, 1984.

Asor Rosa, A. *Storia d'Italia, Dall'Unità a oggi, 2, La Cultura*, Einaudi, Torino, 1975.

Ball, P. *Morbo. The Story of Spanish Football*, London, WSC Books, 2001.

Barrows, S. *Distorting Mirrors. Visions of the Crowd in Late Nineteenth-Century France*, New Haven and London, Yale University Press, 1981.

Bartoli, P., Pasquini Romizi, C., Romizi, R. (eds) *L'organizzazione del consenso nel regime fascista: l'Opera Nazionale Balilla come istituzione di controllo sociale*, Perugia, Istituto di etnologia e antropologia culturale della Universita degli studi, 1983.

Bassetti, R. *Storia e storie dello sport in Italia. Dall'unitá a oggi*, Venezia, Marsilio, 1999.

Beck, P.J. *Scoring for Britain. International Football and International Politics 1900–1939*, London, Frank Cass, 1999.

Bellamy, R. (ed.) *Antonio Gramsci. Pre-Prison Writings*, Cambridge, Cambridge University Press, 1994.

Bellocchi, U. *Il Resto del Carlino. Giornale di Bologna*, Bologna, Società Editoriale 'Resto del Carlino', 1973.

Ben-Ghiat, R. *Fascist Modernities. Italy, 1922–1945*, Berkeley, University of California Press, 2001.

Berend, I.T. *The Crisis Zone of Europe: An Interpretation of East-Central European History in the First Half of the Twentieth Century*, Cambridge, Cambridge University Press, 1986.

Berezin, M. *Making the Fascist Self: The Political Culture of Interwar Italy*, Ithaca, Cornell University Press, 1997.

Berghaus, G. (ed.) *Fascism and Theatre: Comparative Studies on the Aesthetics and Politics of Performance in Europe, 1925–1945*, Providence, Berghahn Books, 1995.

—— *Futurism and Politics: Between Anarchist Rebellion and Fascist Reaction, 1909–1944*, Oxford, Berghahn Books, 1996.

Betti, C. *L'opera Nazionale Balilla e l'educazione Fascista*, Firenze, La Nuova Italia, 1984.

Bianda, R. *Atleti in camicia nera. Lo sport nell'Italia di Mussolini*, Firenze, Edizioni Volpe, 1983.

Bosworth, R.J.B. *The Italian Dictatorship. Problems and Perspectives in the Interpretation of Mussolini and Fascism*, London, Arnold, 1998.

Brantliger, P. *Bread and Circuses. Theories of Mass Culture as Social Decay*, Ithaca, Cornell University Press, 1983.

Brera, G. *Storia critica del calcio italiano*, Milano, Bompiani, 1975.

Bromberger, C. *La Partita di Calcio. Etnologia di una passione*, Roma, Riuniti, 1999.

Burgwyn, J.H. *Italian Foreign Policy in the Interwar Period, 1918–1940*, Westport, Praeger, 1997.

Burleigh, M. & Wipperman, W. *The Racial State. Germany 1933–1945*, Cambridge, Cambridge University Press, 1991.

Cannistraro, P.V. *La fabbrica del consenso: fascismo e mass media*, Bari, Laterza, 1975.

—— (ed.) *Historical Dictionary of Fascist Italy*, Westport CT, Greenwood Press, 1982.

Cantagalli, R. *Storia del fascismo fiorentino 1919/1925*, Firenze, Vallecchi, 1972.

Cantamessa Arpinati, G. *Arpinati il mio padre*, Roma, Il Sagittario, 1968.

Carsten, F.L. *The First Austrian Republic 1918–1938*, Cambridge, Cambridge University Press, 1986.

Castronovo, V. & Tranfaglia, N. (eds) *La Stampa Italiana del Neocapitalismo*, Bari, Laterza, 1976.

—— (eds) *La Stampa Italiana Nell'Età Fascista*, Bari, Laterza, 1980.

Cavazza, S. *Piccole Patrie. Feste popolari tra regione e nazione durante il fascismo*, Bologna, Il Mulino, 1997.

Ciucci, G. *Gli Architetti e il Fascismo. Architettura e città 1922–1944*, Torino, Einaudi, 1989.

Cresti, C. *Architettura e fascismo*, Firenze, Vallecchi, 1986.

Cristofori, F. *Bologna gente e vita dal 1914–1945*, Bologna, Alfa, 1980.

De Donato, G. (ed.) *Carlo Levi 'Coraggio dei Miti. Scritti contemporanei 1922–1974'*, Bari, De Donato Editore 1975.

De Felice, R. *La Conquista del Potere (1919–1925)*, Torino, Einaudi, 1995.

—— *Mussolini il fascista. L'organizzazione dello Stato fascista 1925–1929*, Torino, Einaudi, 1995.

—— *Mussolini il duce. Gli anni del consenso 1929–1936*, Torino, Einaudi, 1996.

de Grazia, V. *The Culture of Consent. Mass Organization of Leisure in Fascist Italy*, Cambridge, Cambridge University Press, 1981.

—— *How Fascism Ruled Women. Italy 1922–1945*, Berkeley, University of California Press, 1992.

Detti, E. *Firenze Scomparsa*, Firenze, Vallechi, 1970.

Drescher, S., Sabean, D. & Sharlin, A. (eds) *Political Symbolism in*

Modern Europe, New Brunswick NJ, Transaction Books, 1982.

Duarte, O. *The Encyclopedia of World Cup Soccer*, New York, McGraw-Hill, 1994.

Duke, V. & Crolley, L. *Football, Nationality and the State*, New York, Longman, 1996.

Fabrizio, F. *Sport e Fascismo. La politica sportiva del regime 1924–1936*, Rimini-Firenze, Guaraldi, 1976.

—— *Storia dello sport in Italia. Dalle società ginnastiche all'associazionismo di massa*, Firenze, Guaraldi, 1978.

Falasca-Zamponi, S. *Fascist Spectacle: The Aesthetics of Power in Mussolini's Italy*, Berkeley, University of California Press, 1997.

Federazione Italiana Giuoco Calcio, *Azzurri 1990. Storia bibliografica emerografica iconografica della Nazionale Italiana di Calcio e del Calcio a Bologna*, Roma, La Meridiana, 1990.

—— *Azzurri 1990. Storia bibliografica emerografica iconografica della Nazionale Italiana di Calcio e del Calcio a Firenze*, Roma, La Meridiana, 1990.

—— *Azzurri 1990. Storia bibliografica emerografica iconografica della Nazionale Italiana di Calcio e del Calcio a Roma*, Roma, La Meridiana, 1990.

Ferrara, P. *L'Italia in palestra. Storia documenti e immagini della ginnastica dal 1833 al 1973,* Roma, La Meridiana, 1992.

Forgacs, D. (ed.) *The Antonio Gramsci Reader*, New York, University Press, 2000.

Galluzzo, A. *Il Fiorentino. Vita e Opere del Marchese Luigi Ridolfi*, Roma, Societá Stampa Sportiva, 1999.

—, Battiloro, C. & Varrasi, F. *La Grande Vicenda dello Stadio di Firenze,* Firenze, Edifir, 2000.

Gentile, E. *The Sacralization of Politics in Fascist Italy*, Cambridge MA, Harvard University Press, 1996.

Ghirelli, A. *Storia del calcio in Italia*, Torino, Einaudi, 1990.

Giuntini, S. *Storia dello Sport a Milano*, Milano, Edi Ermes, 1991.

Gramsci, A. *Gli intellettuali e l'organizzazione della cultura*, Torino, Einaudi, 1949.

—— *Sotto la Mole, 1916–1920*, Torino, Einaudi, 1960.

Gregor, J.A. *Interpretations of Fascism*, New Jersey, General Learning Press, 1974.

Gresleri, G. & Massaretti, P.G. (eds) *Norma e arbitro. Architetti e ingegneri a Bologna 1850–1950*, Bologna, Marsilio, 2000.

Grimaldi, M. *Storia del calcio in Italia nel movimento sportivo europeo. Profili Storici, Sociali E Sportivi (1896–1998)*, Roma, Società Stampa Sportiva, 1998.

—— *Leandro Arpinati. Un anarchico alla corte di Mussolini*, Roma, Societá Stampa Sportiva, 1999.

—— *Vittorio Pozzo. Storia di un Italiano*, Roma, Società Stampa Sportiva, 2001.

Handler, A. *From Goals to Guns. The Golden Age of Soccer in Hungary 1950–1956*, Boulder, East European Monographs, 1994.

Hearder, H. *Italy in the Age of Risorgimento*, London, Longman, 1990.

Hoare, Q. & Nowell Smith, G. (eds) *Selections From The Prison Notebooks of Antonio Gramsci*, London, Lawrence and Wishart, 1971.

Horn, D. *Social Bodies. Science, Reproduction, and Italian Modernity*, New Jersey, Princeton University Press, 1994.

Inglis, S. *The Football Grounds of Europe*, London, Willow, 1990.

Ipsen, C. *Dictating Demography. The problem of population in Fascist Italy*, Cambridge, Cambridge University Press, 1996.

Isola, G. *Abbassa la tua radio per favore . . . Storia dell'ascolto radio-fonico dell'Italia fascista*, Firenze, La Nuova Italia, 1990.

—— *Le immagine del suono: i primi vent'anni della radio italiana*, Firenze, Le Lettere, 1991.

—— *Cari amici vicini e lontani: storia dell'ascolto radiofonico nel primo decennio repubblicano, 1944–1954*, Scandicci, La nuova Italia, 1995.

Instituto della Enciclopedia Italiana, *Enciclopedia Italiana di Scienze, Lettere ed Arti*, Roma, Istituto Poligrafica dello Stato, 1950.

—— *Lessico Universale Italiano di Lingua Lettere Arti Scienze e Tecnica*, Roma, Istituto Poligrafico dello Stato, 1978.

—— *Dizionario Biografico Degli Italiani*, Catanzaro, Arti Grafiche Abramo, 2002.

Jarvie, G. & Maguire, J. *Sport and Leisure in Social Thought*, London, Routledge, 1994.

Koon, T.H. *Believe, Obey, Fight: Political Socialization of Youth in Fascist Italy 1922–1943*, Chapel Hill, North Carolina University Press, 1985.

Kuper, S. *Ajax, the Dutch, the War: Football in Europe During the Second World War*, London, Orion, 2003.

Lanfranchi, P. & Taylor, M. (eds) *Moving with the Ball. The Migration of Professional Footballers*, Berg, Oxford, 2001.

Laqueur, W. (ed.) *Fascism: A Reader's Guide*, Scolar, Aldershot, 1991.

Lidtke, V.L. *The Alternative Culture: The Socialist Labor Movement in Imperial Germany*, Oxford, Oxford University Press, 1985.

Lolli, L. *I Mondali in Camicia Nera 1934–38*, Roma, Ardini, 1990.

Lowe, C.J. & Marzari, F. *Italian Foreign Policy, 1870–1940*, London, Routledge & Kegan Paul, 1975.

Lyttelton, A. *The Seizure of Power, Fascism in Italy 1919–1929*, New Jersey, Princeton University Press, 1978.

Macartney, C.A. *Independent Eastern Europe*, London, Macmillan, 1962.

Mack Smith, D. *Mazzini*, New Haven, Yale University Press, 1994.

—— *Modern Italy. A Political Italy*, New Haven, Yale University Press, 1997.

Mangan, J.A. (ed.) *Tribal Identities. Nationalism, Europe, Sport*, London, Frank Cass, 1996.

Marchesini, D. *L'Italia del Giro d'Italia*, Bologna, Il Mulino, 1997.

Mason, T. *Passion of the People? Football in South America*, London, Verso, 1995.

Mathews, S. *My Autobiography. The Way It Was*, London, Headline, 2000.

McClelland, J.S. *The Crowd and the Mob – From Plato to Canetti*, London, Unwin Hyman, 1989.

Meldini, P. *Sposa e madre esemplare: Ideologia e politica della donna e della famiglia durante il fascismo*, Rimini, Guaraldi, 1975.

Monteleone, F. *La radio nel periodo fascista. Studi e documenti 1922–1945*, Venezia, Marsiglio, 1975.

Mosse, G. *The Image of Man. The Creation of Modern Masculinity*, Oxford, Oxford University Press, 1996.

Nye, R. *The Origins of Crowd Psychology. Gustave Le Bon and the Crisis of Mass Democracy in the Third Republic*, London, Sage, 1975.

Onofri, N.S. *I Giornali Bolognesi Nel Ventennio Fascista*, Bologna, Moderna, 1972.

—— & Ottani, V. *Dal Littoriale allo Stadio. Storia per immagini dell'impianto sportivo bolognese*, Bologna, Consorzio Cooperative Costruzioni, 1990.

Palla, M. *Firenze e il regime fascista (1929–1934)*, Firenze, Olschki, 1978.

Papa, A. & Panico, G. *Storia sociale del calcio in Italia. Dai club dei pionieri alla nazione sportiva (1887–1945)*, Bologna, Il Mulino, 1993.

Parodi, E. (ed.) *Nove colonne in Prima. Gino Palumbo: L'ultima intervista*, Milano, Editrice Portoria, 1989.

—— (ed.) *Giocavamo senza numero: la Juventus che eravamo noi: Piero Rava, un terzino lungo la linea di un secolo*, Torino, Torchio orafa, 1999.

Parola, L. (ed.) *Il fascismo al microfono: radio e politica in Italia, 1924–1945*, Roma, Studium, 1978.

Pennacchia, M. *Il Calcio in Italia*, Torino, UTET, 1999.

Petacco, A. *Il Superfascista. Vita e morte di Alessandro Pavolini*, Milano, Mondadori, 1998.

Piccardi, M. & Settimelli, M. (eds) *Lo Stadio di Firenze. Storia di Ieri e di Oggi*, Firenze, Arnaud, 1990.

Pick, D. *Faces of Degeneration. A European Disorder, c.1848–c.1918*, Cambridge, Cambridge University Press, 1989.

Pivato, S. *Sia lodato Bartali. Ideologia e cultura dello sport cattolico (1938–1948)*, Roma, Edizioni Lavoro, 1985.

Porter, R. & Teich, M. (eds) *Fin de Siecle and its Legacy*, Cambridge, Cambridge University Press, 1990.

Pozzo, V. *Campioni del Mondo. Quarant'anni di Storia del Calcio italiano*, Roma, Centro Editoriale Nazionale, 1960.

Preti, L. *I miti dell'impero e della razza nell'Italia degli anni '30*, Roma, Opere Nuove, 1965.

Quine, M.S. *Population Politics in Twentieth-Century Europe. Fascist Dictatorships and Liberal Democracies*, London, Routledge, 1996.

—— *Italy's Social Revolution. Charity and Welfare from Liberalism to Fascism*, Palgrave, Basingstoke, 2002.

Ragionieri, E. *Storia d'Italia, Dall'Unità Oggi, 3, La Storia Politica e Sociale*, Torino, Einaudi, 1976.

—— *Dalla dittatura fascista alla liberazione 1926–1945*, Torino, Einaudi, 1978.

Rees, P. *Fascism and Pre-Fascism in Europe 1890–1945. A Bibliography of the Extreme Right*, Sussex, Harvester Press, 1984.

Riall, L. *The Italian Risorgimento. State, Society and National Unification*, London & New York, Routledge, 1994.

Ridley, J. *Mussolini*, London, Constable, 1997.

Riordan, J. & Kruger, A. (eds) *The International Politics of Sport in the Twentieth Century*, London & New York, E & FN Spon, 1999.

Rothschild, J. *East Central Europe Between the Two World Wars*, Seattle, University of Washington Press, 1974

Rous, S. *Football Worlds. A Lifetime in Sport*, Newton Abbot, Readers Union, 1979.

Rudé, G. *The Crowd in the French Revolution*, Oxford, Oxford University Press, 1959.

San Pietro, S. (ed.) *1990: Stadi in Italia*, Milano, L'archivolta, 1990.

Santarelli, E. *Storia del movimento e del regime fascista*, Roma, Editori Riuniti, 1967.

Scarpa, R. *Eravamo tutti balilla*, Roma, Ciarrapico, 1984.

Schnapp, J. *Staging Fascism. 18 BL and the Theater of Masses for Masses*, Stanford, Stanford University Press, 1996.

—— (ed.) *A Primer of Italian Fascism*, Lincoln, University of Nebraska Press, 2000.

Setta, S. *Renato Ricci. Dallo squadrismo alla repubblica Sociale Italiana*, Bologna, Il Mulino, 1986.

Simonini, A. *Il linguaggio di Mussolini*, Milano, Bompiani, 1978.

Stone, M.S. *The Patron State. Culture and Politics in Fascist Italy*, Princeton, Princeton University Press, 1998.

Tavella, R. & Ossola, F. *Il romanzo della grande Juventus. Un secolo di vita bianconera nella storia del club calcistico più famoso del mondo*, Roma, Newton & Compton, 1997.

Van Ginneken, J. *Crowds, Psychology, and Politics 1871–1899*, Cambridge, Cambridge University Press, 1992.

Varrasi, F.M. *Economia, Politica e Sport in Italia (1925–1935)*, Fondazione Artemio Franchi, Firenze, 1999.

Veggi, G., Tazzi, G.A. & Delli Colli, L. *Firenze: gente angoli, calcio storico, luci*, Vercelli, White Star, 1988.

Wagg, S. (ed.) *Giving the Game Away. Football, Politics and Culture on Five Continents*, London & New York, Leicester University Press, 1995.

Zangheri, R. *Bologna*, Roma, Laterza, 1986.

Articles

Acquarone, A. 'Violenza e consenso nel fascismo italiano', in *Storia contemporanea*, 1, 1979, pp. 145–55.

Adamson, W. 'Avant-garde modernism and Italian Fascism: cultural politics in the era of Mussolini', *Journal of Modern Italian Studies*, 6, 2, 2001, pp. 230–48.

Agostinelli, F. 'Stadi/Dalle Prime Olimpiadi Moderne ai Campionati del Mondo di Calcio del 1934', *Parametro. Rivista Internazionale di Architettura e Urbanistica*, n.172, May-June 1989, p. 56–65.

Berezin, M. 'The Organization of Political Ideology: Culture, State, and the Theater in Fascist Italy', *American Sociological Review*, 56, 5, 1991, pp. 639–51.

—— 'Cultural Form and Political Meaning: State-subsidized Theater, Ideology, and the Language of Style in Fascist Italy', *American Journal of Sociology*, 99, 5, 1994, pp. 1237–86.

Bonetta, G. 'Dalla ginnastica allo sport', *Italia Contemporanea*, 179, June 1990, pp. 347–51.

Cante, D. 'Propaganda e sport negli anni trenta. Gli incontri di calcio tra Italia e Austria', *Italia Contemporanea*, 204, September 1996, pp. 521–44.

Cerri, R. 'Note sulla politica della bonifica integrale del fascismo. 1928–1934', *Italia Contemporanea*, 137, October–December 1979, pp. 35–61.

Dogliani, P. 'Sport and Fascism', *Journal of Modern Italian Studies*, 5, 3, 2000, pp. 326–43.

Fugardi, A. 'La rivoluzione metodica del sistema. Due scuole tattiche a confronto', *Lancillotto e Nausica*, 5, 1988, pp. 16–21.

Gentile, E. 'Fascism as a Political Religion', *Journal of Contemporary History*, 25, 1990, pp. 229–51.

Giuntini, S. 'Storiografia dello sport in Italia', *Italia Contemporanea*, 179, June 1990, pp. 342–5.

—— 'L'inno ginnastico dall'Unità al fascismo', *Ludus. Sport & Loisir*, I, 3–4, October 1992–April 1993, pp. 41–50.

Grozio, R. 'La 'sportologia' tra antropologia e storia', *Italia Contemporanea*, 179, June 1990, pp. 345–7.

Hill, J. & Varrasi, F. 'Creating Wembley: the construction of a National Monument', *The Sports Historian*, 17, 2, 1997, pp. 28–43.

Holt, R. 'The Bicycle, the Bourgeoisie and the Discovery of Rural France, 1880–1914', *British Journal of Sport History*, 27, 1985, pp. 127–39.

Isola, G. 'La radiocronaca all'italiana: Nicolò Carosio', *Ludus. Sport & Loisir*, I, 3–4, October 1992–April 1993, pp. 41–9.

Lanfranchi, P. 'Bologna: "The team that shook the world"', *International Journal of the History of Sport*, 8, 3, 1981, pp. 336–46.

Marri, F. 'Sistema, Metodo . . . Italiano', *Ludus. Sport e loisir*, 3, 1992, pp. 86–126.

Marzola, p. L. 'Storia economica dei campionati del mondo di calcio dall'Uruguay a 'Italia 90'', *Ludus. Sport e loisir*, 1, April 1992, pp. 34–45.

McCarthy, P. 'The Beginnings of Italian Sport', *Journal of Modern Italian Studies*, 5, 3, 2000, pp. 322–3.

Milza, P. 'Il football italiano. Una storia lunga un secolo', *Italia Contemporanea*, 183, June 1991, pp. 245–55.

Monzeglio, E. 'Il Bologna che tiemare il mondo fa!', *La Grande Storia del Calcio Italiano*, 4, 20/2/65.

Mosse, G. 'The Political Culture of Italian Futurism', *Journal of Contemporary History*, 25, 2–3, 1990, pp. 253–68.

Nello, P. 'Mussolini e Bottai: due modi diversi di concepire l'educazione fascista della gioventù', *Storia contemporanea*, 2, 1977, pp. 335–68.

Panico, G. 'Quando gli italiani scoprirono il calcio', *Italia Contemporanea*, 179, June 1990, pp. 351–5.

Papa, A. 'La memoria senza storici. Sulla storia del calcio in Italia', *Italia Contemporanea*, 176, September 1989, pp. 156–9.

Pivato, S. 'Associazionismo Sportivo e Associazionismo Politico nella Romagna d'Inizio Novecento', *Bolletino del Museo del Risorgimento*,

1987–1988, pp. 167–93.

—— 'Le pigrizie dello storico. Lo sport fra ideolgia, storia e rimozioni', *Italia Contemporanea*, 174, March 1989, pp. 17–27.

—— 'Il football: un fenomeno di frontiera. Il caso del Friuli Venezia Giulia', *Italia Contemporanea*, 183, June 1991, pp. 257–72.

Provvisionato, S. 'Terzini d'attacco. L'alternativa di sport e proletariato', in *Lancillotto e Nausica*, 3, 1986, pp. 66–74.

Rigo, L. 'Cerchi olimpici e fasci littori', *Lancillotto e Nausica*, 2, 1986, pp. 12–35.

Rossi, L. 'Giovinetti pallidi della rivoluzione, L''antisportismo' dei socialisti', *Lancillotto e Nausica*, 3, 1986, pp. 50–5.

—— 'Per la Montagna Contro L'Alcool. Sei anni di alpinismo proletariato in Italia (1921–1926)', *Lancillotto e Nausica*, 2, 1988, pp. 30–5.

Salotti, M. 'Esercizi paralleli: sport e spettacolo', *Ludus. Sport & Loisir*, I, 2, July 1992, pp. 54–61.

Susmel, D. 'Il Ras del Pallone', *Domenica del Corriere*, 69, 36, 29/8/67, pp. 16–20.

—— 'Lo Stalin del Fascismo', *Domenica del Corriere*, 69, 37, 5/9/67, pp. 50–3.

—— 'Lo Sgambetto di Starace', *Domenica del Corriere*, 69, 38, 12/9/67, pp. 16–19.

—— 'Ucciso Senza Perchè', *Domenica del Corriere*, 69, 39, 19/9/67, pp. 37–9 .

Whitacker, B. 'Leandro Arpinati, anarcoindividualista, fascista, fascista pentito', *Italia Contemporanea*, 196, 1994, pp. 471–90.

Index